'ortsmouth
ept Aug 27(1100)
rr March 23 (0906)
a
17
ot 25
INDIAN
OCEAN
Cape Town
arr Oct 16(1829)
dept Oct 25(1130)
Auckland
arr Nov 24
(2034)

LAST BUT NOT LEAST

LAST BUT

NOT LEAST

Robin Knox-Johnston

His own story of the
1978 Round-the-world Race

Angus & Robertson · Publishers

Angus and Robertson · Publishers
Brighton · Sydney · Melbourne · Singapore · Manila

First published by Angus & Robertson (UK) Ltd,
16 Ship Street, Brighton, Sussex, in 1978

ISBN 0 207 95830 0

Printed photolitho in Great Britain by
Ebenezer Baylis and Son, Limited,
The Trinity Press, Worcester, and London

DEDICATION

For those we left behind

CONTENTS

1. PLOTTING AND PLANNING

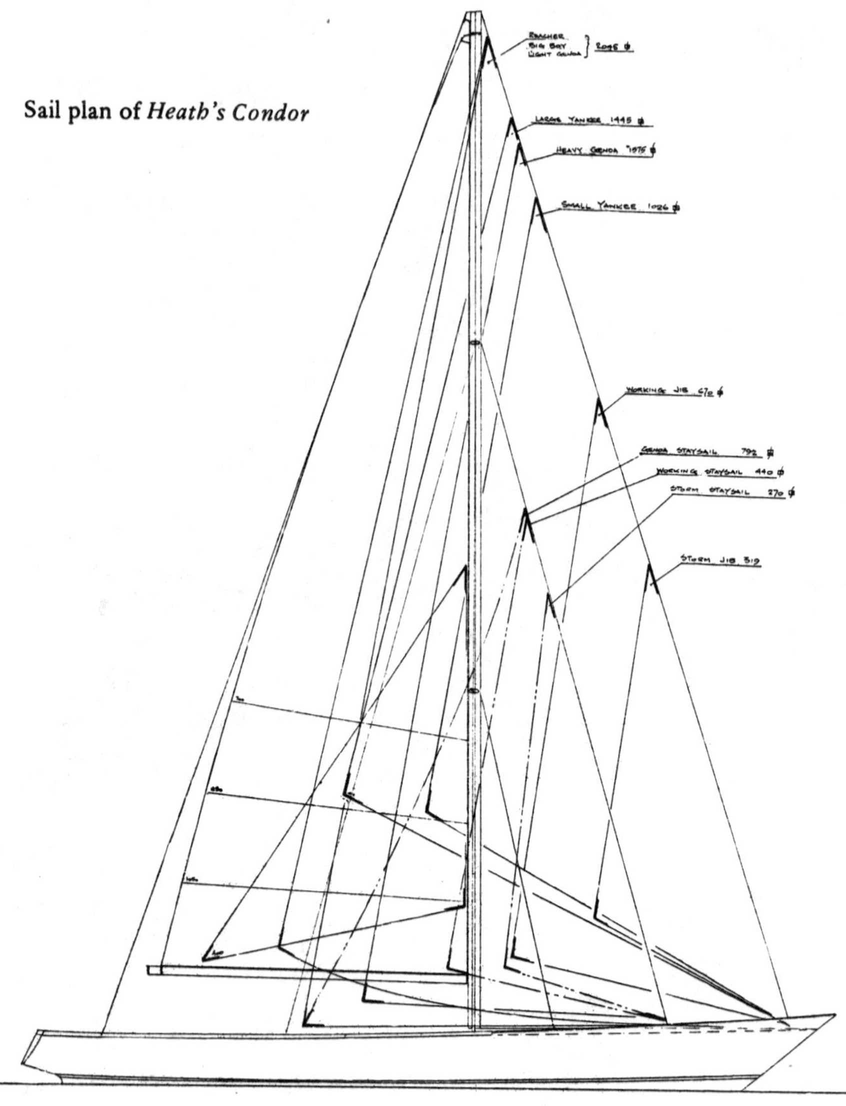

Sail plan of *Heath's Condor*

In 1967 Sir Francis Chichester electrified the sailing world with his single-handed voyage around the world in *Gypsy Moth IV*, with only a month's rest in Australia. People were at once made aware of the possibility of racing a yacht around the world, instead of the normal rather cautious cruising approach, and of course Sir Francis left only one thing to be done—to sail around the world single-handed non-stop. A year later Sir Alec Rose completed his single-handed circumnavigation with stops only in Australia and New Zealand in *Lively Lady*. Even before he reached home, a race was on to be the first person to circumnavigate the globe single-handed non-stop. In all, nine boats entered, but in the end I was the only one to complete the race successfully, in *Suhaili*. Two years later Chay Blythe also completed the same journey non-stop on his own, sailing *British Steel*.

Once someone had drawn attention to the idea of a race around the world, it was only a question of time before a race for fully crewed racing yachts was organised. In 1973 the Royal Naval Sailing Association set up a race with stops in Cape Town, Sydney, and Rio de Janeiro, sponsored by Whitbread the brewers. It was a gamble on the organisers' part, as no one could tell whether sufficient boats would enter to make a real race of the event, the main problem being thought to be the difficulty of getting the right sort of crew who could take a year off to go sailing. As it happened, no one need have worried: fourteen boats crossed the start line at Portsmouth in August 1973, and all returned safely to Portsmouth the following spring, although there had been plenty of incidents on the way, and three men had lost their lives in the Southern Ocean. Inevitably, there was criticism levelled at the organisers because of the tragic loss of life, and the pessimists predicted that the experiment would not be repeated. They were wrong. The organisers can hardly be blamed for events that take place once the boats are at sea. They can and did frame stiff safety regulations, but having done this, the responsibility for sailing safely lies with the skipper and crew of the boat, just as the Board of Trade is not to blame if a British Merchant ship founders at sea—the captain and crew are responsible. The race was won by the only Mexican entry, a Swan 65 ketch named *Sayula* which although not the first boat home, had the best corrected time which gave her a well deserved victory on handicap.

Two years later another fully crewed race was organised, this time by the *Financial Times*. It differed in that it only had one stop at Sydney between the start from London and the finish at Dover. Perhaps it came too soon after the Whitbread Race, or maybe people are attracted to a race because of the pleasant ports of call—but only four boats entered; all, however, reached home safely. The times for this second crewed race, if you took only the time at sea, were faster than the previous ones, which seemed to indicate that people were more confident of pushing their boats now they knew that a race in the Southern Ocean was practicable.

Even before the 1975 race, Whitbread and the Royal Naval Sailing Association had announced another in their series, the only difference being that the middle stop would be at Auckland, New Zealand, instead of Sydney. The race was to start in August 1977, and entries were received almost immediately after the rules were published.

I had been following the progress of these races for some time, and was beginning to think about getting an entry organised when Les Williams dropped in to see me.

Les and I had first got together in 1969 when we decided to buy the first of the Southern Ocean Shipyard's Ocean 71 hulls and fit it out for the two-man Round Britain Race in 1970, and the Cape Town to Rio Race in 1971. We had thought to make the boat pay for herself by chartering in the Mediterranean and West Indies after these races. The whole programme had been an incredible rush from the start. Tyler's had moulded the hull by March 1970, but the deck was not completed for another month, and then had had to be floated down the Medway on oil drums from Tonbridge to Hoo for assembly, propelled by outboard motors. A team of four of us, plus eight Tyler men, had somehow got the boat ready by the middle of June, and we had launched her ten days before the start of the Round Britain Race, calling her *Ocean Spirit*.

The *Observer* two-man Round Britain Race had been the maiden voyage, but we won the race by two days in a new record time. There had not been another boat anywhere near our size, and of course length means speed, but the two of us had been hard pushed to sail the boat efficiently, as we just did not have the reserves of power that a full crew would have provided.

After this initial success, we had sailed for the Mediterranean to do the Middle Sea Race from Valetta, round Sicily and back, mainly because we wanted to race against *Stormvogle*, a boat of similar size and by the same designer, Van der Stadt. We had got off to a good start but in gale conditions all but one of our sails blew out, and we sat sewing hard as *Stormvogle* went past, building up a lead we could not win back.

From Malta we planned to sail to Cape Town for the first Cape Town to Rio Race, which started in January 1971. By this time we were beginning to build up a core of crew, all of whom paid their way as far as food was concerned. Perhaps one of the most notable was Peter Blake, a young New Zealander who had flown direct to Malta from New Zealand just to join us. The voyage to Cape Town was undertaken by Les, and apart from going aground south of Walvis Bay on the dreaded skeleton coast, and getting off again which was a major feat of seamanship, it passed uneventfully. In Cape Town we picked up our full crew including, as cook, Clement Freud, who was to prove to all of us that you could still race a boat and enjoy five-star cooking. It was in Cape Town before the start of the race that we first met Eric Tarbarly, sailing *Pen Duik III* in Class 2 of the race. Clement discovered that Tarbarly's engine was welded upside-down beneath his cockpit floor and had asked the race committee to force a change as the rules stated that the engine must be connected up. A reluctant committee was obliged to put pressure on their 'star' entrant to put things right before the start.

The race itself was a three-week fast cruise, mostly downwind. We took an early lead, and logged one day's run of 286 miles running before strong south-east Trade winds. Then the whole fleet closed up when we ran into the South Atlantic high and for five days we sailed in close company with Lol Killam's new *Greybeard* before we got away to take line honours by twenty-two hours.

This was the end of our racing with *Ocean Spirit*; from then on she chartered until we sold her in 1973. We found that there was little profit in chartering—we just covered the running and mortgage costs, and neither of us was getting time to enjoy the boat so there was little point in keeping her. In retrospect, if we had hung onto her for a couple of years, she would have doubled in value, but it is always easy to be wise after the event. She did not last long with her new owners and was wrecked in the West Indies in 1974.

At least we had had the experience of building a near maxi-rater in the extraordinarily short time of six months, and of sailing her in a number of good races. For both of us it was an interesting and enjoyable experience, and the thrill of steering a really large yacht at sea is not easily forgotten.

Les was very soon involved in another even bigger yacht, *Burton Cutter*, built to enter the 1973 Whitbread Round the World Race. Again he had a rush to finish her but she was ready just in time. Unfortunately, the hull construction in aluminium did not prove strong enough, and she had to limp into port after some large cracks appeared in the forward sections in the second leg. The boat was repaired in South Africa and rejoined the race for the last leg from Rio to home. It was a bitter disappointment to Les, but his knowledge and experience with big boats were increased.

In 1974 we raced against each other in the Round Britain Race, Les in *Burton Cutter* and I in *British Oxygen*, a seventy-foot catamaran. I came in first, and Les was the first mono-hull home.

In 1976, whilst I was sailing *More Opposition*, Les suggested that perhaps we should get together for another maxi-rater and enter the 1977/8 Whitbread Round the World Race. As is usual, our major problem was how to raise the money. A maxi-rater is an expensive beast, and you cannot really think of building one for less than a quarter of a million pounds, and that assumes a stripped-out machine and no building hiccups, and neither Les nor I, even combining our joint assets, were wealthy enough to buy one ourselves. Sponsorship, or a share arrangement, seemed likely to be our best hope, but few companies would spend that amount of money on a boat for one race, as the advertising return just would not be worthwhile. We worked out a share system under which up to fifteen people, including Les and I, would have a share in such a boat. We had barely got the prospectus printed when Les met Bob Bell, an insurance broker with large commitments abroad, who expressed an interest and things suddenly began to move very fast. Bob decided that he would take all the shares in the boat, so suddenly the money was available, and Les and I got down to the business of organising the designer and builder, with just eleven months to go before the race was due to start.

There are a number of well-known yacht designers to whom one can go for a design, and the resulting yacht may not be brilliant but will always be good. There are others, perhaps not so well known, who will give you a good result. With our very short building time we needed a designer who could devote himself fully to the project without any other distractions, and one also that had had some experience with large boats. We chose John Sharp because he had designed *Burton Cutter*, which Les knew well and which had the interesting characteristic in that in strong following winds she had sailed consistently faster than was theoretically possible without planing, and sixty per cent of the Round the World Race is sailed in strong following winds.

We met up with John Sharp in September to discuss the design specification. It was very simple to say what we wanted, but nothing like so simple to provide it. I put it to John that what was required was a two-tonner that rated seventy feet to the International Offshore Rule, that should be sloop-rigged to maximise windward performance, and yet be able to run downwind like *Burton Cutter*. The boat was to be designed purely for racing, with no thought given to conversion later to a cruising yacht. What we wanted was a boat that would out-perform any other maxi-rater afloat, that is, any of the dozen or so other maximum size yachts permitted under the IOR, and would also out-perform in particular *Pen Duik VI* and *Great Britain II* which we knew were likely to be entered for the race. The boat had also to be planned so that she could be maintained without outside assistance for up to forty days at a time. This inevitably meant that we had to allow for extra fittings, so that back-up was available in the event of any one part failing on us.

It was a tall order, particularly with the limited time we had available, but to help out, I introduced John to Phil Stanbury, an ex-test pilot turned boffin with the British Aircraft Corporation, who had been largely responsible for the work on the keels for *British Oxygen* which had been so effective. The relationship between pushing an aeroplane wing through the air and a keel through the water is a complex one, and best left to experts like Phil. When John had produced his preliminary lines he went and spent a day with Phil just going through the basic ideas, and from these discussions a keel and skeg shape was arrived at. It had to be a compromise to a certain extent: for Phil, the ideal keel shape had vertical leading and trailing edges, but John wanted to set the leading edge back at an angle for better downwind performance, and this is how the keel ended up. The trailing edge was also set back, although the latest theory is that a vertical trailing edge is more efficient. I think this was a mistake, as we could have had two foot more depth of keel before incurring a rating penalty, and the extra weight of keel that was accommodated by the swept back section could have gone into the two foot of extra draught. This would have given more stability—or, as the boat was pretty stable anyway, allowed us to reduce the keel weight slightly as the extra lead ten feet from the centre of gravity would have had a greater righting moment than at seven feet below the centre of gravity. At the time, however, we were satisfied with what we had got, and of course there is a problem finding a place to berth a boat that has a draught of twelve feet—ten feet gives problems enough.

John's basic lines looked good. We had a long clean body with a sharp upturn, or bustle, aft. The idea of a bustle, apart from slight rating advantages, is to 'surprise' the medium you are going through, and give the impression to the water that the hull carries on after it has in fact finished. The object is to create a theoretically longer boat, as a boat's length has a direct bearing on its speed. It is easy enough to design a smooth fine bow or entry, but much more difficult to design a really efficient run or stern section. The concept used was as far away as you could get from the old traditional clean upsweep such as is seen on, say, a Dragon, and we would have to wait and see if our stern was better. To go as far as we could to check the hull lines, we asked John to have tank tests carried out at Southampton University, and eagerly awaited the results.

The deck layout was, at my request, left to me. Over the

years I have developed a number of pet aversions in racing boats, and I had also collected what seemed to me some quite efficient ideas from sailing aboard *Frigate* and *Yeoman XX*. These two boats had had, when new, some quite radical ideas in their deck layout designs and although they were a great deal smaller, some of them seemed suitable for a larger boat. To start with, the greatest chaos in a boat always seems to occur when rounding the leeward mark when a spinnaker is being handed and a genoa or jib set for a beat. On these two boats all halyards had been lead aft to the cockpit as this was where the winches, and the musclemen, were, and a halyard could be taken to any winch and when it had been hauled taut, it could be stoppered off thus releasing the winch for another job. The only problem we had experienced was the difficulty of communicating between the foredeck and the cockpit when some other task like handing a spinnaker was going on in between. One solution is to have the halyard winches on the mast just above the deck, but they get in the way, snag sails and sheets, and cannot be operated efficiently. To put them below decks gets them out of the way, but we found on *More Opposition* that with this system, we had even greater difficulty in communicating. The answer on a large boat seemed to be to get the halyard winches as close to the mast as possible, but placed in their own special cockpit. I drew up a plan showing a special cockpit with a coaming around it on which the winches would be placed, and all the halyards came down from their exit boxes on the mast to a turning block on a special platform built out at winch level around the mast. The halyards then passed through another horizontal turning block which had a stopper attached, so that we could use any winch which was convenient. Because of the stoppers, all the winches could be ordinary sheet winches which made them much more useful, but as Lewmar had just brought out a new self-tailing mechanism that went on the top of the winches, we had these fitted as well, both for safety and to reduce the number of people required forward when a sail was being hoisted. To ensure that the winch handles were at an average man's hip level, the most efficient position, I put the deck down six inches in this cockpit which slightly impinged on the headroom below, but this was unimportant.

John Sharp made two alterations to this part of the layout.

Firstly he divided the cockpit into two smaller ones separated by another winch platform; this not only made it far easier to give the halyards kind leads, it also simplified the winching, and meant furthermore that the extra depth required for the cockpits was now on either side of the centre of the boat which gave us full headroom in a central alleyway. He also changed the turning block platform for a collar on the mast which we were not at all happy about, and asked him to change, but when the mast was eventually delivered it had his collar on it and that is what we had to put up with—for a while, anyway.

I had wanted to be able to keep the foredeck as clear as possible and have removable inner forestays so that we would dip the spinnaker pole when gybing. This was not really on because of the sheer size of everything and the strains it would put on the mast, so we had to have two poles ready at any time. Because of the weight of the poles, we arranged their stowage along the centre line of the foredeck so that they could be easily fitted into their cups on the mast track which was lead right down to deck level. This saved having to carry a heavy pole from the usual stowage position at the side of the foredeck when the boat was heeled over and plunging about in a big seaway. We put two hatches through the foredeck, one on each side for sail handling, as apart from the fact that the spinnaker poles were in the way, on a large boat we thought it preferable to have two rather than one hatch.

To handle the sizes of sails we would be carrying, we obviously went for coffee grinders, and we got four. Two were of the normal Lewmar type; the other two, a new type, we chose because they could be backwound, which made easing the sheets safer. We planned originally to have all four linked together on deck between the halyard cockpit and the main cockpit, but there just was not the room. We chose instead to put the two normal coffee grinders in this space, but not cross linked, and the two backwind ones went abaft the helmsman, but were cross linked. The after pair were for genoa and spinnaker sheets, the forward two for staysail sheets and spinnaker guys. The arrangement of all these winches was planned so that in the event of one breaking down, we could always easily use another one that would take the loads. Thus if the after coffee grinders packed up, we moved to the forward ones. If these were not in use, a Lewmar 65 on the halyard winch platform was placed so that it could be used. This interchangeability is useful in short races, but absolutely vital in a boat where no back-up is available for a month at a time.

The mainsail sheeting arrangement gave us some food for thought. Originally we looked at a main sheet on one track forward of the helmsman, and a hydraulic kicker halfway along the boom on its own circular track. This presented rather too many problems, and so in order to provide support for the main boom at its mid point, where an awful lot of its strains are experienced, we had two tracks for the main sheet, one forward of the helmsman and one forward of the main cockpit, but one sheet rove through blocks on each. This provided the support we felt was necessary and was manageable, although it had the disadvantage that a great deal of sheet was required, and a great deal had to be wound in for just a small movement of the boom.

The helmsman steered from the aft end of the main cockpit, in a section separated off by a large aluminium structure designed to take the instruments, steering mechanism and compass. Both Les and I felt we wanted to give the helmsman the best possible view with the minimum of interference from crew activity which could be controlled by a crew boss or mate. Had we been able to keep all the coffee grinders amidships this would have been achieved, but having the headsail sheet winches behind the helmsman meant that at times the helmsman was bound to be surrounded by activity and distractions, which was a pity.

We considered having some sort of dog house for crew protection, but ruled it out as it would have got in the way and hindered the view. This meant more exposure to the elements for the watch on deck and the helmsman, but we felt that some form of screen could be fitted if necessary.

A number of different track systems for adjusting sheet blocks were considered, but we decided to use these only for the smaller sails such as staysails, and we put a heavy aluminium toe-rail along each side of the boat with holes drilled through to take heavy blocks for the headsails. This aluminium was made up of two sections: a flat plate and a corner section welded together so that it could be fastened both into the sheer strake at the top of the hull and down through the deck at the sides. Although this system left less initial scope for sheet trimming, it was immensely strong, and any adjustment to the sheeting angles could be achieved by rigging barber hauls to strategically placed reinforced eyes on deck. We considered running the aluminium toe-rail right forward, but later decided to stop it just forward of the mast, and a mini bulwark was fitted from there forward which gave the foredeck more protection when we were in a big sea.

Below decks we discussed having the boat on an open plan, but decided against this as although bulkheads add weight, they also add strength. In fact the below decks arrangement was not finalised until near completion; there were other more important things to sort out before we got on with that. Firstly, for instance, we needed a builder, and one that could build the boat within eight months.

Because of the time available we had little choice in hull material. Aluminium, which was our first choice, was out as none of the yards experienced with this material had the spare capacity. Foam sandwich GRP could have been built, but personally I am not over-fond of this form of construction, although it avoids the need for a mould. A normal GRP hull required a plug and a mould, and although Tyler's had completed *Ocean Spirit* this way in this sort of time scale, they were not prepared to guarantee such results again. This left wood, which was our second choice to aluminium, but we needed a yard with experienced and enthusiastic shipwrights who had the time available. We saw a number of yards before we heard that Larry Baker of Bowman's in Emsworth was interested. I went to see him with John Sharp, and having discussed the project and got a rough figure for the costs, went back to Les and Bob Bell. We realised that time was short, and to find a yard keen to do the job was a lucky break, and agreed to go ahead. First, however, we needed some sort of guarantee that the boat would be ready by the following June, as it was essential that we had time to try the boat before we departed, not just to make sure that everything was all right and give ourselves time to sort out any gremlins, but also so that we could get to know the boat and work up the crew. Even with this schedule we would have only just over two months to work up, which was little enough. When I asked for an assurance that the boat would be ready in early June, Larry hedged a little, and eventually we agreed on late June, provided, he said, that he got all the drawings from John in time. Since John had agreed to concentrate solely on this boat, we were all reasonably happy about this and so the contract was signed.

By this time we were into October 1976, but work on lofting the boat started immediately under the supervision of Eggo Dridge, the foreman of the yard. This is the job of drawing out the lines of the boat full size from the drawings and table of offsets provided by the designer. The need for such full-size lines is so that the shipwrights can measure off the frames for the boat directly, but they also serve another purpose—that of checking that all the boat's lines are fair.

Work got off to a flying start and within three weeks the keel and frames were set up upside down and battens were being laid along them. These frames were purely for shaping purposes, and the battens provided stiffness and support for the hull veneers as they were applied.

Cold moulding is a fascinating method of construction, and looks terribly easy—until you try and do it yourself. It basically consists of laying a number of thin planks from the keel, round over the battens to the vicinity of the gunwale and stapling them in place to the battens. These planks are not laid either fore and aft or athwart, but diagonally across the hull, as this makes them easier to lay, and allows the timber a longer run to be bent three-dimensionally. Once the first layer of quarter-inch mahogany planks had been laid, the second layer was fitted. They were glued down over the first layer, diagonally, but at right angles to the first layer. To hold the second layer firmly in place whilst the glue hardened, staples were used to hold the first and second layers together. Before the third layer was put on, all these staples had to be removed, and the planks were planed down to give a good surface. The third layer was glued to the second and stapled, and laid in the same line as the first layer, and a fourth layer was put on in the same way but in line with the second layer. When these four layers were glued in place we had a very strong inch-thick plywood hull, with each veneer of quarter-inch-thick Brazilian mahogany. A final layer of hull veneer was yet to be applied, but this time the veneers went fore and aft, so that when in place, the hull looked as if it was made of planks. There was some talk of the hull being painted, but Eggo and I both agreed that the only finish for this style of construction was varnish, and that is how she was finished.

Once all five layers were glued on, the whole hull was faired off and planed down to give a good smooth finish.

The next job was to turn the hull over, and this took a whole day. Eggo asked us to keep quiet about the date chosen as he did not want gawpers whilst he and the men were doing it, and I did not blame him. I stayed at home on the chosen day chewing my nails, as it only wanted one small slip and the boat and our hopes would be shattered. I need not have worried, and when late afternoon the phone rang I knew from Eggo's voice that all had gone well.

The frames had then to be fitted, and these were laminated in place in the boat as the shaping frames were slowly removed. By late February the deck frames were going in, but we were running short on drawings which were threatening to hold us up. John did not seem to be able to keep the drawings coming in fast enough for the yard, and although the yard was capable of finishing the boat without them, it was better if detailed drawings were available. We had one incident that lost us time when John decided that he would prefer the forward bulkhead to be made of aluminium. Unfortunately, his earlier drawing showed it in wood, and lacking further detail the yard built it in wood. John ordered the wood bulkhead removed, and the yard did this but morale took a blow. No one, especially when they are working as hard as they can on a project they know is short of time, likes to pull perfectly good work to pieces, and the men at Bowman's were no exception. When I heard about this I went to the yard and stopped the ripping out, and told Eggo that he was never to remove anything he had put in unless I specifically said so. I then saw John and told him what I had told the yard and asked what the problem was; we had been promised all the drawings in time and were not getting them. The fact of the matter was that the drawings were taking John all his time and he could not keep ahead of the work, so we asked Stuart Rogers to come in and help out on the details, and this improved matters considerably.

With bulkheads going in, the interior arrangements had to be finalised; we sketched these out and Stuart provided drawings as the work progressed. The boat was divided into four main sections. Starting from forward we had the sail lockers with a cut away fore and aft bulkhead down the centre line. At the aft end came a small workshop to port and a rope store to starboard, either of which could be passed through on the way forward. The centre of the boat was split down the middle by a four-foot-wide passageway which led off to two cabins to port and a cabin and WC to starboard. We made the passageway this width as we wanted to have room below for sail repairs, and for this you need space. It also meant that there was a good long area for re-packing sails below when this could not be carried out on deck. It also gave us space to stow sails at sea. The three cabins each had four bunks, as we planned to have three watches of four people, and it seemed sensible for each watch to have their own cabin as they would all be disturbed at the same time. If the watches are split up between sleeping spaces, a light sleeper gets awakened at each watch change and so does not get his proper rest.

The main saloon and galley came next, stretching right across the whole width of the boat with the galley occupying the port side. We put the calor gas stoves outboard, the sink forward and the deep freeze inboard of the galley area. This meant that the deep freeze top could be used for serving into the saloon, and also provided something to stop the unfortunate cook from being thrown right across the boat if she lurched suddenly to starboard. It is bad enough trying to cook in a galley being thrown around all over the place—it is even worse if you cannot brace yourself, and it is downright dangerous if you can loose your grip and tumble fifteen feet.

The calor gas storage was in a special locker under the cockpit. This kept the weight reasonably low down, but also enabled the locker to have a gas drain overside. The locker was sealed all round, but we had a watertight opening into each side down below so that cylinders could be switched without having to open up the cockpit. Unfortunately, the builders put the generator exhaust immediately forward of the gas locker drain on the starboard side at the waterline. This was fine when we were heeled to port, but when we were heeled to starboard with the generator running, the exhaust fumes went straight up the gas locker drain and the locker quickly became black with soot.

The saloon area—you could hardly call it a saloon as it really consisted of a U-shaped cushion seat—was approximately fourteen feet by ten feet. The central passageway divided it from the galley, thus giving a clear run through the boat from the companionway which came down from the cockpit at the aft end. Outboard of the settee was storage space and shelves, and forward was a locker for the deep freeze machinery, powered by electricity, and space for a sewing machine. The machine was positioned so that it could be slid out into the alleyway, and then a long repair could be led to it. A sewing machine may seem a bit of a luxury, but hand-sewing repairs to a sail takes a very long time, and we had to be prepared to repair any sail we carried, possibly very quickly if it was needed.

The saloon had no table in it. We planned that the crew could eat off their knees, which may not be too convenient, but a table is not easy to eat off either in a seaway, and it meant that we had more room and people could move about easily. In fact I do not think anyone really missed a table, so one could save a little extra weight like this in any boat.

On the starboard side aft of the saloon was the navigatorium, which contained a large chart table, shelves for the Admiralty Pilots, the main radio set, a Dancom 400 watt SSB radio telephone and a small Dancom VHF set. Some duplicate instruments were arranged on the aft bulkhead. We put in a settee cum bunk as well, as I like to sleep where I am close to the centre of things, and when someone comes down to write up the log, you can ask how things are going without anyone else being disturbed.

Amidships from the navigatorium was the engine room which housed a Savage Ford diesel engine and the G. and M. generator. To drive the boat we had a two-bladed Martec folding propeller, which folds flat when not being turned by the engine, thus reducing drag, but the moment the engine turns, its blades are thrown out by centrifugal force.

On the port side we had an oilskin locker, and in the remainder of the space one large bunk. This space could have been better used, and with a bit of thought two bunks could easily have fitted in to it.

Aft was a large empty space, that later had two pipe cots fitted. It was planned to use this space for dry food storage. There was also another WC here. Astern of this was the lazarette which could only be reached via a hatch through the after deck, and in which was the rudder stock and emergency steering gear. Because of a number of obstructions it was not possible to fit a tiller on the emergency steering, so it was designed to operate from an extension to the rudder stock that came through the deck and was then controlled by lines to the two aft coffee grinders. If we had to use it, it would mean stationing someone permanently on these.

We had ordered an aluminium mast and spars from John Powell in Emsworth during October. In deciding to go for a sloop rig, we had told John Sharp to put the maximum length of mast he could get on the boat whilst keeping her within the rating of seventy feet. Frankly we rather hoped that this would give us over one hundred feet of mast, as *Windward Passage*, an American maxi, had a hundred-foot mast and we did not want to be smaller. We ran into problems over mast sections, however. John Powell reckoned that we could use a Swan 65 mast section up to ninety-three feet, but we would need a heavier section if we went above that. The use of a heavier section would mean we would lose stability or heel more to a given wind, unless we increased the keel moment by either making it heavier or deeper. Since we were trying to keep the boat as light as possible, we ruled this out.

About this time the question of a carbon fibre mast was first raised. Vickers had been making mini submarines for North Sea oil work for a couple of years using special resins and glass fibre with carbon fibre strands added. They were quite keen to try their hand at a mast so John gave them the design specifications and asked for approximate weights of a 93- and 102-foot mast so that we could draw up a table of comparisons and evaluate which would best suit the boat and our purpose. John drew up a table as shown on the following page.

The choice was interesting. If we went for the 102-foot rig with the carbon fibre glass mast we had our nearly maxi rating, but in the event of the mast failing, our performance

Comparison of mast/rig factors

Factors	*Displacement tonnage*	*Sail area in sq ft*	*GM in ft*	*Righting moment at 25° in ft/ton*	*IOR rating in ft (appx)*
93 alloy	36.60	2496	6.464	80.916	66.5
93 carbon fibre reinforced plastic	36.38	2496	6.781	84.374	68.5
102 alloy	36.96	2762	5.733	72.471	67.5
102 carbon fibre reinforced plastic	36.41	2762	6.581	81.953	69.5

was going to fall off badly if we stepped a sufficiently strong aluminium 102-foot replacement. If we went for the 93-foot solution, we failed to have a maxi rating, but whatever happened, we should have a good performance. The discussion as to which solution to have continued for some time. I think we were all intrigued by the thought of having a mast made of a new material, particularly as it would enable us to sail more upright for a given strength of wind, but at the back of Les's and my mind was the thought that a race around the world was not the event in which to experiment with a mast. Eventually things polarised a little. Les and I felt that if the carbon glass mast was to be fitted at all, it should be 102 feet long and if that failed we would fit the 93-foot aluminium replacement. It would mean an emergency re-cut of the sails if this had to be done, but we got the best of the alternatives this way. Bob Bell was undecided; John Sharp and Larry Baker were for carbon fibre, but at ninety-three feet to save re-cutting the sails and altering the rigging. While everyone was trying to reach agreement I contacted John Powell and told him to get on with the 93-foot aluminium mast, as whatever happened we were all agreed on that, and he promised delivery May/June. Ultimately it was decided that we would have a 93-foot carbon fibre glass mast, with the aluminium mast as standby, but we asked for compression tests to be made on a forty-foot section. The results given showed that the material was nearly one and a half times as strong as aluminium in this respect, which made Les and me a little happier with the decision.

At least the decision resolved one thing, and that was the size of the sails. We could go for more than 150 per cent overlap on our headsails and thus put our rating back up near the seventy-foot limit, but we felt that we would only rarely be able to use this extra area, and it would be preferable to have a lower rating instead. For a while Butler Verner had been concentrating on storm sails and staysails which would fit either rig, but now they were able to get on with the full set. The storm jib, staysail and mainsail—we decided against a storm trysail—were all hand-sewn of 14.5-ounce cloth. The rest of the sails were machine-sewn but we asked for a few hand stitches every yard on the working sail seams so that if a seam started to go, it could only rip for one yard and we would have an easier repair. The final wardrobe was:

	P in ft	*E in ft*	*Area in sq ft*	*Weight in oz*
Mainsail	86.0	29.0	1247	12.5
Storm mainsail (hand-sewn)	72.0	25.0	900	14.5
	Luff	*LP*		
No. 1 light genoa	94.0	43.5	2045	6.0
No. 1 heavy genoa	94.0	43.5	2045	9.0
No. 2 genoa	83.5	37.75	1576	10.0
Small yankee	78.5	27.0	1060	9.0
Ribbon yankee	76.0	18.0	684	10.0
Storm jib (hand-sewn)	44.0	14.75	325	14.5
Genoa staysail	49.0	33.0	809	8.0
Working staysail	48.0	18.5	444	10.0
Storm staysail (hand-sewn)	40.0	13.5	270	14.5
Reacher	94.0	43.5	2066	8.0
	I	*SPL*		
Floater tri-radial spinnaker	93.0	29.0	4314	0.8
Light tri-radial	93.0	29.0	4314	1.5
Heavy tri-radial	93.0	29.0	4314	2.3
Gale tri-radial	93.0	29.0	3404	2.75
Storm tri-radial	—	—	1000	2.75
	Luff	*LP*		
Blooper	94.0	43.5	2045	0.75
Blooper	94.0	43.5	2045	1.5
Tall spinnaker staysail	76.0	25.0	950	5.0

All the sails were supplied in long turtle bags, so that they could be flaked out ready for hoisting in the bag, and when stowed, would be easier to handle than a normal sail bag. The spinnakers were to be supplied in long, full length turtles sealed with velcro, so that they could be hoisted under control in the turtle which could be pulled apart to release the sail when we were ready.

We decided to order a special spinnaker that could be set from the upper spreaders using a staysail halyard for use in really heavy weather. Being smaller than the others, it required a specially short spinnaker pole, but the plan was to hoist this sail, within the main forestay, in storm or worse conditions, as it could be strapped right down and enable us to keep pushing the boat along. Les had had one on *Burton Cutter* which he found most useful, and we felt we could benefit from this experience.

By the end of April 1977 things were coming together quite well, although Larry was beginning to talk about July for launching which worried us, as he was biting into our work up time. One could not blame the workmen—they had their hearts in the job and were pushing on as fast as they could—but it was a big project and time was short, and we only needed a few items to fail to arrive on time and delay was inevitable. In this sort of situation, however, the crew of a boat always come out worst, as apart from losing the time needed for tuning, fault finding and just building up as a team, it probably means that the unworked up crew will have to tune up and put faults right during the race; but of course it's the crew who, whatever happens, get the rap if the boat does not seem to be going fast enough.

For some time, I had been badgering John Sharp for the towing tank test results. All his basic work had been modelled upon modifications made to *Burton Cutter*'s lines based on some previous tank tests, but what we wanted to know was how our hull would perform. Because of the time taken to have the tests made there was little by way of modifications that could be carried out, but if the tests showed a potential disaster, we could at least have more tests made to find out if any drastic action, such as strategically placed wedges, would improve matters.

The eventual results, which we got in May, were fascinating. The basic comparison was made with *Burton Cutter* which had a waterline length of sixty-nine feet as compared with our design's waterline of sixty-four feet. Our design also had a greater displacement to length ratio and displaced five tons less, and had a plain sail area three hundred square feet larger.

The tests showed that, in the testing tank anyway, our design had a reduced resistance at higher speeds, which meant that we would have a better windward performance, and our single-masted sloop rig, as opposed to *Burton Cutter*'s ketch rig, would only enhance this. The general performance could be expected to be better at hull speeds up to nine knots, identical from nine to twelve knots, worse between twelve and eighteen knots, and better again at speeds above eighteen knots.

Quite where this left us we were not sure. We had hoped that

John would be able to improve on *Burton Cutter* and give us the ability to blast through the theoretical maximum speed governed by the waterline length as he had done before; but this point was reached between eleven and twelve knots, and did the worse performance between twelve and eighteen knots mean we would not be able to do this? In that case we would never get up to eighteen knots where we ought to do better. In fact the curves of resistance of the two boats were never very far apart, and so we had to hope that if we hung onto sail we would be able to match the performance, and of course we had more sail to hang onto with our larger rig. It was encouraging to know that we could expect a good performance up to nine knots though, as this indicated that the boat would be quite good in light weather which was important when you consider the areas of calms we would have to sail through. All in all, these results were not disappointing, and we looked forward to being able to check them out practically.

Choosing a crew is always an interesting job. To start with you are selecting the people you are going to have to live with in a confined space for nearly a year in sometimes very trying conditions, and so one goes for people one has sailed with and enjoyed sailing with before. Thereafter you have to interview people and see if they shape up to the requirements. I think an ideal age for a crewman is twenty-nine. At this age a person is old enough to have learned about himself, and has lived long enough to find out how people tick and adjust to different personalities. A person of twenty-nine is also sufficiently young to get and remain fit. The aches and pains and brittle bones come along later, and if there was one thing we needed it was a healthy, fit, troublefree crew. Having established a norm however, it must not be set in concrete. There are plenty of healthy, fit people a lot older, and many experienced and well-adjusted people a lot younger. On the whole, however, Les and I favoured the older person because they work in more easily, and accept that they have to give on a boat, not just by giving up a few of their pet likes and dislikes, but by offering to help with the chores when the necessity arises, even if it is not their turn.

Having established this, you then have to take into account the other properties you consider desirable. Sailing ability and experience is an obvious one, and we did not restrict ourselves to those with big boat knowledge. A person who has raced a dinghy will find that everything is a lot larger, but the ability to adjust the sails to a given wind is just as important. We had already decided not to take anyone who did not have sailing experience, however, so this became a natural filter and ruled out those who had not sailed before. The Southern Ocean is not the place to be giving sailing lessons. A sense of humour is vital. The over-intense person who cannot make or take a joke becomes a bore, and then starts to get on people's nerves. The ability to laugh and see the funny side of even a quite serious situation, somehow makes the problem more bearable, and a solution much easier to work towards.

I think the most important attribute we were looking for in our crew was motivation. We wanted people who were set on going in the Round the World Race, but in the winning boat, and who would put everything aside before and during the race to achieve that end. If a person was determined to be on the winning boat, and wanted to come with us, we could count on them to push as hard as us to get the boat round first. You do not want a crew that has to be spurred on the whole time, you want a crew who are leaping in ahead, as this makes you push harder yourself, and the end result is a faster boat. Motivation in this respect includes determination and a commitment to success. We used to have a motto on *Frigate* that said 'Winning is not everything, but coming second is nothing'. One cannot always win—there are times when one must accept defeat, however unpalatable it may be—but a person who is really motivated to win stands a much better chance of crossing the finishing line first, and that surely is the whole reason why one enters a race in the first place.

So our crew would be selected for their sailing experience, determination, compatibility and sense of humour, but above all else, their desire to be on the winning boat.

It is partly because I do not believe that you should make things too easy for people that we decided that the crew would pay their way as far as food was concerned. Bob would have paid the food bills, but I came out against it, for if everything is given to a person he seems to lose the feeling of responsibility towards the boat and the race, and adopts the attitude of pampered pet. If people have had to pay, even just for their food, they feel that they have made some contribution to the project, and they feel more involved and more committed as a result. In fact our crew had to pay for their food and clothing, the bill at the end of the day coming to about nine hundred pounds a head for the whole race. The sum did not include spending money in port, just what was required from each person for what we as the crew decided we wanted to eat and wear.

Our crew was going to have to be made up of a hard core who would do the the whole race, and about three each leg who would be on board for one leg only. We were inundated with requests to crew the boat by people who wanted to do odd legs, but again we largely chose those we knew.

By the end of May the crew selection had been completed and we were arranging crew uniforms, inoculations, photographs and potted histories for Race Control. Les and I had started the crew selection by making a list of the positions we wanted to fill, which were: mate, two more watch leaders, a doctor, sailmaker, radio operator and engineer, all of whom had to have sailing experience. We decided to have an all-male crew, as had we taken females with us there was always the risk of attachments developing during long periods at sea, and although this is very pleasant for the affected parties, it is unfair on the remainder of the crew and can lead to rows and ill-feeling which could affect the performance of everyone. One can always say that it will not happen, but having served on passenger ships, I have observed that it often does.

The most important person, since Les and I would be skippering alternate legs, was the mate. We needed someone whom we both knew who would provide continuity and act as crew boss. When we discussed this appointment it was quite obvious that we both had someone in mind, so I told Les I was for Peter Blake, the twenty-nine-year-old New Zealander who had sailed with us both on *Ocean Spirit* in the 1974 Round Britain Race. Peter is aggressive when it comes to sailing, a hard worker, and at six foot four inches tall, very strong. Les said that he had been about to suggest Peter anyway, so that was settled. Our next problem was to find him. I had last heard of him in Beirut, skippering a large yacht, but this had been about the time of the beginning of the Lebanese problems, and

I did not know where he had got to since. Les thought he was back in Auckland, so we sent a cable out to a local spar-making company who we thought would know him, and got a reply back almost immediately saying 'Yes'. The reason for the quick reply, we discovered, was that Peter was working for the company. We arranged that he would come to England in June so that he would be around during the fitting out stage to give a hand. In fact, when the time came both Les and I were very busy, and Peter took charge.

We next turned our attention to finding two more watch leaders. We contacted all the people we knew who might fit the bill, and got the men we wanted, Julian Gildersleeves and Chris Edwards (the latter better known as the Major because he had been in the army).

Julian had worked for me in my boatyard at Hamble and later had been part of *Burton Cutter*'s crew, and stayed with her when as *Kriter II* she had taken part in the *Financial Times* Round the World Race of 1975/6. He was currently skippering her in the south of France. Although not particularly tall, Julian is strong, has a very calm disposition, and has packed a great deal of experience into his twenty-eight years. He is also very good at fixing broken things like radios, engines and instruments, and his acceptance meant we had our engineer as well.

Chris Edwards, aged thirty-five, was working out in Saudi Arabia when we found him. He also had been a part of *Burton Cutter*'s crew. Perhaps he had had enough for a while of burning, waterless sands, and the contrast appealed to him, but he accepted, and we had, although we did not realise it at the time, one of the real characters of the crew.

Recruiting a doctor proved surprisingly easy. Most young doctors are hard at work at their careers, and it is not simple for them to take time off. We found David Dickson through Larry Baker, who had built a boat for his father, Wilfred, a rare bird who had started life in the Merchant Navy, got his master's ticket, and then decided to become a doctor himself. David was twenty-three and had not yet qualified, but was due to take his finals in May. Working on the principle that as he was working hard for his examinations, his theoretical knowledge at least would be up to date, and the fact that both his parents were doctors so some of his home environment must have rubbed off on him, we accepted him subject to his exam results being positive. Fortunately for us all, they were, and we had another of our positions filled.

Finding a sailmaker was a little more difficult, but I bumped into Chris Ratsey and he told me of one of his young employees who was keen to find a berth for the race. Paul Newell was twenty-two, a bit younger than we were looking for, but he has a fairly serious and responsible outlook on life. He is a native of the Isle of Wight, and like so many others from 'the Island' had grown up in boats. Chris vouched for him, and we never had cause to question his recommendation. We arranged for Paul to leave work at the end of June and go to work with Butler Verner for a couple of weeks so that he could be there when our sails were being finished—the idea being that he should acquaint himself with any differences between their methods and those of Ratsey's before we left.

We had tremendous difficulty in enlisting a radio operator. I started out by asking Marconi if they had anyone they would like to release but they were not interested. The Navy came next, but they said that anyone good enough for us was going in one of their crews on *Adventure*. This exhausted our search for a professional who could listen in to the morse traffic and get us weather reports. We decided that we would have to find a gifted amateur, and if necessary help his talents by means of a two-speed tape recorder. I mentioned our requirement to Captain Norman, the Race Secretary, and one day he phoned to say that although he did not have a radio operator on his list of people looking for a berth, he did have a British Airways pilot named Graham Carpenter who might just be 'trainable'. I took the name and address and wrote off. The reply was prompt, and we arranged a meeting in London. Graham was thirty, had sailed quite a lot in Scotland, and said his morse was rusty but he would brighten it up. Les and I liked him from the outset and offered him a place in the crew. The fact that he had dropped everything to come and see us proved his keenness, but we found out later that he had all the qualities that make for a good companion in a small boat. Within a very short space of time his name was changed to Golf Charlie by the rest of the crew, the two phonetic letters for his initials, because he had to make so much use of the phonetic alphabet when using the radio.

The last member of the crew to join us from our circle of sailing friends was David Alan-Williams, who had been on *Burton Cutter* and now was working for Jeremy Rogers in Lymington. David was one of the last to arrive because he was part of the crew of *Moonshine* in the 1977 British Admiral's Cup team. He joined after the Fastnet Race with his sail trimming expertise well brightened by a hard summer's successful racing.

John Sharp introduced me to Herman Vanura, an ex-German Naval Officer, who had done his training in the German Navy's square rigger. I was not at all sure that we ought to introduce one foreigner into what was basically a British, or British and New Zealand crew, but Herman seemed willing enough to accept this, and he had plenty of sea experience, and I felt that another professional seaman on board would be no bad thing. Herman's English was excellent—in fact those who tried to crack a joke at his expense soon discovered to their cost that his knowledge of colloquial English was as good as anyone else's on board. He was hardworking, willing, and had a great sense of humour, and I always attach great importance to the latter.

Graham Pearson was a twenty-seven-year-old trainee accountant who was about to qualify, having entered accountancy from university where he had captained the sailing team. He was sufficiently keen to throw up his job, although I was not at all sure that was a good thing to do—obtaining leave of absence would have been a wiser choice; it is what I used to get from my employers when I wanted to go sailing when I was at sea. He was the first of the crew to arrive, and I arranged for him to spend some time with Butler Verner as there was little else for him to do, and the experience of sailmaking would come in useful later. He also helped me with the clothing and food procurement, and very soon, because of his profession, found himself appointed treasurer of the crew account.

The last member of what one might call the permanent crew was an eighteen-year-old named Justin Smart. He came with us because of his sheer persistence. He started writing to us the moment the news was out about the boat, but we thought he was too young. Eventually, six months and five letters later, we agreed to interview him and we told him we thought he was too young. Politely he asked us why that should count against him and we said that he was not old enough yet to have found out what life was worth, and we were worried that he would take unnecessary risks through lack of experience. He said he did not think that was necessarily the case, and he was mature enough. The discussion carried on for half an hour and eventually Les and I decided we would take him as we liked his style. Justin joined up as soon as he had finished his 'A' levels at school and we never regretted our decision to take him along.

For the first leg Andy Cully, a Customs Officer who had sailed on *Burton Cutter*, and John Carter, who had managed St Katharine's Yacht Haven with me and subsequently built Troon Marina with me, were enrolled. Herman was meant to be first leg only, but we had a vacancy in Cape Town, and as he was the reserve crewman he stayed on with the boat. In Cape Town we added Les Best, a New Zealand engineer and friend of Peter Blake, who also remained the rest of the voyage; Barry Buchannan, a car salesman who had sailed on *Burton Cutter* and who stayed with us as far as Rio; Bill Abram from Scotland where he worked in the family paper business; and Ronnie Roos, a South African solicitor. On the third leg, Roddy Coleman, one of my partners at Troon; Peter Visick, an engineer from Falmouth; and Allan Prior, a New Zealand accountant, filled out the crew, and on the final leg Allan Prior stayed with us, and Ianto Jones, a Welshman who skippered a charter boat in Scotland, joined the boat.

We had finished programming our crew when we suddenly had a message that an American had arrived in London to sign on. No one knew anything about him, but we subsequently discovered that a colleague of Bob's had sent him over. Jack Keyhoe came from San Francisco, and was reputed to be an experienced sailor, and to avoid any difficulties we took him.

Originally all the crew were asked to report by the last week in June, but as May progressed it became obvious that if they arrived then, there would be no boat to sail. Larry now said that it would not be ready until August, which was totally unacceptable, but he supported his claim by saying that there would not be sufficient depth of water to launch her before the end of August. I felt that this point could have been raised before, but there had to be a way round it. We considered, with Joe Brooks, a diving and salvage expert, lifting the boat with flotation bags, but eventually plumped for launching her without a keel which removed all the arguments about tidal heights, and we would fit the keel round at Port Hamble boatyard of which I was a director. All sorts of problems were raised of course, most of them perfectly valid, but the fact remained that we had to have the boat in time for some trials, which we then planned would consist of Cowes Week and the Fastnet Race. It would be unwise and unseamanlike to set off around the world in an untried boat, so we simply had to have the boat launched during July, and even that gave us little enough time.

Once a deadline has been set, I think it concentrates people's minds, and they automatically start to programme their work loads so that they can be finished on time. There was still a great deal to do. The interior work was hardly started, the deck was not finished and we still awaited drawings for the deck structure which was to be made of aluminium by Bowman's. The immersed part of the hull was cascovered in early June to protect it further, but the topsides were left clear for varnishing which, because Bowman's did not have the men available, was done by Peter, Julian, Graham, Justin and Jack, who later on also filled and anti-fouled the bottom. We fixed up a caravan in Emsworth for them to live in whilst they were working on the boat.

As we entered July things began to come together. As fast as Jess, the welder at Bowman's, finished pieces of coaming, winches and cleats were fitted. The deck was all laid in marine plywood and a full layer of glass fibre put over it before the Treadmaster non-slip surface was put on top. Below decks, Malcolm, the foreman, was fitting tanks and piping. We had six water tanks in all, two in each cabin under the pipe cots, and these were piped through to a twenty-five-gallon feeder tank by the gallery. We considered putting in an electric pump to top up this tank, but decided that a hand pump would be preferable. Because it is harder to work, people are less willing to pump it, and therefore we would use less water.

Along the keel inside the boat a great aluminium backbone

was being bolted together; this served three purposes. It acted as a stronger series of floors along the centre of the boat; it gave a strong point to which the seventeen-ton keel would be bolted; and it acted as an anchor for some large aluminium straps that connected it with the chain plates. Ever since during my first trip in *Suhaili* from Bombay to Muscat, when the hull had opened up because the strain upwards of the rigging was not firmly connected to the downwards pull of the keel, I have made a slight fetish of seeing that these two opposite strains are connected.

We decided not to make too much of the launching because the boat was going into the water without keel and masts; we considered that a commissioning party would be more appropriate. On 20th July, with all the crew in attendance, Bob Bell's wife Dee cracked a bottle of champagne over the bow and christened the boat *Condor*. The name had been decided upon long before when we had first got together. We felt that a big bird's name would be suitable, and for a while considered 'Albatross' as that is the largest sea bird. But it has been used before, so we looked for another bird and the only larger one was the condor which lives mainly in Peru and has up to an eleven-foot wing span. Having decided on the name, we thought we would use the bird as our insignia, and I wrote to Sir Peter Scott and asked if he would draw the bird for us, just as he had done for *Frigate* four years before. The drawings that arrived a couple of weeks later were magnificent and we had them printed on our T-shirts as badges, and enormous ones put on the spinnakers. To carry the big bird theme even further, we discovered that K707 was a free sail number at the Royal Ocean Racing Club; perhaps 747 would have been better but we were quite satisfied.

Once *Condor* had been launched she motored under her own power for the first time round to Port Hamble where a large crane had been ordered to lift her up and over the keel which was held in place on the big slipway. The keel was made of a steel shell filled with lead, and had made a long journey from Falmouth to be joined up. Despite the fact that the two parts had been made two hundred miles apart, all fourteen keel bolts fitted through the holes in the hull and were soon bolted on firmly. We had planned to be off the slipway as soon as possible to get across to Spencer's at Cowes to be rigged, but the mast had only arrived that week, and although it was in Cowes the rigging was not yet ready, so we stayed on the slip and improved the finish on the hull.

The mast had looked most impressive when I first saw it on two railway wagons in Southampton docks. Measuring ninety-three feet and painted orange, it had, unlike most masts, a very noticeable taper along its whole length, and when lifted on slings bent a great deal. For one used to wood or aluminium masts, the way this one bent was most alarming, but we had been warned that this would happen and were not too worried. It was incredibly light and four of us could lift it.

The mast was eventually ready to be stepped on Wednesday, 4th August, in the middle of Cowes Week. We motored over to Cowes in the morning and by lunchtime our mast was clearly visible sticking up way above everything else. We motored to the Trinity House wharf, and for the rest of the afternoon we worked away at setting up all the rigging. The following day we motored back to Hamble, swinging the compass on the way, and got on with finishing the boat and preparing for the Fastnet Race which was all that was left for us by way of work up.

Before we could do any racing, however, we had to be measured for our Rating Certificate under the International Offshore Rule. Much of this measurement had already been carried out whilst the boat was on the slipway, but waterline lengths and breadths, freeboard and stability could not be measured until we were in the water with the mast stepped and sails on board. This was carried out on Friday by the Royal Ocean Racing Club, and the results came through the following week, so we started the race with a provisional rating. John Sharp had estimated that our rating would be about sixty-five feet, and in fact we came out just above this at 66.8 feet owing to the lighter mast which gave us more stability. We were somewhat surprised to learn that although this was our rating, we had an extra three per cent mast correction factor because we had a mast made of an exotic material. This meant that our rating would be 68.8 feet. Apart from the fact that no one had mentioned that the carbon fibre mast would cause us to have a penalty, it seemed to us that we were being penalised twice, once because our rating went up due to our lighter mast which gave more stability, and then an exotic penalty because the mast was lighter than aluminium.

Our crew for the Fastnet was augmented by a number of people: some of the crew who would be with us for various legs, Bob himself, who despite a busy schedule was not going to miss the first real sail, and a team from Southern Television—in all a total of twenty-one. We did not expect wonders from the race, but we hoped to be able to sort out the boat and perhaps be lucky enough to take line honours. There was some good competition. *Great Britain II*, one of our competitors in the forthcoming Round the World Race, was entered, and there were large boats from Italy and Australia, so we had plenty of boats to work up against.

Because of the large numbers of boats that enter the Fastnet Race, the start is staggered and the biggest boats start last, which was a relief as there were not too many of them, and I did not fancy the rapid manoeuvring necessary in a competitive start with a brand-new boat and crew who were still organising sheets. The wind at the start was moderate southwesterly, and we tacked down the Solent, slowly working through the smaller boats. The wind began to die and it did not rise properly again for six days. The 1977 Fastnet Race was one of the slowest on record; it became a drifting match with most boats spending hours becalmed with next to no movement. This was not what we wanted at all. We wanted plenty of wind to try out everything under strain, to see that nothing would break, but we just did not get it. We were fortieth round the Fastnet Rock, which even accepting that it was our maiden voyage was very poor. Slightly more wind on the way back helped us to gain a little, but we finished third, an hour behind the first boat home, *Ballyhoo* of Australia, and half an hour behind the Italian *Moro de Venezia*.

The race did not enable us to find out how *Condor* would behave in rough weather, but it did give us some encouragement. No boat can move without wind, but the moment we got a little breeze *Condor* picked up speed very quickly. All the gear and equipment had behaved well, apart from the aluminium main boom, which was not strong enough, and we had been a little worried to see the way the top panel of the mast had bent in a breeze. Peter Ramage from Vickers was with us for the race and he had watched the mast closely the whole way. He felt that the amount of bend was acceptable and to be expected from the material, which was reassuring. The crew had come together well, there had been no discordant notes, and Les and I were confident that, with more sailing time, we would have a good team.

We had one week before we had to be at HMS *Vernon*. Ideally we would have liked to have spent a fair proportion of this week at sea, but there was far too much to do. Apart from ordering a new main boom, we also chased the four aluminium spreaders which could fit either the carbon fibre or aluminium mast. We had knocked out some temporary spreaders, but they were round instead of the more efficient aerofoil shape which we had ordered with the aluminium mast.

You cannot set off on a 7,500-mile voyage which will probably take at least five weeks without a great deal of preparation. Every item that you would normally need in a home over five weeks has to be listed, ordered, delivered or collected, and if anything has been forgotten there is no nipping down the road to the nearest supermarket—you just have to go without until the voyage has ended. Chris Edwards had offered to take on the job of organising the stores for the first leg, a thankless task which seldom gets the praise it deserves. We had been collecting food for some time, and had been fortunate to receive gifts from a number of firms, among which were Ryvita, Anglia Canners, Smedley HP, Batchelors, Booker Health Foods and Jacquet, but we still had a huge shopping list for the local supermarket. The task of storing the boat was really too big for one man in just over a week and Chris was fortunate to get the full-time help of Jane Blakemore, Midge Young and Midge Culley. Much of the food was stowed on board before *Condor* went to HMS *Vernon*, but the fresh food was left to the last moment.

We now knew that there were to be fifteen starters on 27th August. Of these, six were British: *Condor, Great Britain II, King's Legend, ADC Accutrac, Debenhams* and *Adventure*. Two were from Holland: *Flyer* and *Tielsa*. One was a European Community entry, *Treaty of Rome*, which had the unique national identification letters of EUR 1. The Swiss entered a Swan 65, *Disque D'Or*; the Italians *B & B Italia*; and the

French *Neptune, 33 Export, Japy Hermes* and *Gauloises II*. In addition *Pen Duik VI* was due to enter the race in Auckland, although Les and I were not satisfied with the Race Committee's assurances about her rating. We had our three per cent penalty for having a mast made of an exotic material, and we could not see why *Pen Duik VI* did not carry a penalty for her exotic keel made of exhausted uranium, a material twice as heavy as lead which meant she could have a smaller keel, and therefore less water resistance, for the same weight.

The boat we had to beat was *Great Britain II*, skippered by Rob James, a slightly larger boat with a proven record even if she was four years old and this was to be her third circumnavigation. Boats we felt we would have to watch were *Flyer*, a new Sparkman and Stephens boat launched in April, which had been working up ever since, and *King's Legend*, a Swan 65 with a very tall sloop rig. But of course in a race, especially a long one, anything can happen, and one cannot afford to ignore any of the competition.

Shortly before the race started, *Condor* was rechristened *Heath's Condor* by Mrs Holland, wife of the chairman of C. E. Heath, the Lloyd's insurance brokers. It was quite a simple ceremony, but we had a large power boat alongside for a party afterwards which everyone enjoyed. During the final week a number of firms contacted us about possible sponsorship, not all of them from Britain, but Bob decided to go for Heath's offer, as he ran the marine side of their business.

2. PORTSMOUTH TO CAPE TOWN

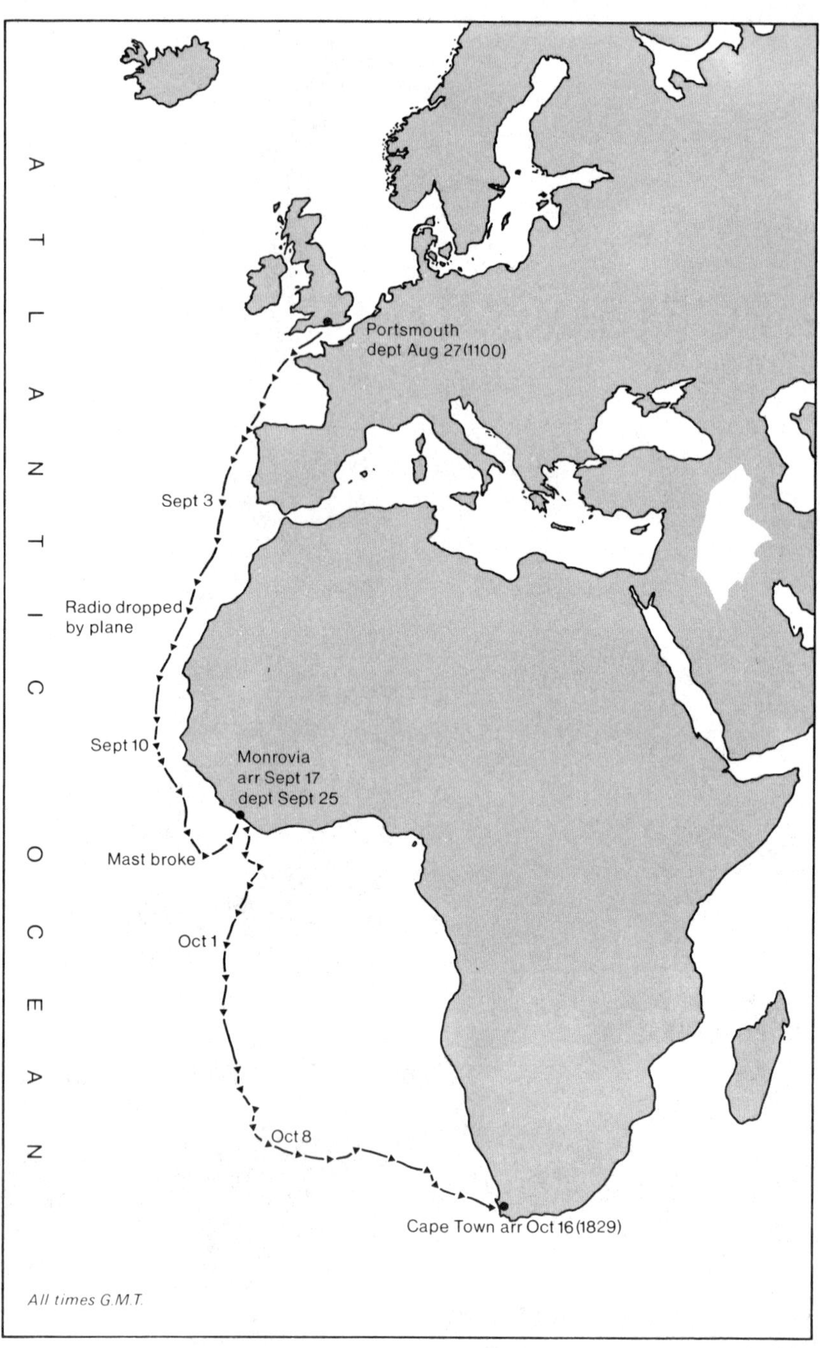
ATLANTIC OCEAN
Portsmouth
dept Aug 27(1100)
Sept 3
Radio dropped
by plane
Sept 10
Monrovia
arr Sept 17
dept Sept 25
Mast broke
Oct 1
Oct 8
Cape Town arr Oct 16(1829)
All times G.M.T.

Heath's Condor had been far from ready when we sailed her round to HMS *Vernon* in Portsmouth to join the other competitors a week before the race was due to start. For the lucky crews who had had time to get their boats worked up, this last week was a merry social occasion. For us and a few others, it was a last-minute rush to get the boat finished. As most of the crew had been working pretty solidly for a couple of months, we made this weekend a free one so that they could spend some time with their families, but they all had to report back on board first thing on Monday morning; to their credit, everyone did.

While Chris Edwards fussed over his catering supplies and where to store them, Julian took us through the Race Committee's scrutiny, an inspection to check that we had all the necessary life-saving, radio, and other safety equipment on board, and the rest of us got on with finishing off the boat. We still had no proper mast spreaders although they were promised; we also awaited a new, stronger main boom. Deck leads and cleats had to be positioned, the navigation instruments needed adjusting, the radio needed to be checked out by the GPO, the deep freeze had still to be connected up, no one could make the generator work, and so on and so on.

By Friday evening, when most of the competitors were beginning to complain about the constant round of parties, we were almost ready apart from the spreaders, and they arrived at 19.00, and then only one, not two sets. We debated leaving them off as we were all tired and there were only seventeen hours left until the start, and if we did change them all the rigging would have to be set up again. But they would improve the efficiency of the rig, so, while the crew had a last supper at the Dolphin Hotel, Malcolm from Bowman's, Roger from David Carne Hydraulics and I removed the upper spreaders, fitted the new ones in their place and then swopped the lowers around. We finished at 04.00. Peter turned to at 07.00 and retuned the rigging—not exactly a job to be doing five hours before the start of a race.

At the skippers' briefing two days before the start we had been assured that this time the start area would be kept clear for competitors only. But when Les motored out of Portsmouth harbour at 11.00, he could hardly make his way through the vast fleet of spectator craft. Eventually he got up to the line as the fifteen-minute gun went at 11.45. *Heath's Condor* motored back from the line, hanking on the No. 1 genoa as a panic sail, and preparing a spinnaker for hoisting. At 11.53 Les put her about and thirty seconds after the five-minute gun the spinnaker broke out. Watching from another boat my heart was in my mouth, for there is nothing worse than being early over the line and having to get all the sails in somehow and go back to recross it again. I need not have worried; Les had timed it perfectly and *Heath's Condor* creamed across the start line making eight knots about five seconds after the start gun had sounded.

Within minutes a gap had opened between *Heath's Condor* and the rest of the fleet as they headed for the only mark of the course, Bembridge Ledge Buoy. The blooper was hoisted after clearing the Forts, but could not be left up long as the wind backed and the spinnaker had to be gybed. By the time the fleet were passing St Catherine's lighthouse on the southern side of the Isle of Wight, *Heath's Condor* had worked up a lead of about two to three miles over her nearest rival, *Great Britain II*, and the rest of the fleet were spread out astern. The race had begun at last, and as I watched the fifteen yachts sail off into the south-west, I could not help wishing I was with them on the 7,500-mile leg to Cape Town.

To follow the sailing ship route to Cape Town, one heads west from the English Channel until one clears Cape Finisterre, the north-westernmost point of Spain, and then one tacks and heads south until the full north-east Trade winds are picked up about the same latitude as Gibraltar. In a modern racing yacht which can sail much closer to the wind, it is usual to head straight across the Channel for Ushant, and then steer across the Bay of Biscay to Finisterre. The only reason for not doing this would be because of a bad forecast. Once round Finisterre fresh northerly winds are usually experienced down the Portuguese coast and these carry one very nicely into the north-east Trade winds. The Trade winds carry one down to the Doldrums, an area of calms which lies around the Equator, separating the north-east Trade winds in the northern hemisphere from the south-east Trade winds of the southern hemisphere. After the light weather work of the Doldrums, the boat is hard on the wind in the Trades for the final 2,500 miles to Cape Town. The total distance is 7,500 miles and should take from five to six weeks depending upon your luck with the Doldrums.

After dropping St Catherine's light astern, the last sight of England that many of the crew could expect for a good few months, Les set a course straight for a point ten miles off Ushant, and handed over to the watches.

The first night at sea is always an exciting one. No one really wants to go below and sleep as they have not got into a routine, and they hang around on deck, leaping willingly to tackle any job that comes along. It is all very well having this enthusiasm—the trouble is that come midnight when the watches are due to change, the new watch is tired instead of being refreshed by four hours' sleep. In part this is probably due, for many of the crew, to the change in environment, but I think even the most experienced sailor feels some sense of excitement at the start of another long voyage. You are off at sea at last, all the hard work and preparation is done, and the feeling of anticipation that has been building up in the preceding weeks has to have some form of release. Normally by the second day things are beginning to sort themselves out, people have settled into their bunks and stored their gear around them, and can start finding out where everything is stowed.

I usually allow for not having all the crew available for the first two days, as some people take a day or two to adjust to being in a heaving, rolling home, and even if they are not physically sick, the motion makes them feel tired. Of course to a certain extent our crew had been able to adjust during the Fastnet Race, and symptoms of seasickness were not apparent. Being one of those fortunate people who does not suffer from seasickness, at least not since my first trip to sea in the Merchant Navy, I have always felt sorry for those who do. It is not a sign of physical or mental weakness, just a question of luck as to whether you do feel sick or not, and usually after a couple of days the body adjusts and you feel all right for the rest of the trip. I always console sufferers with the thought that Nelson was seasick for his first few days at sea, and try and give them a complicated job on deck that requires concentration and makes them think of other things. The worst possible action is to lie on your bunk—somehow the motion seems worse below, and the inevitable bilge and other unpleasant shipboard odours do not help. There is one consolation: a sailing boat is much steadier than a power-driven vessel; it may be heeled over, but the wind pressure on the sails takes most of the rolling out of the motion.

At daybreak on the second day, the boat was tacking off Ushant in very light airs, trying to beat round into the Bay of Biscay. One thing was very quickly becoming obvious; our plan for three watches of four people did not give enough men on deck at a time to tack the boat efficiently, and Les decided to reduce to two watches led by Peter Blake and Julian so that there were at least six men on deck at any time. Watch on, watch off is hard work, but to break it up the day was divided into two six-hour watches from 08.00 till 14.00 and 14.00 till 20.00, and the night which is colder was divided into three four-hour watches. This meant that a watch was on duty at different times every other day and gave the crew some variety.

Ushant is not a particularly nice place to be becalmed as it is a point for which all North European shipping heads both inwards and outwards, and the last thing a yachtsman likes is to be slow moving in the middle of a mass of commercial traffic. With depressing slowness *Heath's Condor* tacked her way clear of the shipping lanes and round the corner into the Bay of Biscay. If there was any consolation it was that the other boats in the race would be similarly affected, and the only sails in sight were astern, the nearest of them, of *Great Britain II*, about seven miles away.

For the next four days, light variable winds were experienced as the boat slowly made her way across the Bay of Biscay. The Bay of Biscay has a bad reputation for weather because when it blows, a boat within the Bay has a lee shore in any wind from south-westerly to northerly, and the seas are short and steep. When the wind is not blowing, the Bay is just like any other sea area, calm with a low ground swell that comes in from the Atlantic. Contrary to popular belief, it is these calm conditions which give a crew the most work, as the sails have to be trimmed to every slight variation in wind direction, or changed if the strength varies by more than a few knots, and all this work is being done for very little progress.

Between noon on 31st August and noon on 1st September the boat covered only thirty-five miles in frustrating conditions off Finisterre. The light floating spinnaker, which was the right sail for the wind, was hoisted early on but ripped almost immediately when it caught on the rigging as the boat rolled in the swell. For nearly the whole twenty-four hours sails were changed to suit each little puff of wind in the hope that it would prove to be the beginning of a steady wind at last. All the time, at regular intervals, came the crash of the mainsail banging over from one side to another, causing the whole boat to vibrate and preventing the off-watch crew from obtaining their much-needed sleep.

It is sometimes possible in these conditions to move weight in the form of sails, stores and people over to one side to give the boat a list. If the sails are also flopped over on one side so that they take up a slight aerodynamic shape, the effect will be to give a little power the moment some wind appears. Once some motion has been achieved the boat's passage through the air creates a wind that can further help to produce momentum and eventually the boat is able to sail at three or four knots purely on the wind generated by its own movement. This will work in a calm sea, when the boat can be held reasonably steady for a while, but in a swell, as soon as the boat is settled and a small breeze is beginning to work on the sails, the boat rolls, the sails are thrown aback and all movement is lost. The result is that you can never even get started, and you are tempted to take all the sails down to save wear and tear, except that you are racing and your conscience would never allow you to do this. So the boat drifts, sails slatting, and the only consolation for everyone on this occasion was that a school of whales appeared during the night, providing a welcome distraction.

Still, there were some advantages from having light weather: there was ample opportunity to finish off a lot of the jobs that had not been completed in the mad rush before the start. It also meant that conditions were easier for the crew struggling to put right all the inevitable faults that developed which would normally have been sorted out by the boatyard before the boat was handed over. At times it seemed to Les that he was being overwhelmed by the trivial things that kept going wrong, and as fast as he sorted out one problem, another appeared. During the first two weeks of the race he spent more time fault finding and effecting repairs than he did actually sailing, and the temptation just to sail and ignore the electrical, mechanical and structural problems must have been very strong.

During this painfully slow progress across the Bay of Biscay, Les had been trying to report in on the radio, but was having considerable difficulty with the set. Sometimes he was able to get through loud and clear and on other occasions he could pick up nothing. After two days of trying to raise Portishead unsuccessfully, he decided to close Corunna and see whether he could get through to me via the port VHF system. He was eventually successful and was able to explain that the tuning had gone on the receiver. We arranged that he would try and maintain contact with *Great Britain II* on VHF and I would get messages through to him that way while he sorted out the problem. I contacted Race Control and explained that Les would not be able to report his position directly as required from then on, and discussed the possibility of sending a replacement unit to be picked up in Las Palmas. This was the nearest large port to the proposed route which meant that the boat would deviate as little as possible from course. Bob Bell decided that with *Heath's Condor* in the lead we did not want to lose any time and the answer was to have a replacement receiver put on board by helicopter as the boat passed Teneriffe. Race Control agreed to this provided the transfer was carried out within territorial waters, which were defined as fifty miles. I asked them if they could have a message sent to Les to inform him of this decision and they agreed. Although the message was sent to *Great Britain II* it was never passed on to Les, who in the meantime had rounded Finisterre and was beginning to pick up speed down the Portuguese coast, occasionally being reported by *Great Britain II* or *King's Legend* who were in VHF contact.

The boat was obviously doing well to keep ahead of *Great Britain II*, and in fact Les was widening the gap slowly day by day. Some of the other competitors though, like *King's Legend* and *Flyer* and the other two Swan 65s, *Disque D'Or* and *ADC Accutrac*, were keeping up well, and it was quite obvious that everyone was treating this as a real race and pushing their boats as hard as they could, instead of holding back a little to reduce wear and tear. In the 1973 race people had worried more about gear failures, and had worked much more on the principle that it was all very well to race hard, but if anything broke it would be a major job to make repairs. This time the attitude was much more one of pushing hard the whole time as there had not in fact been that many breakages on the previous race.

I could not help comparing this press-on approach, typical of round-the-buoys racing in the Solent, with the cautious way I had sailed down the Atlantic on my own in *Suhaili* eight years before. One obvious difference was that I had been on a non-stop circumnavigation attempt then, and a major breakage would have made the difference between success and failure, but even though these boats had only a quarter of the distance to cover in one hop, they were still pressing on with racing rather than cruising determination. A lot had happened to attitudes to round the world sailing since *Suhaili* and I had struggled back into Falmouth after 312 days at sea in 1969.

Heath's Condor picked up the Trade winds just north of Gibraltar, and her speed southwards began to increase. The fleet had been quite close together at Finisterre, not surprising with the light winds that everyone had experienced, and in fact one night another boat had been sighted close to, thought to have been *King's Legend*.

As we were unable to get the message through to Les regarding the radio, we could only hope that as he approached Teneriffe he would call me. In the meantime, we had a new receiver sent out to Las Palmas and a helicopter was put on standby.

At 22.30 on Tuesday, 6th September Les came through via Santa Cruz port radio station and I was able to explain the arrangements. Les made contact with the Lloyd's agent in Las Palmas who said that the helicopter would be with him by 08.00. A schedule was arranged for 07.00 so that the boat's position could be passed on to the pilot.

Ideally, helicopters like to lower things so that there is no risk of an entanglement; a yacht hove-to is likely to roll quite a lot, so to avoid risk it is usual to trail a dinghy well astern and make any deliveries or collections into it. Justin and Jack were put in the dinghy at the end of a two-hundred-yard tow line, but it took five attempts before the receiver was safely unhooked. The pilot did not wait to take a package that had been prepared to send home—as soon as the receiver was on board he gave a wave and was off. The dinghy had been blown all over the place by the down draught from the helicopter, and Jack and Justin were like drowned rats when they were hauled back on board.

The next day the receiver was installed, and with great ceremony switched on. Almost unbelievably it was duff as well. Whereas in the previous set the digital readout had moved but no tuning took place, in the new one tuning took place but the digital readout did not work, so they had very little idea of which frequency they were listening to. Eventually it became possible to tune the set roughly, but we did not think we were getting our five thousand pounds' worth from it.

The new radio had been delivered within the restrictions imposed by the Race Committee, although they subsequently changed their terms which was a bit unsporting, and Les had lost hardly any time. Once clear of the lee of Teneriffe he was back into the Trades and continued to pull out on the other boats.

Trade wind sailing is probably the most pleasant sailing one can have. The wind is relatively steady in direction and strength, usually averaging about force four. The Trade wind belts lie between about five and thirty degrees north and south of the Equator, so are generally warm and allow a crew to sail in very little clothing; if one does get wet, one quickly dries in the warm winds. Herman delighted everyone by shaving his head once the Trades were reached; this let him in for a fair share of good-natured ragging, but fortunately his English was fluent enough for him to give as good as he got.

Down below, however, the warmer weather was not so popular as it was discovered that the ventilation system refused to function at all, and sleeping was almost impossible in the small, hot, airless cabins. In desperation an electric saw was produced and two holes cut in the deck above the forward crew cabins, and hatches were fitted over them to allow more air below, but it was still not circulating properly. The saw came out again and holes were cut in the bulkheads between the cabins to try and create a draught through them. It was sheer butchery, but a crew who are trying to put all they can into racing a boat must sleep properly. The alternative was to sleep on deck, but there are not many places where a person can lie out safely, and not be disturbed by the other watch working the boat.

The Trades also gave Les an opportunity to find out just how well *Heath's Condor* compared with *Burton Cutter* in a following wind. So far we were fairly convinced that we had a better windward boat, but we wanted to discover whether she would break through the natural barrier imposed on all craft for their top speeds. This is roughly the square root of the waterline length times a factor which varies from boat to boat, but can be taken on average to be 1.4. This formula gave *Heath's Condor* a theoretical top speed of 11.29 knots, and to drive her any faster, an almost impossible increase in power would be required. *Burton Cutter*, however, had for some reason been very easy to drive through this limit and we had hoped that by going to the same designer, he would be able to repeat the magic. Unfortunately it did not appear that *Heath's Condor* had the same ability, and perhaps we had expected too much. To have produced an exception to a well established and tried rule once in a lifetime was miracle enough; to hope to repeat it was being over-optimistic. *Heath's Condor* would drive up to eleven knots easily, but to get her to go any faster, except in a brief surf down a wave, proved impossible. Trying to press her by holding on to all the sails when the wind rose did not increase the speed, it just made the boat very difficult to control and risked breaking the gear.

Just occasionally twelve knots was exceeded, but only when the boat caught a good size following wave, and began to surf. In these conditions the log once showed as high as twenty knots, but after the wave had passed it fell back to eleven or twelve again.

On 8th September, when about twenty degrees north, the first flying fish were sighted, much further south than usual. They are not really flying fish in the sense that they can flap their wings to give themselves movement through the air. They are gliding fish, and achieve flight by swimming rapidly towards the surface and extending their delicate, almost transparent wings once they break surface. They cannot stay out of the water for too long, as their wings dry and harden and become unusable, so their glides are usually of only fifteen- to thirty-foot duration. They normally only fly to escape predators, but of course to them a boat looks like a potential enemy, so they often take off as a boat approaches. Their sense of direction cannot be all that good out of the water, as they frequently glide straight into the boat they are trying to avoid, and if the freeboard is low enough, they will land on deck and provide a very tasty breakfast.

Whilst the boat was still in the north-east Trades, Les called all the crew together and pointed out that the next few days would be the last chance to practise running and gybing before the Southern Ocean. He set up one or two drills so that people could have a good think about what had to be done and how best they played their own part in it. The subsequent conference led to the construction of one or two new items of equipment to make gybing safer, like permanent wire main boom fore guys kept lashed along the boom when not in use, which were to prove a godsend in the Southern Ocean.

The north-east Trades began to ease on 9th September when the boat was lying about fourteen degrees north and twenty degrees west, and the wind became light and variable. They had reached the Doldrums at last and the only person who was in the slightest way pleased was Paul Newell, the sailmaker, who had had to work pretty solidly for the previous ten days repairing spinnakers and bloopers, all of which were proving a bit lightweight for the boat. On one of his radio schedules Les mentioned this, and I ordered an extra, special heavy, full-sized spinnaker to be sent out to Cape Town.

On 10th September, when there was no longer any doubt that the Doldrums had been reached, Les decided to give morale a boost by holding a 'two weeks at sea party'. Chris Edwards, the Major, mixed a vicious brew of which the whole crew partook unwisely and too well, with the result that most of them were suffering from hangovers the next morning. These were soon sweated out as a south-east force two became a northerly force one, and then anything from nothing to thirty-five-knot rain squalls prevailed. The only consolation with this sort of weather is that it is possible to have a proper wash in the rain squalls.

The sun can be intensely hot near the Equator, and if a crew have not slowly tanned themselves whilst passing through the north-east Trades, severe sun burn and even heat stroke can be experienced. When I first went to sea as an apprentice, the 'first trippers' were forced to keep themselves covered when working on deck, as the average English skin is not accustomed to such intense heat. Once we had achieved a reasonable sun tan, which was usually a deep nut brown, we were allowed to do deck work without shirts and wearing shorts instead of jeans, but we were told when we had reached this point. Even the senior apprentices, though, were forced to wear sun hats. One has to see that people allow themselves to burn brown slowly and evenly and not rush at it intending to resemble mahogany in two days—they won't, they will just burn the top layer of skin away which is very painful.

It is never easy to predict how long it is going to take to get through the Doldrums; one just keeps plugging away keeping the boat moving as much to the south as possible, and thinking that every time the wind turns south-westerly, one has got through to the southern hemisphere's Trade winds at last. After a couple of days of variable winds, Les picked up a light but steady southerly on 12th September. This veered round to the south-west the next day and built up from force two to three in the morning to force four and higher gusts that evening. The next day, the 14th, it eased and backed south, south-west, but never fell below force two, and on the 15th, at about 5½ degrees north, they eventually found the south-east Trades.

This was a very fast run through the Doldrums, and they were very lucky to pick up the light southerly early on so that they could keep the boat moving. It had been depressing for them on the 10th and 11th to listen in to the 'chatter net' and hear all the other boats, still in the north-east Trades, whilst *Heath's Condor* was nearly becalmed. But by the evening of the 14th the remainder of the fleet were becalmed a good 180 miles astern, and Les was sailing steadily south opening up a greater and greater lead. If *Heath's Condor* was to win this leg on handicap, here was her chance as she sailed for Cape Town at ten knots, with none of her rivals doing more than two knots in the Doldrums. It was almost as if fate had decided to give Les a hand at last; he was sufficiently far ahead to guarantee breaking the record from Portsmouth to Cape Town, which he held anyway with *Burton Cutter*, and then his luck changed.

The south-east Trade winds, blowing force four, were the first serious headwinds that *Heath's Condor* had been in since she was built, and so no one knew how well the experimental mast would do in these very different conditions. As the boat lifted her bow into the first wave, she shuddered and then swooped down to meet the next one. The speed hardly altered, and the clock flickered from ten down to nine knots and then quickly went back up to ten again. The most alarming aspect of it all was the way the rigging slackened as the masthead, which was steady, was swung forward by the slight de-acceleration as the boat hit the wave. On the next wave the mast's behaviour was watched carefully and it was seen to bow forward in its upper section as the boat was checked, and then spring straight again, each time loosening and then jerking the rigging straight. We did not know how much of this the mast would take, but the tightening and slackening of the rigging was not going to do it any good at all. To reduce the strain two reefs were put in the main, and the double-headed rig of yankee and staysail set, but it did not make much difference. Nervously the boat pressed on, but at 13.25 on Thursday 15th September the almost inevitable happened: with a tremendous crack the mast suddenly broke at just above the upper cross trees, and then fractionally later it broke again just above the lower spreaders. With horrifying speed, nearly a ton of mast, fittings, sails and rigging crashed down onto the deck, miraculously missing everyone.

For a moment the whole crew were stunned. As the watch below came up to see what was going on, they just gazed disbelievingly at the mess as the realisation of what this meant to them dawned. All the hard work to get the boat finished in time had been thrown away in a moment. Gone was any chance of getting to Cape Town first on handicap or even just getting there first. Gone perhaps were our chances in the whole race—they lay in a tangled heap on deck.

Slowly people began to pick amongst the wreckage and start to tidy up, and then suddenly, the whole deck was full of bustling people hauling the top section back from overside where the masthead fitting was knocking a hole in the side, and unhanking sails. Our prospects were not too good, but the boat could not just sit there in a mess.

Once the deck was tidied up, an assessment of the damage could be made, and then a decision had to be reached as to what should be done next. The lower third of the mast was still standing firmly and would obviously take a sail, but the remaining pieces could not be grafted back on, so only a small jury rig was possible, certainly nothing efficient enough to think of using to hold the lead, and not really good enough to get to Cape Town either, unless one had about five weeks in which to do it. Les got out the chart and had a good look at the nearest coastline, the west coast of Africa. The nearest port was Monrovia, about four hundred miles away, and with a south-easterly wind, a reach. He decided that his best bet was to head there and try and repair the mast using whatever facilities might be available. A north-east course was set, and under storm jib and a staysail set on the stump of the mainmast, the boat was soon making 6½ knots on a beam reach.

Once underway, Les got on the radio and managed to pass a message on to me via *King's Legend.* I knew that I could not expect any real information until Les and I were able to speak directly to each other, but I very much doubted whether a really good repair could be made to the glass fibre mast in Monrovia.

The most urgent problem was to get the boat to Cape Town as fast as we could, as until she crossed the finish line, our time spent making repairs was counted in our time to sail the course. So first thing Friday morning I went round to Powel masts in Emsworth to see what was the state of the aluminium mast that should have been ready for us the previous April. There was no aluminium mast, but there were the materials to make one, and I gave instructions that it was to be made, working twenty-four hours a day if necessary. A rough completion time of Tuesday was given. Larry Baker at Bowman's got on with finding transport out to Monrovia, and came up with a small airline which operated one flight a week there, usually on Thursdays, but they thought that they might be able to bring the flight forward to Wednesday morning.

In the meantime the boat sailed slowly towards Monrovia.

Monrovia is the capital city of Liberia, perhaps best known these days as a flag of convenience, but an interesting country in that it was established in 1847, with the support of President Monroe of the USA, as an independent republic, its population composed largely of freed American negro slaves. This part of west Africa at this time of the year was having its monsoon, which brings torrential rainfall and reduces visibility down to a few yards. There are no prominent landmarks, and the only aid to navigation is an aero beacon about thirty miles south of Monrovia. Les, as a result, made a rather cautious approach for without the sun he could not get a fix. They were getting close to the shore when out of the rain appeared a dug-out canoe with three native fishermen quietly paddling towards the boat. They must have been somewhat surprised at the sight of this strange vessel looming up out of the rain, but after some time shouting 'Monrovia' at them, Les got all three to point in the same direction, and within ten minutes found himself in the port's outer anchorage. No navigator would have been unhappy with that landfall particularly in view of the conditions. *Heath's Condor* entered port at 11.15 on Saturday, 17th September and was made fast alongside a large lighter.

Les phoned me at midday to say that he had arrived and that they intended repairing the mast with materials available there. He did not think it would be a brilliant job, but at least it would get him to Cape Town. I was able to pass on the news that a twenty-four-hour shift was being worked on the aluminium mast, and it looked as if this would be with him by Wednesday. We decided to allow both plans to go ahead, and reconsider our options on the following Monday.

In Monrovia work started immediately. The lighter's derrick was used to haul out the stump of the mast, which was laid on the lighter's deck as there was more room available. Then the three sections of the mast were cleaned up and a plan worked out for joining them up again. We were lucky that Peter Blake was a professional mast maker, so the expertise to carry out what is a major rebuilding job was ready to hand. The basic plan was to shape up two long wooden plugs which would be placed inside the mast at each break and then the whole mast would be resecured with fibre glass. By Saturday evening the plugs were made and the rigging checked, despite the almost continual downpour.

On Sunday the lower plug was fitted. The actual fibre glassing was left until the evening as the rain usually eased up then, but this one evening it did not, and so a human screen was formed to protect the glass fibre, plugs and joins, and the job was completed by midnight. It took longer because of the conditions of course, but even so, to clean out the inside of the mast, pack chopped-strand mat heavily resined around the plug, and push it four feet into one end of the broken mast, and then push the next section of broken mast four feet down over the other end of the plug until the two ends of mast were together, was no easy job.

On Monday, the aluminium mast was on schedule, and on the phone Les and I decided that it would be best to ship it to Monrovia, rather than fit the repaired carbon fibre mast and have to struggle to Cape Town with that. It meant that all the crew's work repairing the carbon fibre mast was wasted, but they would be able to race to Cape Town, and the new mast would have a good trial before going into the Southern Ocean.

It seemed that within minutes of Les and I agreeing that he would await the aluminium mast, things started to go wrong. The mast was finished just after midnight on Wednesday morning, and in its three thirty-foot sections taken up to Luton airport where the aircraft was due to take off at 06.00. I also sent off some new rigging to replace that damaged when the mast broke, and wonder of wonders, I found the other two spreaders that had not been ready at the start, so I included them in the shipment as well. The mast got to the airport all right, but the aircraft did not take off. We were phoned and told that because of the size of the three sections, which had been advised in advance anyway, the aircraft would have to be re-stowed and an extra payment of three thousand pounds was required. Bob Bell's comments when he heard this can be imagined, but we were over a barrel, and had to agree. For some reason it took two days to reload the aircraft and the mast did not arrive in Monrovia until Friday morning. Unfortunately no one told us about this further delay, so Les and the crew made two abortive journeys out to the airport with a special truck. This waiting, in a climate that alternated between one hundred per cent humidity when dry and torrential rain otherwise, was the worst part of the stay in Monrovia which offers little by way of distraction. The climate sapped everyone's strength, and they had to sit still, not knowing where the new mast was, but knowing that our rivals in the race were all pushing on for Cape Town. The mast arrived eventually, unheralded, but the transport party was at the airport just in case.

With an incredible effort the crew got it back to the docks, assembled, all the halyards rigged, and spreaders and rigging fitted by Friday evening. On Saturday morning the mast was stepped using a merchant ship's cranes, and the rigging set up. Just after midnight on Sunday, *Heath's Condor* re-entered the race having lost some ten days since the failure of the carbon fibre mast, and with another two days yet to lose before a position was reached the same distance away from Cape Town as when the mast broke. All in all twelve days were lost, and although we did not like to admit it, we all knew that there was no possible way we could recover that amount of time in a race that was being so closely contested. *Heath's Condor* now had no chance of winning the race on handicap; all we could race for were line honours for the other three legs, and see if we could end up some way from last on handicap overall, but that would be difficult.

It was heartbreaking for the crew who had put so much faith in Les and me to sail them to a victory in the race, and here we were, only an eighth of the way round the course and they all knew that our chances of winning were nil. I think it says everything necessary about them that they continued to give us all their loyalty and hard work.

Not surprisingly, with an exhausted crew and a new mast, and half the rigging new and therefore unstretched, Les decided to take things easy for the first night, and the boat was sailed by two men at a time on two-hour tricks in a light southwesterly breeze until daybreak. The cool wind was gorgeous, and absolutely every deck hatch was left open to allow the fresh air to work its way through the boat, blowing out the stale air and bugs as it did so. This was the first decent night's sleep anyone had had for more than a week. Throughout Sunday they tacked slowly south, taking up the slack in the lee rigging each time they went about, and gradually beginning to get the boat tuned up once more. But yet again, just as it seemed as if things were looking up, lady luck turned her back again. Early on Monday morning there was a tremendous bang that brought everyone out of their bunks in alarm with the common thought—the mast has gone again. The watch on deck had no idea of the cause, but the mast was still there although all the sails were hanging slackly. The cause was soon discovered. At the base of the mast a large aluminium band was bolted on which acted as a holding point for all the blocks taking halyards from the mast, and turning them to go to the winches. This band had disintegrated and all the blocks were dangling, and the spray guard had been torn upwards. We were fortunate no one had been near when it shattered, because there were always a few tons of tension in the band. Les could only fume. Neither of us had wanted a band on the mast for these turning blocks, we had wanted an extension to the winch platform that could be bolted down through the deck by means of long bolts to the keel structure. Our instructions had been ignored, and here was the result. A temporary fixing was arranged for the blocks, but it would not take the real strain necessary to get the luffs of the sails as tight as they should be, and this of course meant that *Heath's Condor* could not sail as efficiently as she should and yet more time would be lost. Once fate turns against you, it turns with a vengeance, but it is rubbing salt in the wounds when the cause of your problems, in this case both the mast and mast band, would not have been in existence if one's opinion had been regarded.

Although living conditions on board had improved beyond measure with getting back to sea again, and morale was boosted by being on the move, after a couple of days the whole crew began to go down with what one could only describe as Monrovian belly. The symptoms were a feeling of lassitude, and difficulty in doing anything but sleep, accompanied by sharp stomach pains. The doctor was kept pretty busy because nearly everyone suffered, and for almost a week there were only six half-fit people available at any one time to sail the boat. Inevitably, this meant that the speed was down yet again.

Despite having half the crew unfit, it was decided that crossing the Equator could not be ignored, especially as nearly half the crew had not 'crossed the line' before. To have crossed the Equator by aircraft or on land does not count, as King Neptune desires to meet and test anyone who has not crossed the line before at sea. The ceremony is usually fairly simple. Each of the novices is brought before a court made up of trusted subjects, tried for their shipboard sins, found guilty, and the punishment administered completes their initiation. It is a good excuse for a bit of light-hearted fun, at the end of which each of the novices is issued with a certificate that proves he is one of Neptune's loyal subjects and as such immune from treatment on a future occasion. Unfortunately the eight certificates my wife had laboured to produce got left behind, and were not handed out until Cape Town.

The line up for line crossing was:

Golf Charlie:	Sometime paltry pilot of BOAC or something.
Graham:	Unknown assistant to an assistant low class accountant.
Jack the Lad:	A Californian cutie of outrageous background.
The Nipper (Justin Smart):	Timorous teenager with low class morality.
Ratsey Paul:	Needless needler from the Needles.
Doc:	A medical miracle with pill-pushing traits.
John:	An anonymous advocate of obscure pastimes.

The trial is always the most interesting part of the whole ceremony, with a prosecutor thinking of anything that has occurred on board as evidence of guilt, and the defence strenuously finding no defence. With half the crew ill, and with half the crew to initiate, there was a risk that the initiates would rebel, but fortunately steps were taken to split them up before they realised what was going on and all were successfully tried.

The origins of the line crossing ceremony are steeped in antiquity, but it is one of those nautical traditions that has hung on. In the days of sailing ships it provided a break from the tedium of everyday work, and an opportunity to deal with all the newcomers of whatever rank and remind everyone that regardless of position they were sailors first. Twenty years ago when I first crossed the line on a cadetship, fanciful haircuts such as the 'hot cross bun', 'Mohican', 'monk' and 'Hindu' were still performed on initiates. When Neptune said 'Seven times seven' as a punishment you got ducked forty-nine times by the bulls in the pool in an attempt to wash off some of the filthy muck with which you had been coated, but this was only partially successful, and it was usually a few days before one was really clean again.

With all the novices initiated a party took place which bucked everyone up. The boat was now well behind the last boat in the fleet. But even though there were no line honours and no good handicap position to aim for, the sooner the boat could be got to Cape Town the better as the second leg might prove more successful, provided there was time to do the necessary repairs.

The southerly winds at the Equator could be expected to back round to the south-east and steady up, as these are the south-east Trade winds. To make Cape Town one has to sail hard on the wind which makes for a bumpy ride, and hope that the westerly winds of the northern edge of the roaring forties will give one a favourable wind into Cape Town. But it all depends upon what weather pattern is prevailing at the time, and from news being received from the other boats it appeared that the centre of the high pressure system was south and east of Cape Town, so they were able to sail fast in with a favourable wind. The leading boats were *Flyer* and *King's Legend*, lying about two miles apart and having the race of their lives, eventually won by *Flyer* which arrived at 07.54 GMT on 5th October, two hours ahead of *King's Legend* and a new record for the distance. If only the mast had not broken perhaps *Heath's Condor* could have been in before. She should have been, but it is no use coming up with 'ifs' after the event, it is results that count. Nevertheless, despite losing twelve days, and ensuring last place on handicap, there was a chance of coming in before the last of the fleet arrived, and a new target was set to see how many could be beaten in. The main competition was the whole race after all, and although it would be nice to win each leg, if we could not do that we could at least try to claw back the twelve lost days.

Instead of sailing on the port tack and taking a long left-handed curve into Cape Town, which is the old sailing ship method, and the one favoured by most of the yachts, Les decided to tack every time he was forced round to west of south. The danger with this is that it keeps one to the eastern side of the south-east Trades where they are more south-easterly, rather than further west where the winds have backed a bit to the east and one can sail east of south. It is a calculated risk, and it had paid off before so Les decided to try it again, banking on the high pressure centre remaining where it was to give him a good run in as well.

The wind proved to be quite variable in strength and it also varied a little in direction, so that constant sail changes were necessary and this, with a weakened crew, meant hard work for those fit enough to stand a watch. It is times like this when people show their true colours, and it brought matters to a head as far as American Jack was concerned. Ever since leaving Portsmouth people had wondered whether he was really pulling his weight. Before Monrovia Les had spoken to him about his habit of reading through his off-watch period and then falling asleep on watch. He had complained of tiredness, which was not surprising, and had been given sleeping pills to give him a twelve-hour sleep to try and break the cycle he had got himself into as he did not seem capable of breaking out of it on his own. As far as most of the others were concerned the last straw was when, short-handed through illness, they were struggling with a headsail, and Jack was in the sail locker reading and refused to help as, he said, he was not on watch. On his next watch he was asleep in the cockpit when two buckets of water were emptied over him and immediately everyone leaped about in alarm at the appearance of a 'freak wave' that appeared to have just landed on Jack and nowhere else. Jack went along with it—what else could he do?—but the situation was not one that could be allowed to continue. He was not a good deck-hand when he was awake, and now the others were openly going for him. Les had a quiet chat with Jack, the upshot of which was that he ceased to be in a watch 'owing to illness', and all he was asked to do was to take films. As a source of friction he was now out of the way, but it was quite obvious that he was not suitable or safe and would have to be dropped from the crew in Cape Town as no one was prepared to risk hanging onto a rope if Jack had the other end. Les made this clear and Jack agreed. The problem of getting him physically off the boat in Cape Town remained, however. It was not that Jack himself was likely to prove difficult, but the Immigration Authorities in South Africa insist that a boat is responsible for its crew, and if Jack left *Heath's Condor* they would insist that he had an air ticket from South Africa to his home, the USA. We knew he did not have one, and we could not afford it, so this problem was shelved until the boat got in to Cape Town.

On Wednesday 5th October, when *Flyer* and *King's Legend* finished, *Heath's Condor* still had 1,900 miles to go, ten days if all went well. The boat was sixteen degrees south and the southern cross was sighted properly, which cheered up Peter Blake who was glad to see some more familiar stars at last. But the wind was becoming light as the high had moved rather rapidly back to its more usual position, roughly in the centre of the South Atlantic, and the boat was soon becalmed. Sitting on deck with his watch, drinking tea, Peter saw the slight rippling of the surface which indicates a zephyr. Getting to his feet, he told them to be ready to take advantage of whatever came along. The zephyr arrived. 'Right,' said Peter, 'spinnaker gear, it's from the starboard quarter.' As the watch started to move forward he called to them to wait a minute. 'No, it's not,' he said, 'it's from the port bow. Oh S . .t,' and he sat back down again and picked up his tea mug. Realising that any manoeuvre had been cancelled, his watch wandered disconsolately back to the cockpit. In these sort of conditions it is very difficult to tell where the wind is really from. The rolling of the boat causes the masthead instruments to swing all over the place, and the slatting of the sails creates a local puff which is much stronger than any natural wind. So until there is enough wind to see what is happening, it is not always easy to know how to set the sails.

To boost morale, Graham made a cocktail consisting mainly of rum, which was immediately christened Doris Bong after a lady in Monrovia whom no one now wished to remember. Andy got his guitar out, and led a sing-song which helped raise spirits. No one likes drifting around in circles, particularly when you are meant to be racing.

October 6th offered a complete contrast. A south-easterly

gale set in with heavy rain, and soon a nasty swell had developed. From being warm and dry one day, thirty-six hours later everything was wet and the weather had turned distinctly colder. As if to welcome the boat to the colder southern latitudes, the first wandering albatross was sighted at about twenty-five degrees south. It is not generally realised that the seawater in the southern hemisphere is as cold as a latitude ten degrees further from the Equator in the northern hemisphere. Thus the seawater temperature at thirty-five degrees south of the Equator is roughly the same as the seawater temperature at forty-five degrees north.

During this bad weather five sharks were sighted quite close to, but could not be clearly identified. One wonders what food they find right out to sea, as few sharks can swim fast enough to catch a healthy pelargic fish, and have to resort to picking up the injured or whatever they can find floating on the surface. Quite often they will rub themselves alongside a yacht as if to remove parasites on their skins. This is not dangerous to a large well found yacht, but they look frightening, and a large shark will rock a small boat. A shark's skin, known as shagreen, is rough. In the old days it was used on sword handles as it gave a good grip even when covered with blood. It is made up of denticles, small in size but nevertheless produced and replaced like teeth. It is no wonder that a shark scraping alongside a boat will remove the anti-fouling, and I suppose, if it kept at it, it could eventually wear a hole through the hull. There are numerous species of sharks and much still to learn about them, so it is always useful to identify them if you can. Sharks are known to have existed sixty million years ago, and the fact that their general shape has changed little in that enormous expanse of time indicates the efficiency of the original species. The most dangerous and as far as anyone knows the largest species around today is the white pointer or white death shark. The largest seen in recent years was forty feet long, but teeth five inches long have been dredged up which would indicate a shark one hundred feet long with a mouth six feet across—large enough to swallow an ox in one gulp. One hopes that sharks of this size no longer exist, but so little is known about what has survived that it is not beyond the realms of possibility that they may still be lurking around somewhere. The coelacanth was considered to be extinct for forty million years, until one was caught off Madagascar in 1938; and an eel cell measuring over two feet in length was caught by a research ship at the turn of the century—this, if scaled up, would indicate an eel eighty feet long, although such a creature has never been seen. There is still a great deal that we do not know about the sea and the fishes that swim in it, and man's research so far has barely scratched the surface.

The men sailing in ships hated sharks, and would always try to catch them if they could and kill them, as they believed that every shark had killed some poor sailor. The contents of the stomach were always examined with interest as sharks have been known to eat bottles and even saucepans, the theory being that the smell from the object eaten attracted them in the first place. An eighteen-foot white pointer caught by a ship was found to contain a human foot, half a goat, two pumpkins, a wicker-covered scent bottle, two fairly fresh fish and a small shark. Once a shark was cut up, certain parts were much prized as curios. The cartilaginous backbone, if stiffened with a piece of wire, will harden up and make an attractive walking stick. The jawbones with their evil rows of teeth can be mounted, and the fin was usually nailed to the jib-boom. Shark meat is edible, but it is advisable to soak the flesh in salt water for twenty-four hours before cooking it as this removes the strong ammoniac flavour. Shark livers are particularly rich, and should be avoided as they can poison people. It is worth remembering that a diet of fish without plenty of water can kill through protein poisoning as the body just cannot take the quantity of protein in fish on its own and needs water to wash away the surplus. One method of killing sharks was to heat up a whole melon or pumpkin in boiling water and toss it overboard. A following shark would eat the pumpkin whole and the internal heat would then kill it. The trouble with this method is that a shark does not have a swim bladder, and is heavier than water, so if you kill it without getting a hook or harpoon into it, it will sink. To keep afloat, sharks have to keep swimming. If one comes in close enough, aim for a point where the apex of an equilateral triangle, with the eyes as a base, occurs back from the snout. The brain is roughly here, and a harpoon or bullet in the brain kills it outright. One has to be careful though. A shark's brain is not large, and it is advisable to remove the barbs from a harpoon before throwing or shooting it, because if you miss the shark will take off and you will lose your gear. It cost me five spears and nearly a spear gun before I caught on to this. The only effective method is to swim around until the shark passes beneath you, then you get a clear shot at the target. If however the shark has abandoned his rather beautiful slow sinuous motion, and appears to be swimming in a more agitated manner, get back into the boat fast!

By 8th October, the boat was twenty-eight degrees south and seven degrees west. The gale force winds of the previous two days which had slowed things up had eased, and the high appeared to have passed west as a south by east wind came up enabling the course to be set for Cape Town on a reach. *Heath's Condor* was catching up slowly and it looked as if she might not be last into Cape Town despite the delay. Already one other boat, *Japy Hermes*, had problems, and had had to pull over towards Brazil to drop off a sick member of her crew. The Brazilian navy frigate kindly rendezvoused and took him off, but this had lost her a few days. However, it was not really very satisfying to be second from last owing to someone else's misfortune and it was the other tail-enders that were the real target.

The period of good speed under reaching sails passed all too briefly, and a day later a gale from the south-east came up again. Ever since stepping the new mast, it had been necessary to adjust the rigging for each sail change. Part of this was due to the fact that some of the rigging was new and had therefore to stretch, but part was also due to the fact that the baby stay was not strong enough to balance the two huge lower shrouds which should have had another pair leading forward to balance them. The result of this was that the baby stay's deck fitting was being slowly pulled aft through the deck and a temporary arrangement was set up to stiffen the base by lashing it forward to the intermediate stay's position. This was still not totally satisfactory, but it did give a little more support to the mast.

Les managed to get through to me on the radio telephone and explain this problem. He felt the deck fitting could be reinforced in Cape Town but it would be advisable to fit a stronger baby stay. He also detailed the problems with the rigging on the mast. I talked the matter over with Ben Bradley of Spencer's Rigging in Cowes and he agreed that a stronger baby stay would help but the long-term answer was more likely to be to move the lower shrouds forward, or fit another set forward. We did not think that we would have time for this in Cape Town as we would be arriving so late, but we got a new stronger baby stay ordered, and I suggested that Ben fly out with me to Cape Town to check the rigging properly as few people know as much about it as he does. The trouble with wire rigging is that it will stretch—even thick heavy stainless steel wire stretches slightly—and we would have been better having stainless rod rigging for a mast of our length, but there just had not been time to get it made before we left.

Although Les had got through to me on the radio telephone we were still having problems with the set, and at a range of five thousand miles it was not that easy to make contact with Portishead any longer. Portishead works on a first come first served basis, so if you get through on a particular frequency, you will then be given a turn and you have to wait, listening in the whole time, until your turn comes round. This can be quite quick, but on occasions it was as much as five hours by which time we would be low on battery power and the radio propagation conditions might have changed so that to be heard properly, or at all, one had to shift frequency. If you moved to another frequency, you had to start in the queue all over again. This made radio communication with the UK rather difficult, and it would have been easier for us if we could have booked a time as was possible with Cape Town radio, but Portishead handles so much traffic I do not think they could really alter their system. Once we got through the operators were more than helpful, and on occasion even asked other ships if they would not mind us jumping the queue as they knew we had power difficulties, but it all rather depended on who was on duty at the time.

On 11th October a ship was sighted which passed about one mile to starboard, going on roughly the same course. She was in sight for several hours but no one was seen on deck, nor did she respond to calls on the VHF or with the signalling lamp. This is a major worry to yachtsmen, most of whom sensibly accept that the large merchant ships cannot manoeuvre in a hurry and it is best to give them plenty of space. But what do you do when you are becalmed and one comes straight at you? If your motor is working you have to start it to get clear, and most race committees will not penalise you for that, but suppose your engine will not function? A modern cargo ship would not even notice the bump as it rolled over a yacht. The problem lies in the fact that lookouts are not being properly kept on merchant ships these days. In any case it is difficult to tell at a distance whether the bridge is manned or not, so one is never sure how dangerous the situation is until it is probably too late. A yacht does not go to sea to get in the way of other shipping, neither do merchant ships go looking for yachts to frighten. It is the unseamanlike behaviour of some watch-keeping officers who do not keep a proper lookout that is the cause of worry to the yachtsman, and bringing their own profession into disrepute. This vessel appeared to be bound for Cape Town as well, still nine hundred miles away where twelve of the race fleet had already docked. It was depressing that only three boats were left to finish—*33 Export, Heath's Condor* and *Japy Hermes*—and the date for the start of the second leg had been set for 22nd October which left very little time to carry out repairs once the boat arrived. Still, the longitude was east at last, and it only required a slight freeing of the wind for the boat to race in. It never happens of course, and it took another five days of constant sail changes as the wind direction altered and the strength rose and fell before there appeared on the horizon the long-awaited fixed cloud which indicated high ground underneath it. This was the Tablecloth, the orographic cloud that frequently covers Table Mountain which, being three thousand feet high, is visible quite far out to sea.

Heath's Condor slowly worked up to the finish line in Table Bay, crossing just half an hour after *33 Export*, and then motored in to the Royal Cape Yacht Club where moorings had been organised for all the competitors. Although the crew immediately started a party in the club, it lacked the zest an arrival party should have had. *Flyer* had finished eleven days before, and the harsh fact was that our first leg, because of the broken mast, had been a disaster, and had probably removed any opportunity that might have existed of doing well in the handicap stakes.

Fortunately, owing to the late arrival of some of the other yachts the start of the race had been put off until the 25th, which gave us nine days to clean out the boat, get a new system for holding the halyard heel blocks in place, work out a method of stiffening up the mast, get the sails to a loft so that they could be checked, and re-provision the boat.

Golf Charlie agreed to organise the food for the 30–35-day run to Auckland and it took him all his time to work out his lists, get things ordered, delivered and stowed. Paul took off to a sail loft, re-cut our ribbon yankee which was not setting at all well, and repaired all the sails. He also fitted a new type of cringle into the mainsail reefing points on the leach, as the usual cringles were not proving at all satisfactory. On large heavy sails, cringles are stainless steel and are either pressed into the sail cloth under considerable pressure, which grips the edge of the cloth but all too easily pulls out, or they are sewn into the cloth and the stitching gets worn by the reefing line. Paul's solution was a ring within a ring. The outer ring could be sewn firmly onto the sail and the inner ring takes all the wear. They worked very well.

I flew in to Cape Town with Ben Bradley on the 19th and we got straight on with stiffening up the mast. We started at the keel and worked up. The first thing we did was get some shaped mast wedges so that the mast was held firm at deck level. Next we fitted the new baby stay to a reinforced deck fitting. The rest of the rigging looked all right, but Ben was unhappy about the thirty-foot spans between the spreaders and we decided to fit small shrouds from eyebolts halfway between the spreaders and the upper spreaders and the top of the mast which ran from the spreader ends. This meant removing all the spreaders and having eyes welded onto them, and the whole job took three days.

Our new halyard heel block fitting was made ashore and fitted perfectly. It was a bracket extending forward from the winch platform, and to counter the upward pull, it was fastened with stainless steel rods through the deck to the keel supported web. It looked workmanlike and strong, and gave us no trouble.

With all the repairs and re-storing going on, there was not much time off for anyone, but I tried to allow everyone at least half a day to get into town and, if they wished, climb Table Mountain.

Cape Town has always been my favourite port outside Britain ever since I first visited it in 1957 as an apprentice. The great mass of Table Mountain, flanked by two large hills, Lion's Head and Devil's Peak, completely dominates the old town and harbour and gives a setting that is unequalled anywhere else in the world. The port itself is always bustling with movement, whether it be fishing boats or huge supertankers, and its air of busy efficiency has always appealed to me. Since I had last visited it in 1971 there had been tremendous changes. A new raised motorway ran along between the docks and the town, and high-rise flats and towering office blocks had appeared along what used to be the front of the town facing the docks. A massive new port extension, designed to take the new container ships, which would have dwarfed all but the largest tankers when I went to sea, was nearing completion. Cape Town has always been a strategic port. From the first Dutch East India Company settlement set up by Van Riebeeck to supply provisions and a refuge to the ships making the long passage out to the East Indies from Europe, through British ownership for the same purpose, it has provided the key to the route to the East. Its importance has not changed today, when massive supertankers carrying Europe's lifeblood in oil, and too large to transit the Suez Canal, still stop off at the port to take on mail and supplies. Although busy enough with its own trade, whenever the Suez Canal has been closed Cape Town has managed to cope with a huge increase in traffic with a political impartiality that would amaze South Africa's detractors. It just gets on with its job of being a port. This attitude appeals to merchant seamen, who belong to the most international of professions, bound together by their common task of dealing with an impartial element that shows no respect for any flag.

To stand on the deck of a vessel in Cape Town harbour, breathing in the fresh crisp air and looking up at Table Mountain, gives one a tremendous feeling of well-being, and even the smoke from the steam engines that are still being used by South African railways, adds to the character of the place. I had promised myself that I would try and climb the mountain again this time. It's a pleasant energetic day's climb, and a much more satisfying way of getting to the top for the incredible views offered, but unfortunately there was just not the time available. Still, I am sure there will be another opportunity in the future.

The hospitality of the South Africans lived up to its usual high standard. Parties were available most evenings and, having worked hard all day, the crew were glad to get away from the boat and relax for a while.

Rear-Admiral Otto Steiner, Chairman of the Race Committee, was in Cape Town, and shortly after arriving I asked him if, as we no longer had a GRP mast, our three per cent penalty could be removed, and he agreed. He also told me that we had been given a seventeen-hour penalty for motoring back to Monrovia after the mast had broken, and for taking on a new radio receiver. I protested strongly about this, as we had motored away from the finish line, but he did not agree. I was particularly incensed about the penalty for receiving a radio as I had been assured by Captain Norman that this was all right. Indeed he had put it in writing, but minds had obviously changed. This was the first of a number of contradictory decisions by the committee which were ultimately to cause a great deal of confusion amongst the competitors.

The last couple of days were chaotic, but we managed to get half a day to go out and test the strengthened mast and give the new members of the crew their first chance of learning their way about the deck when sailing. They had had plenty of time to get to know the deck layout during the frantic overhaul and repairs, but it always seems different when sails are set. Apart from myself, Bill Abrams, from Scotland, and Les Best, a New Zealander, had flown out to join up, and we picked up an ex-crew member from *Burton Cutter*, Barry Buchannan, who had settled in South Africa. At the last minute we were approached by a South African lawyer, Ronnie Roos, and as I felt we could use another crewman we took him along as well. John Carter, Andy Cully, and Les left us, but all stayed around to help get the boat ready and see us off. Jack Keyhoe disappeared on arrival, and we had to alert the immigration people that we had lost one of our crew. He turned up just before we left, and Bob Bell was faced with no alternative but to put up the money for his air fare back to California.

Bob threw a party for the crew the last night, but many of us did not stay long as we wanted a good night's sleep; however, the gesture was good for morale, and enabled people to relax and forget the hard labour of the previous nine days, and get them thinking about the race starting tomorrow.

With everything ready, I did not rush down first thing the following morning, but had a leisurely breakfast at the yacht club and arrived on board at ten, just as the last items of equipment, two large lifeboat oars, were being put aboard, much to everyone's amusement. These were not to be used for rowing, however; that is not allowed under the rules. I wanted them on board in case we had a rudder failure. One of the most efficient ways of steering a boat is by means of an oar over the stern. In fact man's earliest rudder was just that, and they are still issued as part of the equipment of a ship's lifeboat; I wanted them on board, just in case.

3. CAPE TOWN TO AUCKLAND

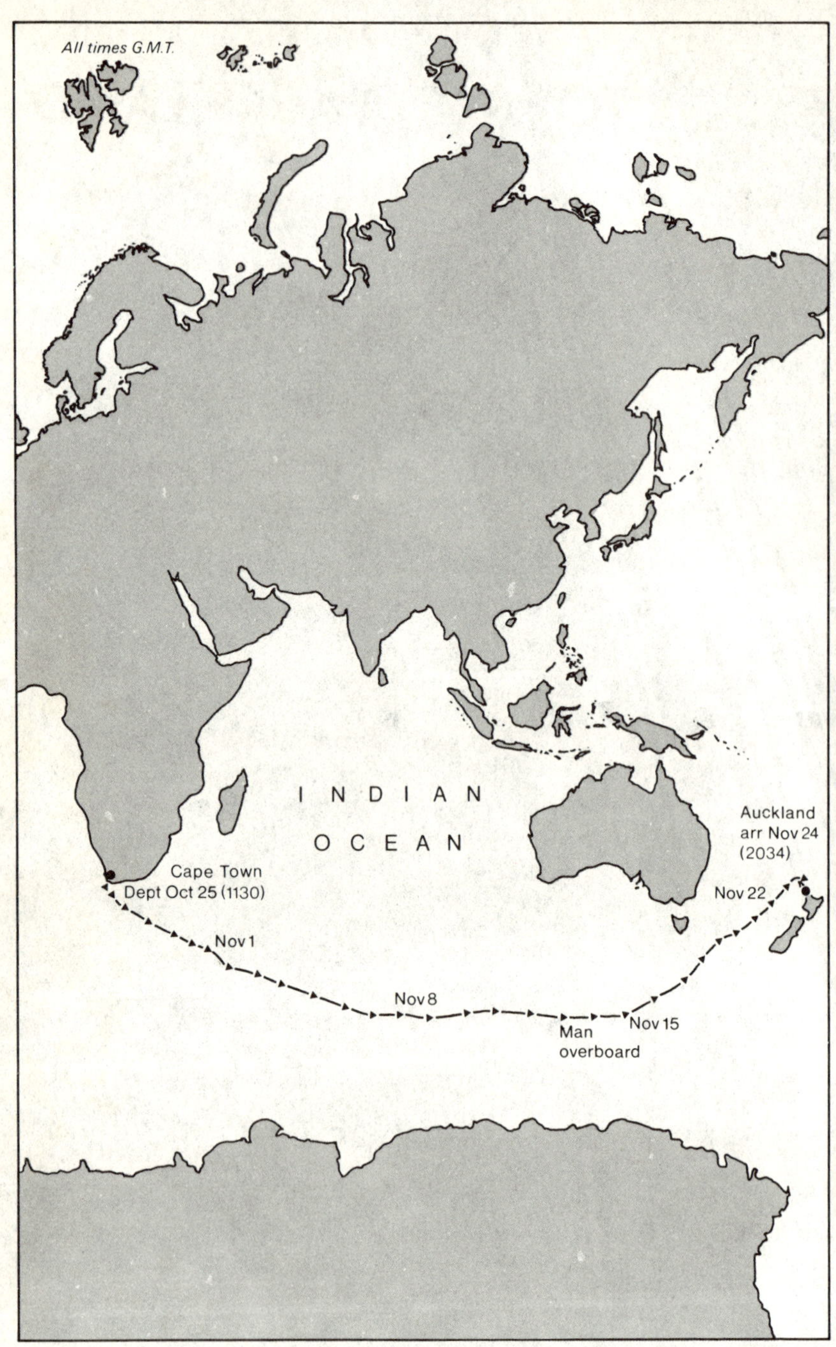
All times G.M.T.
I N D I A N
O C E A N
Cape Town
Dept Oct 25 (1130)
Nov 1
Nov 8
Man
overboard
Nov 15
Nov 22
Auckland
arr Nov 24
(2034)

1. *Heath's Condor* streaking away with the Big Yellow set minutes after the start

2. The jury rig set from the stump of the experimental mast to get to Monrovia

3. Clearing the decks after the experimental mast had broken

4. The new mast being lifted up after assembly prior to being stepped

5. The Major steering as we surf down a wave in the Southern Ocean. The rooster tail behind the boat reached a height of 20 feet when we exceeded 30 knots

6. The helicopter, carrying the spare radio receiver, approaches to make the drop to Justin and Jack in the dinghy

7. Saying goodbye an hour after the start of the second leg. The Twelve Apostles, the chain of mountains to the south of Table Mountain, in the background

8. Herman re-reaving a reefing pennant from the foot of the mainsail

9. The Doctor (David Dickson) filling one of Ronnie Roos's teeth

10. Off the east coast of New Zealand sailing down to Auckland. Taken from Bob Bell's aeroplane

The second leg of the race, from Cape Town to Auckland in New Zealand, took us down into the Southern Ocean, that vast expanse of water that circles the globe between the southernmost capes of Africa, Australasia and America, and the northern shore of Antarctica. The Southern Ocean is the only area of sea in the world where no land intervenes and the sea is free to circulate the globe without interference. In the northern hemisphere, the great oceans of the Atlantic or the Pacific are limited by the continents on either side of them, and although very large seas can build up, they must sooner or later meet land and be broken up. There is no such restriction in the Southern Ocean. A wave formed in one part of the ocean can, provided the wind keeps generating it, roll right around the world, and this leads to much larger waves being formed in the Southern Ocean than anywhere else.

There are two sorts of waves formed at sea, swell waves and sea waves. The swell waves are created by a constant wind over a great distance which will not heap the seas up but will generate a long low rolling wave. In the Southern Ocean these can build up to a height of about thirty feet and the distance between wave crests to over three hundred feet. These low swell waves have little effect upon a small craft, apart from gently lifting it up and down, as the height is not that great relative to the length, and the slope of the wave is not steep. Swell waves are always present in the Southern Ocean and even when the wind that generates them has been light for days, the slow gradual rise and fall of the sea's surface is still present. The other waves are sea waves which are built up locally by the wind. These are much shorter and sharper than swell waves, the distance between crests being as little as thirty feet, and it is these waves that throw a yacht around. Now and again (one expert has calculated it as being one wave in every 300,000, but it is probably less frequent), a larger sea and swell wave will combine to form an enormous, almost vertically faced, wall of water over sixty feet in height. These freak waves are rare, but a small boat caught by one has every chance of being rolled over completely. The fact that one of these waves could be met in the Southern Ocean makes it a sobering place to sail. Also, if the boat was rolled and was lucky enough to remain afloat, the area is so infrequently sailed through that the chances of obtaining any outside assistance are almost negligible.

But if the Southern Ocean is a frightening place to sail let alone race through, it does have one advantage for the sailing ship. The winds are predominantly westerlies and there are usually plenty of them. The area of ocean between latitudes forty and fifty degrees south had been christened the roaring forties by the old sailing ship men because they usually found strong winds there, and I see no reason to argue with them. The area south of latitude fifty degrees south has an even higher wind average, but few of the old sailing ships went that far south.

When I planned our course, I considered sailing through the Southern Ocean at about forty-two to forty-five degrees south, the same latitudes I had sailed alone in *Suhaili*, and this gave us a distance between start and finish of about 7,450 miles, or fifty more than the race committee had decided was the handicap distance. Unfortunately the great circle route (the shortest distance between two points on the Earth's surface) between Cape Town and Auckland passes through Antarctica, which is a fairly hefty land mass, and apart from this is surrounded by some pretty impenetrable ice, so the shortest practical route is a composite great circle course. This means that one would sail down a great circle to a chosen latitude then level off on this latitude until one met the great circle from that latitude to one's destination. The question is which latitude to choose. The further south one can go the shorter the distance there is to sail, but one wants to avoid the iceberg areas if possible as at night and in a rough sea one can not always be certain of seeing an iceberg in time to avoid it, and the psychological effect of knowing that there are, or might be, icebergs in the vicinity, would cause one to press the boat less and we were in a race.

We were unable to obtain information about the ice limit before we sailed, but it seemed to lie somewhere south of fifty-five degrees south on average, so I chose this latitude at which to level off. The distance we would have to sail using this route was 6,876 miles, a saving of 524 miles over the handicap distance, which could save us a couple of days. This worked to our advantage only if all the other yachts took the course expected by the race committee. If they decided to take the same course we were at a disadvantage in a race being handicapped on a time on distance basis, as the shorter distance of almost ten per cent meant we would have to sail ten per cent, or a knot, faster than if we sailed on the longer more northerly course in order to hold the smaller boats on handicap. I discovered later that most of the other boats had planned to come further south anyway and things would have been even more to our disadvantage if we had stayed north.

This more southerly course carried with it the risk of worse weather from the stronger winds close to Antarctica. Some very deep low pressure areas form along the Antarctic coast. Provided we kept north of these we would be guaranteed westerly winds, but the closer we got to them the stronger the winds would be.

Ever since I had been forced to go fairly carefully in *Suhaili* because of her small size, I had always had a hankering to go down into the Southern Ocean again with a larger boat and see if it was possible to hang onto sail in those seas in a real blow and sail fast enough to keep out of danger from the waves behind. Here I had a brand-new boat two and a half times *Suhaili*'s length and a good fit young crew plus the added impetus that we were in a race, so I would never get a better opportunity of testing out the theory to my own satisfaction.

Only two of us on board had sailed through the Southern Ocean before, myself in *Suhaili* and Julian on *Kriter II* in the *Financial Times* Clipper Race of 1975–76. Two more, Peter and the Major, had been into the Southern Ocean with Les in *Burton Cutter* in 1973, but because the boat had been damaged and forced to withdraw, they had not got very far. Of the remainder, none had any experience of the area at all and this worried me far more than the fact that they had not sailed in very large seas before, because in view of the reputation of the Ocean, they might tend to be cautious and not push the boat to the limit.

I probably did not help to overcome any caution they may have felt by giving a lecture, as we motored out to the start line, on safety on board, the importance of wearing safety harnesses at all times on deck, and running through the man overboard drill. However it was the first opportunity we had since arriving in Cape Town to have all the crew together without interruption and we had four new crew members as well. We allocated liferaft positions and the two watches at the same time. Although all the members of the crew got on well together, certain people work better with each other and we tried to put these sort of pairs in the same watch, at the same time maintaining a balance as far as experience was concerned. The watches chosen were:

Peter Blake	Julian Gildersleeves
Chris Edwards (the Major)	David Alan-Williams
Graham Carpenter (Golf Charlie)	Graham Pearson
Les Best	David Dickson (Doc)
Barry Buchannan	Paul Newell (Sails)
Justin Smart (the Nipper)	Herman Vanura (Herman the German)
Bill Abram	Ronnie Roos

As before, like Les, I kept myself out of the watch system so that I was free to navigate and join in at any time a manoeuvre required an extra hand. With good watch leaders there is no need for the skipper to be interfering the whole time, and this leaves a bit of time to think about the race and consider the possible alternative courses of action to take when the wind changes or the weather pattern looks like making a dramatic alteration. In fact, later on I found it paid if I did the morning watch for Peter or Julian to give them a good lie-in periodically, as they inevitably worked harder than the rest of their watches and did not get the uninterrupted sleep that everyone else got once every six days when on cooking duty. The three of us did not appear in the cooking rota, which took one from each watch every day so that two people were, apart from emergencies, effectively off deck each day. These two were responsible for preparing three meals a day, doing the washing up and galley cleaning, and also for peggying out the saloon. In return they were given a lie-in the next night.

One aspect of life at sea in a boat that cannot be given too much attention is feeding. Apart from the need to keep everyone well fed so that they have the energy to work the boat hard, and the energy to keep warm when the weather gets really cold, meals become an important event in a daily schedule otherwise restricted to sail changes, keeping a look out and the occasional trick on the wheel. The crew look forward to mealtimes as a break in the monotony, and the cooks were always guaranteed a full restaurant of satisfied customers, regardless of the quality of the food. In fairness, it must be said that the cooks did well and only once during the whole leg was a meal not fully eaten.

Stocking up with sufficient food for fifteen hungry males for a voyage of thirty-seven days plus a fortnight's reserve takes considerable planning and, having placed all the food on board, the commissar for the leg, in this case Golf Charlie, had to ensure that the food was used according to a fixed plan. There is nothing worse than finding towards the end of the voyage that there are only two tins of meat left, but masses of fruit, carrots and curry powder. Each day, the duty cooks were given a list of the raw materials they could use and it was up to them to decide how imaginatively they could produce the three meals for the day from what was allocated. If they wanted to vary things at all they had to have Golf Charlie's permission. Basically we had porridge or muesli followed by eggs-and-something for breakfast. Lunch could be two or three courses depending upon whether the cooks produced soup and a pudding, and dinner was the same. In between coffee or tea would be served up for the watch on deck and anyone else who happened to be around. The wise cooks soon discovered that it was best not to offer a choice of hot drinks, as they would end up having to produce coffee with and without milk, with and without sugar, tea the same, and then cocoa, Bovril and anything else people could think of. If people are just handed up a steaming cup of something they are usually grateful to have anything at all, but given a choice they are amazingly difficult to please.

At the start of the voyage we instituted water rationing, forbidding the use of fresh water for anything but cooking or where required by the doctor. Teeth can be cleaned just as effectively in salt water as in fresh, and beards would provide a bit of facial protection once things got cold. Having a twenty-five-gallon header tank that was hard work to pump up acted as a natural check on fresh water usage and also enabled us to keep a check on the rate that water was being used up.

The start gun was fired at 13.30 on 25th October 1977, most of the boats making a reasonable go for the line. We had been advised to stick offshore and so started at the leeward end of the line with five others, going about onto the port tack almost immediately after crossing to beat clear. We headed out to sea for an hour and then, seeing the boats inshore appearing to be making better progress, tacked back. *Flyer* and *Great Britain II* held on out to sea, which turned out to be the wrong thing to do. By nightfall we had worked our way past the boats which had stayed inshore leaving only one ahead of us. Acting on local knowledge we tacked offshore again at nightfall to avoid the calms that we were told always fall inshore, and the next morning after a very quiet night, we were once again forced to work our way past all the smaller boats we had left inshore to be becalmed. So much for local knowledge!

The wind remained a light southerly or south-easterly for the first two days, during which we covered a total of 194 miles, an average speed of four knots, and I eventually decided that, in these conditions, we could afford to turn east early instead of continuing south to get clear of a west going current and to avoid the Aghullas Bank, the area of comparatively shallow water that lies to the south of Cape Province.

Most seamen are aware of the short choppy seas created when the wind and tide are going in opposite directions. Off Southern Africa, the Aghullas current, a very strong current of water up to a hundred miles wide and a thousand feet deep, runs at up to five knots south-west down the south-east African coast, sweeps west and then a part of it turns south to join the Southern Ocean current and another part carries on round Cape Point to join the Benguela current. With the passing of a cold front across the area, the north-easterly winds, which blow in the same direction as the Aghullas current and help it on its passage, back round to the south-west. This change in direction occurs very quickly, within four hours or less, and a local wind-generated sea with waves of up to ten feet in height and a wave-length of two hundred feet can appear within an hour. Where this local effect is combined with a fast current moving in the opposite direction, the wavelength of the local waves is decreased and the height increased. Combine this with fully developed swell waves, and a combined wave of up to sixty feet in height with a very steep leeward edge is created upon occasion. A number of large modern ocean-going ships have been severely damaged or even sunk by freak waves of this sort in recent years, and the prudent mariner keeps well clear of the Aghullas Bank in a south-westerly wind. In our particular case, however, the winds were southerly or south-easterly, and no fronts were forecast, so I felt that we could reasonably safely head east or south-east across the Aghullas Bank. Of course within a few hours of making that decision the wind veered round to the south-west, and the sea got up a nasty chop, but it did not last longer than six hours and by that time we reckoned to have cleared the Aghullas Bank. The only way we could tell for sure that we were still getting the effect of the current was by feeling the temperature of the sea, which was warm enough to wash in on the aft deck.

Washing at sea is always a bit of a problem, as it is never possible to carry enough fresh water for even a shower. The result is that one has to use seawater. I am one of those lucky people whose skin does not object to salt water so it is easy for me to have a wash once we get out to sea. Some are not so fortunate and they just have to go without washing. On the second day out, Ronnie Roos and I took a wash. You get the water by throwing a bucket attached to a length of rope into the sea and then trying to fill it from the water rushing by. If the boat is going really fast and the mouth of the bucket suddenly bites, the handle will as often as not come off the bucket. If the handle says on, you get a huge jerk and either you go in or you get your bucketful of water. The next part is the most painful, tipping the water over yourself, particularly in a temperate climate. In the Tropics, washing like this is a pleasure; in a cold climate it is impossible, and in a temperate climate, best completed as soon as possible. By the third day the water was far too cold and I decided to put off outside washing until we got to New Zealand. Ronnie was a bit hardier, but after his third wash he went down with a cold. After that, no one seemed very enthusiastic.

All this light weather in an area that is called the Cape of Storms was exceedingly frustrating, but almost anything can happen at sea. The first time I rounded the Cape in 1966 we sailed from Durban to Cape Town with easterly winds. The second time in 1968 I got caught in a series of lows and had six gales in ten days. This time we were tacking to try to keep to weather of the lines of cloud as that appeared to be the only place we could find any wind at all.

The Southern Ocean as a weather system is dominated by a series of low pressure centres that base themselves at about sixty degrees south, and the varying highs and lows that move in an eastward direction between thirty-five and forty-five degrees south. The wind generated by the southern lows is a westerly, whilst the wind to be found further north can vary quite considerably. Provided one could keep north of the lows at the latitude I had chosen, it was obviously going to be more predictable if we went south which was another good reason for going down to fifty-five degrees. If, however, we went too far, and got south of a low pressure area, we would get easterly winds and probably sixty knots' worth at that, which would drastically cut down our speed.

The whole success of the plan was dependent upon accurate weather information, and this was again dependent upon the radio. Golf Charlie had managed to pick up the morse 'canal' broadcasts on the previous leg, and by sitting patiently and playing the recording back at half speed, he had been able to decode the weather and give us a pretty good plot. The canal broadcasts are the commercial shipping forecasts put out internationally. The trouble is that a plot is only as good as the information upon which it is based, and down in this part of the world there are very few weather recording stations, so the plot was bound to be a bit unreliable. We also had another problem on board in that Golf Charlie was tired after the rush to sort out the food in Cape Town, ordering new food, and arranging stowage on board. Quite how he achieved as much as he did without a nervous breakdown I don't know, but the job got done. It did leave our weather decoder a bit flat though for a week or more.

Fortunately, in the meteorological briefings before the race, it had been mentioned that if one of the boats had a ham radio operator amongst the crews, there was a ham stationed on one of the little islands that lie between South Africa and Australia. This operator, Gordon Proctor, at the South African station on Marion Island, was prepared to re-transmit the general weather synopsis and forecast issued from Pretoria provided we could receive his frequency. The Italian boat *B & B Italia* had a ham in their crew, so a system of schedules was set up. This system worked very well. *B & B Italia* received the weather synopsis and then passed it on to the other boats to start with. Later the frequencies were changed and we were all able to receive the synopsis and talk to Marion Island as well. Receiving a plain language broadcast like this gave Golf Charlie a bit of a break.

Eventually Gordon Proctor was able to extend his forecasts to cover the area beyond sixty degrees east, the limit for Pretoria, which made a tremendous difference, as otherwise there is a gap between where the South African forecasts stop and the Australian forecasts start. With these regular forecasts at our disposal, and by double checking by keeping a good eye on the barometer, we were able to make sure that the lows passed to the south of us.

On the third day out the wind began to pipe up a little at last. *Heath's Condor* was proving to be rather slow in really flat conditions, but once we got a force two to three wind she began to move, and we were soon logging between seven and ten knots every hour. As if to share our enjoyment of some speed at last, a school of dolphins appeared towards dusk and did their usual leaping about around the bow and on our bow wave. Some of the dolphins appeared to be calves as they were considerably smaller than the rest of the school.

The forecast indicated a front on the way, but the barometer showed very little sign of an abnormal fall, and in fact only fell about four millibars throughout the fourth day when the wind increased steadily. Remembering my previous experience, when falls of twenty millibars preceded a front, I could hardly believe we were sitting in the path of one at all, although the wind increased slowly through the night until we were running southeast before a force six or seven north-westerly wind at daybreak.

Despite the fact that both watches had gybed the boat on their own during the night, after breakfast when another gybe was necessary, we called all hands on deck and went through the procedure in slow time so that all the crew, but particularly new members, could take in everything that had to be done. Gybing on a small boat is a comparatively simple job, but on a large one, where the sails and gear have to be much bigger and stronger and therefore handled with considerably more respect, everything has to be planned out in advance.

Gybing, in effect, means turning the boat's head so that the wind which has been blowing from one quarter is brought right aft and then round to blow from the other quarter. All the sails, the spinnaker, staysail and mainsail, have to be changed round. The spinnaker is being held out in place by a long pole, the spinnaker pole, on the windward side. Another pole has to be set up on the leeward side, clipped onto the guy, the rope or wire specially clipped onto the spinnaker clew for the purpose, and hauled up and out so that when the wind direction changes the spinnaker will not collapse. The staysail is lowered and re-hoisted once the boat has been gybed. The mainsail boom is hauled in amidships and at that moment the boat is steered round so that the sails fill from the other side.

In a small boat gybing is a comparatively fast operation, but in a large one like *Heath's Condor* where the mainsail is 1,200 square feet and the boom weighs six hundred pounds, the mainsail has to be kept under control all through the manoeuvre. If it was allowed to swing across out of control it would smash everything in its path. To keep the mainsail under control we had three tackles on it at any time in addition to its main sheet, but even so, when it went across, it went with a considerable bang, which always made me worry about the strength of the fittings on the boom.

All we discovered in this particular gybe was that we could not strap the mainsail right in before gybing as it caught on the steering wheel; still, that in itself was a useful lesson, and we always took the flattening reef in before gybing thereafter. The flattening reef was the first reef in the mainsail, and was much smaller than the other reefs, its purpose being to take the fullness out of the mainsail rather than reduce its size.

The wind continued to rise, and we had to change down spinnakers, from our full size heavy to the gale kite, as the boat became unmanageable with too much sail up. Even this proved too much for the gear, and in mid afternoon, the spinnaker guy broke. The siren was sounded and Peter's watch came tumbling on deck to help get the spinnaker down. We rigged up a new guy and set up our storm spinnaker, a very small heavy spinnaker that set on a staysail halyard from the upper spreader, inside the forestay. It was the first time we had set this sail, and we played around with it for a while until it seemed comfortable.

All this time the sea had been getting up and the boat was speeding along averaging well over twelve knots. Towards nightfall, as the seas began to get really large, we began to surf. This was what I had been waiting for. On the first leg the boat had taken off now and again in the north-east Trades, but they are light puffs compared with the winds of the Southern Ocean, and what we had to find out was whether we could safely surf down these waves and maintain our directional stability. The danger is that once the boat starts to surf down the front of a wave she will get out of control and broach in front of the oncoming wave which will then roll right over her, certainly knocking her down but, even worse, perhaps rolling the boat right over. In *Suhaili* I had not taken this risk, and when the waves had got really large I had taken in all sail but a forty-square-foot storm jib and streamed six hundred feet of warp astern so that the boat was effectively braked when she wanted to surf. But *Heath's Condor* was built for speed, and was over two and a half times *Suhaili*'s length, and I wanted to see whether we could continue to hang onto sail and surf down every big wave that came along, trying to keep the boat's average speed up as high as possible.

The first few surfs were encouraging; we switched the log to double reading, and watched it climb to seventeen knots. The boat seemed quite safe and held course straight down the wave. The fear of the bow digging into the water and sending a wave back along the deck was also unfounded, because although it dipped as the stern was lifted, and the boat reached an angle of fifteen degrees or more by the head, the buoyancy of the bow quickly lifted it up again and we only took a few gallons on board forward. As the boat was lifted bodily by the forward slope of the wave she tended to run downhill, and it was when we were in this situation and travelling at not far short of the wave's speed that we were able to surf. Standing at the wheel one could feel the boat surge forward and then we were off. The bow waves on either side came aft in a welter of hissing foam, rising up well above the level of the deck and coming well back behind the mast. The noise the hull makes as it slips through the water rose to a higher note, and the hull gave off a low vibratory sound similar to that of a tube train. The prow of the boat was completely clear of the water, the bow wave rising on either side from beneath the bow, but everywhere else the boat was surrounded by white, curling, hissing water, culminating in a rooster tail four feet high that appeared about fifteen feet astern. Once surfing, the boat seemed very steady; there was no tendency to yaw at all and we were able to control her by keeping the helm held amidships and nothing more. This sort of surfing can only be compared with riding down a hill on a motor bike with the throttle jammed wide open and no brakes. In both cases all one can do is hang on and keep the machine steady. The slightest yaw means disaster, only in our case the nearest help was four hundred miles away.

Slowly our surfs got bigger and lasted longer. It was an exhilarating experience and, despite the risk, one that we all enjoyed. What puzzled us was that despite our very high bursts of speed—we were getting up to twenty-five knots at times—our average speed was not rising above 12½ knots. This in part was due to the boat wallowing a bit after each rush as the wave eventually overtook us and sometimes we found ourselves tipping backwards down the reverse side of the wave. Nevertheless I felt that we should be able to make a faster average.

As the seas built up it became more and more difficult to hold the boat on course. To surf we had to have the stern pointing at the oncoming wave. If we did not achieve this position at the right moment, the boat would be picked up and pushed at an angle to the wave and the helmsman would have to wind the wheel frantically to prevent a broach. We would then have to let go the mainsail to bring the head round downwind, but, unless the turns were wound off quickly once the boat began to answer her rudder, she tended to swing round too fast and we risked having an unplanned gybe which, in those seas, could have taken the mast out of the boat.

Remembering back to my previous experience in these waters, and the size and power of the waves that eventually developed, I decided that our yaws were becoming too frequent and reluctantly ordered the spinnaker down and a headsail set in its place. A week later I would not have given in, but I was remembering how difficult it had been for me in *Suhaili* in these conditions, and I could see that the crew were beginning to get worried about the situation. And having broken a mast in the first leg, it was important to build up confidence in the new mast on this leg, and risking the gear was not going to do that. I was probably a bit cowardly, but no race has ever been won by a boat that lost her mast. As it happens, once the sails were changed, we lost no speed at all, and the boat was a lot more comfortable and much easier to handle as well. We still had our surfing, not to quite the same top speeds, but our hourly average speed did not go down at all, and as dusk fell, we were still averaging 12½ knots.

Each day we had a set time and frequency when all the boats would tune in and exchange positions and information. The degree of information exchanged depended upon the tactical situation at the time. For instance, if one had found a good patch of wind one did not particularly want to say so directly as the other boats would head for it and pick up speed as well. They could work it out from the position one gave if they wanted to. I always enjoyed the 'chat show', and, provided people were giving accurate positions, it enabled us to settle down and work out how we were doing relative to the fleet. The first two days of the race had been very confusing, and those who were lucky enough to get under a bit of cloud had had the wind for a while. The result was that no particular pattern had developed, and there was no indication as to how the boats would really go once we all got down south to the real wind. It appeared that we had pulled up and although *King's Legend* claimed to be ahead of us, after our day's surfing, according to the position given us by her the previous day, we had taken sixty miles out of her in twenty-four hours, an average of 2½ knots. I thought she had been going rather too well at the beginning of the race according to her claims, and I did not believe we had done 2½ knots more than her for a whole day. Either their navigation was out or they had overclaimed the second day, or, of course, they were further on than they said. With this number of choices it was not worth bothering about—sooner or later the truth would have to come out, even if it was at the end of the race. The bad news that came over was that *Gauloises II* had damaged her rudder and was heading for Port Elizabeth for repairs. This was a great pity, as she had been sailing very well up until then. Apparently, she and *Adventure* had been only a couple of miles apart when the accident occurred, but *Gauloises* had not asked for assistance. They must have had great fun racing along in a gale in the Southern Ocean prior to the accident.

Peter's watch went on duty at 20.00, to be treated to a bowl of porridge made by Golf Charlie. The porridge we ate varied from a good thick dumpling-like mixture to a thin watery gruel, depending upon who made it. This was the first attempt at porridge this trip and its creator was treated to a fairly rough reception. Bill, being a Scot, was looked to as an expert and said after a thoughtful spoonful that apart from being uncooked and lacking in salt it was not bad. Barry said the building trade would welcome it. Golf Charlie retired hurt, but I noticed that it was all eaten.

As the night wore on the wind began to lessen. It is always easy to avoid putting up more sail at times like this, as the seas are still rough and the conditions feel a lot worse than they are because the boat is underpowered and so gets thrown about more. In fact the best thing to do is hoist more sail and keep the boat moving as fast as possible as the speed of the boat gives it a fair amount of stability. It is just like riding a bicycle: if you go too slowly you start to wobble, only instead of wobbling the boat starts to roll and pitch more.

A second front followed quite quickly after the first, but it was not as aggressive, and the wind did not rise as much. Nevertheless we got some good surfs from it and it was while surfing at nineteen knots that the big heavy spinnaker suddenly took off. Fortunately we were preparing to take it down at the time, and so we had everyone on deck and another headsail already bent on, but we were still lucky to recover it without damage. Once we had it below, we discovered the cause. The head swivel of heavy cast bronze had been pulled apart! As we carried spares it was not a tremendous problem, but it had been a bad day for Paul, the sailmaker. He will always say that his problems started when Golf Charlie said he was looking miserable and needed something to do. Within five minutes, our big yellow tri-radial spinnaker split down a seam. We set the big heavy spinnaker in its place and two hours later that was down for repairs as well. We could not afford to be without our two largest heavy spinnakers, so whilst Ronnie helped Paul to repair the yellow, I put a new swivel on the heavy. Sailmakers use a heavy terylene woven tape for this job, and having wound it round the eye of the swivel and the ring on the sail a number of times, stitch it together. Paul explained how it was done and when I had finished he had to agree that his instructions could have been interpreted that way but he had never seen it done quite like that before! All I can say is that it did not break again.

Paul worked on through the night sewing away at the repairs. The great thing about having a sailmaker in the crew is that he gets a repair completed in a quarter of the time, the repair looks right, and usually stays together. Having him working full time on sails deprived one watch of a hand, but if we had only carried out repairs when Paul was on watch we would have been without vital sails for too long. As it was, he worked through until the job was done, and then disappeared into his bunk for about twelve hours. For a young man in his early twenties, Paul has the knowledge and ability in his profession to match that of many older men, and he has a conscientious, hardworking approach to the job. Combine this with a pleasant personality and deep interest in sailing and you realise how lucky we were to have him on board.

All through the night we kept up an average of over eleven knots, and by noon when I took the latitude we had managed a day's run of 253 miles, our best to date. We had now covered a total of 878 miles from Cape Town in five days' sailing, a not too good average, but badly brought down by the first two days of variable winds. At dusk we saw a light to the south of us, which caused us some concern as *King's Legend* reckoned she was sixteen miles north and ten miles east of us, having done another of her sixty-mile jumps in position. We passed slowly ahead and she acknowledged that she had us in sight, so we had got into the lead at last. However variable *King's Legend*'s navigation was, one had to acknowledge that they were sailing well. It was interesting to see that the two biggest sloops in the race, and not the ketches, the rig generally favoured for sailing in the Southern Ocean, were up in front together. Frankly I like a ketch for cruising or short-handed races, where sails in smaller parcels make sail handling easier, but for racing with a full crew I cannot see the logic of it. A mizzen invariably does little when sailing to windward, and gets in the way when running. It only comes into its own when reaching. Against this, a sloop, usually with a bigger mast, gets all the advantages of a higher aspect ratio and can set a much larger spinnaker.

The next morning *King's Legend* put herself ahead of us again by dead reckoning and we decided that they had an optimistic log.

Navigation in a small yacht differs little from that in any large ship except that, in races, one is not allowed to use Satellite Navigation systems and navigators are basically allowed to use a sextant, or when close to a coast, Radio Direction Finding. The use of a sextant in a small boat requires considerable practice, as one is not very far above sea level and the horizon is pretty close, just over three miles away. This means that in rough weather when there is a heavy swell running, the horizon is frequently difficult to find between swell waves, and one really has to wait until the boat is on top of a wave to get a good reading of whatever heavenly body one is using, be it the sun, moon, planet or star. The trouble here is that the boat is lifted up and then dropped back down again quite quickly, so one only has a very short time to adjust the sextant to the exact altitude, check that it is steady, and yell stop to the person taking the time on the chronometer. A second out in time can make a difference of a mile in the result, and of course a second out in one's sextant reading is exactly a mile of error. Having taken the altitude, one has to apply a number of corrections from tables, the most basic being the height of the eye of the observer above mean sea level at the precise moment the reading was taken. This has to be a matter of judgement as far as the boat is concerned, because if you have taken the observation at the top of the swell, your height of eye is going to be half the swell height, plus the boat's freeboard, plus your own height above mean sea level. To average these out, I always take three quick readings in a row and work them all out, and then take the average of the three as my answer. I usually work them out the long way using the Marc St Hilaire method, but just before the race I had been approached by Basil D'Oliveira who had produced a series of navigation programmes to suit an HP 67 pocket calculator, and had agreed to try them out. It took me a bit of time to understand the programmes but, once I had got the hang of them, I was whistling out the answers in no time, and taking a sight became the job of a few minutes instead of a quarter of an hour. I usually took a longitude in the morning and a latitude at noon, followed by another longitude in the afternoon. If we were close to land I would take a star position as well. Most boats carry separate navigators, but as Les and I enjoy doing it, it means we do not have to carry an extra person. If anything had happened to me we had four others on board who could have navigated perfectly adequately.

I had intended going south of Marion Island, the first of a series of small groups of volcanic islands that are scattered across the Southern Ocean at about forty-six degrees south, between South Africa and Australia. Our course lay south of all of them except Marion Island, which it went straight through, but in the event, sailing for the wind rather than an exact course, we passed about a hundred miles north.

None of these islands—the Prince Edward Islands which includes Marion Island, The Crozets, the Kerguelens, Heard and McDonald Islands—is inhabited, apart from research teams. During the nineteenth century they formed bases for sealers from Europe and America, but no permanent settlements were established. Fitful surveys have been made from time to time, but it is only during the last few years that we've begun to know them properly.

The coastlines are most inhospitable, and in many cases bordered by large fields of kelp, perhaps the largest plant on Earth which can grow in depths of up to a hundred feet. The bladder kelp, or nereocystis, which likes a rocky bottom near active waves or currents, has tremendously long tendrils as thick as a man's leg at the base, and will soon jam up a keel or propeller; few sailors will risk taking their ships into it. Kelp is often broken off and floats away into the Southern Ocean, so one does not only see it near land. The first time Justin saw some he called out that a large stick of rhubarb was going past, and I suppose rhubarb is the closest we get to kelp on land in Britain.

Nowadays South Africa runs the Prince Edwards, Australia the Heard and McDonald Islands, and France the remainder. Large tracts have been designated National Parks. It is good to see that in even a remote area like this, the cause of conservation has not been ignored. The French Navy often keeps a warship based on the Kerguelens, as the waters around the island teem with crayfish and these crustacea are so valuable nowadays that it is well worth travelling the distance to pick up a holdful, and if there were no controls we humans would soon fish the place out.

Although there are no indigenous human inhabitants, the islands form breeding grounds for a wide variety of seals. Elephant, leopard, crabeater, Kerguelen and southern fur seals breed here in what appears to us to be a very inhospitable environment, but must be a paradise compared with their only alternative, Antarctica, a few hundred miles to the south.

An attempt was made on one of these islands to breed sheep, but it did not turn out to be successful though a few remain. Rabbits are found on most of the islands, probably put there by seamen years ago to provide food in the event of shipwreck. All the islands have huts with food stored in them for use by shipwrecked mariners. These stores were set up in the nineteenth century, it being the custom of ships to establish such stores in remote areas regardless of nationality or cost—an example of the cooperation amongst men to whom the shared danger and perils of their common element overrode nationalistic considerations.

In fact, despite their starkness, and the snow that covers them during the winter months when the average minimum temperature hovers around freezing point, a surprising amount of vegetation exists, the most interesting being the Kerguelen cabbage which has excellent anti-scorbutic properties.

Penguins are quite common and we found them swimming around in the ocean swell over a hundred miles away from Marion Island. Their peculiar agitated method of swimming, popping under water and popping up again a short way off for a quick breath and look around before abruptly disappearing again, is both attractive and amusing, and it would have been pleasant to stop for a while and watch them.

I think there is a streak in all of us that creates a desire to stop and have a look at a remote and partly explored area, and these islands appeared very romantic to us. So much so that I was always having to go off in search of the Admiralty

Antarctic Pilot when I wanted information, because someone had it out of the chartroom and was reading it. I will have to make time to visit them someday.

Gordon Proctor on Marion Island, who apart from giving us weather information was reporting our positions back to Cape Town, used to tell us about the island and the research team of fourteen—mainly meteorologists and biologists—who stayed there for up to a year at a stretch. At this particular time it was just in the middle of the breeding season; there were about 650,000 penguins, mostly the rockhopper, macaroni and king species. The team estimated that 70,000 king penguin eggs had hatched out that year. They also had a lot of elephant seal pups. Vegetation consisted of grass and bogs and of course the Kerguelen cabbage; trees could not survive the conditions.

We passed the latitude of Marion Island, about forty-six degrees south, on 1st November, having had a poor day's run the previous day of only 190 miles, due to a light westerly wind that never rose above force four. In this sort of conditions, where it is easy to manage the boat, I like to get the crew up in the cockpit at about 17.00 for a 'happy hour'. Some boats do not believe in carrying alcohol on board during a race, but Les and I have always felt that it is good for morale to have a time during the day when as many of the crew as possible can get together in relaxing circumstances. It is not always possible to do this in a race, as pushing the boat must take priority, but when it can be done I think it worthwhile. Usually a couple of drinks each are consumed which is enough to relax people, and tensions between them which might otherwise become a problem are often eased. I found that although there was absolutely no drink rationing, and anyone could help themselves when they liked, our consumption of alcohol was not very great. We had enough beer on board to allow each man a can a day for forty days, but only a third of this was drunk. Spirits were more popular, but even then we only got through just over four cases, an average of two bottles a day for fifteen people. We had started out with a dozen bottles of sherry, but it was soon clear we should have taken more as the 'Major' had a preference for it, and we caught him concealing the stock so that he could make it last out longer. His plan failed, and we ran out in a fortnight. It is quite impossible to be a secret drinker or hoard a personal stock on board a small boat, because if one person feels like a drink, the odds are that someone else will see it and ask for one as well. Poor Major, he is not a secret drinker, but however much he tried to conserve the sherry, it kept disappearing.

On this particular occasion nearly all of us were in the cockpit, despite the cold, as our polar suits kept us insulated from the worst of the temperature. At times like this it was almost impossible to stop Barry Buchannan from story telling. He had a fund of tales, not all brilliantly funny, but the way he told them, with full quadrophonic effects, was hilarious.

Ronnie Roos had developed toothache during the day, due, someone suggested, to his habit of washing. But the doctor discovered that he had a filling missing and put in a temporary one. On previous trips I had carried spirit of cloves to deal with troublesome teeth, and if that runs out or fails, one can always fall back on whisky which will at least make the pain bearable. On balance I think it is better to carry a doctor. As he had only recently qualified, I was never sure how much depth of knowledge he had, but he was never caught out by anything that occurred on board. Not only did he know what to do, but he had remembered to bring along all that was necessary to do it with—all packed into half a dozen Tupperware containers. It gives one tremendous confidence to have a person like that in the crew.

Another casualty at this time was Paul, who went down with sinusitis. I think this may have been due to a general weakening as a result of overwork. He had had no time off in Cape Town, and had then worked hard on sail repairs since we had left, and he must have needed a rest. He had had a motor cycle crash just before we left Cape Town, which left him bruised and shaken, and I don't think that helped much, either. We put him off deck for a while to give him time to rest.

As if to compensate for the poor winds on 31st October, much of the next twenty-four hours was spent with winds of force seven and eight. The wind, although it was westerly, had been south-south-west in this area as we found there was quite a sea running from this direction, which, as the westerly sea built up, gave us a confused cross sea which was not at all comfortable. No fronts had been forecast, and the predicted isobars hardly tied in with what we were getting so we watched the sky astern rather anxiously. Because we had two spinnakers under repair again, we had changed down to a boomed out headsail as the wind got up, but once it appeared to steady at about force seven we hoisted the storm spinnaker and took off, yawing all over the place. As if to spite us, the wind got up again once the spinnaker was up. We held on for a while, partly because it could have eased and partly to see how the boat would handle, but when the wind reached over forty-five knots across the deck, which meant about sixty knots of true wind, we called all hands and let go the weather sheet and guy and hauled it down. I was standing by the shrouds as the sail came in, hauling away with about ten others. Unfortunately the sail was grabbed on either side of me and I was slowly pulled backwards until I fell into the port winch cockpit and was promptly covered with sail. It was very comfortable, but I was a bit upset that no one noticed I was missing!

We kept under boomed out headsail all night, averaging a steady twelve knots according to the log, and occasionally surfing a great deal faster. David Alan-Williams managed to get right off the clock on one wave and as we were on double reading this meant we had hit over thirty knots. I had been lying down fully clothed in the saloon, but as he went off down this particular wave I had got up and put my head through the hatch. We had huge ten-foot-high white hissing waves on either side of the boat, only restricted to port where the waves were hitting and backfilling the mainsail. The noise woke everyone, and even Ronnie's yell that we were off the clock was drowned out. When the wind eased, we set the bullet-proof storm spinnaker, and managed to end up at noon with a run of 267 miles, our best so far. As the wind took its time to ease, we managed 257 miles the next day which put us well ahead of the other boats.

One of the best side effects of these two good runs—apart from the obvious delight we all felt at travelling 524 miles in two days—was the fact that everyone began to feel really confident in the boat, her mast and gear, and our ability to push her hard in rough weather. It was noticeable that I had to chivvy people a lot less after this to hold onto sail, or put more up earlier, and our day's runs showed a steady improvement.

November 3rd saw us cross into the fifties which was the cause of celebration, the Major getting at his sherry. Having had a couple of glasses he got energetic, and insisted upon personally supervising the changeover of calor gas cylinders as we had finished our first one. He took Bill with him as assistant, mainly, it was claimed with some ribaldry, because he was unable to insert a screwdriver into the screws that held the calor gas locker lid. After half an hour of abuse, the lid came off, and then an argument developed as to which of the three cylinders was empty. Bill was eventually ordered to remove one that appeared to all of us to be a bit heavy for an empty, but the Major insisted. Having struggled to and from the lazarete with cylinders and reconnected them, the Major then announced that gas was restored to the galley. There was an outraged yell from Golf Charlie who was on duty as no gas came through, and the lid was unscrewed again and the real empty cylinder disconnected and replaced. The Major refused to have anything to do with the second changeover. He retired below muttering about the low standard of intelligence with which he found himself confined. I noticed half an hour later that he was writing his log with no difficulty at all and, when I accused him of hamming, he grinned happily. Lunch was three-quarters of an hour late as a result of all this mucking about, but it gave everyone something to laugh at.

Crossing the fiftieth parallel of latitude seemed to have a psychological effect upon the weather. A low, centred only six hundred miles to the south of us with a pressure of 948 millibars, got active, and its associated front began to chase us rather quickly. Normally these fronts move eastwards at an average of about seven hundred miles in twenty-four hours, but this one came up on us a lot more quickly. Added to this, it suddenly became a lot colder. We measured the seawater temperature and it was down to three degrees Celsius, and the air temperature was even colder. It became so cold down below that our breathing showed up as a white cloud, and anyone using the heads lost sight of them in a cloud of steam. Everyone took to wearing polar gear full time, even when sleeping inside a quilted sleeping bag. The cold alone was bearable but Leslie's comments about the ventilation system were proved more than accurate. Water from waves coming inboard seemed to have no difficulty finding their way below, and I for one had a soaked sleeping bag before I was aware of the danger and jammed the ventilators above my bunk with towels. The trouble with the ventilation system was that it just did not ventilate. It created no movement of air within the boat and neither brought in fresh air nor evacuated the stale air. The inevitable result was that water vapour in the air condensed on everything, and then dripped down onto sleeping bags, settees, the alleyway—everywhere. I had felt aggrieved when my sleeping bag got soaked, but within a day everyone's bags were wet and there was nothing we could do about it. They dried out a bit when one was in them but soon returned to being cold and damp when one got up. Coming off watch frozen, and then having to crawl into a cold and damp sleeping bag, is not exactly comfortable living.

To try and improve things, I put my sleeping bag inside a large plastic bag and slept inside it there. This had the advantage that it warmed up a lot more quickly, but the moisture that would normally have left the sleeping bag only condensed inside the plastic bag and was re-absorbed. I gave it up as a bad job and resigned myself to being wet and cold when going to sleep.

The front when it caught up with us on 5th November was not as bad as we had expected but gave us our first snow, enough to give a depth of nine inches around the winch cockpit, which was irresistible to the older members of the crew like Peter and myself who promptly began throwing snowballs at each other.

The wind that came with the front also gave us our best day's run of 270 miles, and we found we had pulled out to two degrees of longitude ahead of the bigger *Great Britain II*. It was obviously paying us to keep going south, despite the cold, which I think helped in a way as everyone was keen to be active to keep warm and we changed sail very aggressively. I was glad that we had taken the trouble to put everyone on the helm during the first few days, as we could now let anyone steer the boat, even in really rough conditions, and steering was the warmest job going. Apart from this of course, everyone wants to steer, and feels encouraged if you trust them to do it.

Every day after leaving Cape Town, we had been followed

by sea birds: Cape pigeons, petrels and of course the giant wandering albatross. As we moved further south, the wandering albatross left us, and we only had the smaller sooty albatross in its place. Some wit suggested that this proved the intelligence of the wandering albatross who had more sense than us and did not go further south than fifty degrees. Whatever their reason, about fifty degrees south is where we stopped seeing them, which did not tie in with what is thought to be the normal behaviour of these birds. Furthermore, when we eventually started to come north a fortnight later, we were all looking for the wandering albatross, and the first one was sighted at about fifty degrees south again.

People who go to sea in a sailing ship have a much better opportunity of seeing the natural life at sea than those aboard power-driven vessels, because their progress is dependent upon natural forces, and there is no thump of machinery or propeller vibration to frighten marine and bird life away. To all sea birds, who subsist largely by scavenging what they can from the surface of the sea, we were initially something large and possibly edible in those otherwise deserted waters. On closer investigation, they noticed that from time to time we threw food overboard, and we were thus a fairly reliable food source for them, and so they followed us. Usually they glided about in our wake but occasionally an albatross would sweep past us, not more than a few feet away and then, with a scarcely perceptible wing movement, bank and glide round in a wide circle to resume its station in our wake again. The albatrosses only rarely flapped their wings: they seem to have discovered a form of aerial perpetual motion, and can glide for hour after hour in their endless search for food.

We could not tell whether we had the same birds with us day after day, as we could not pick out any individual characteristics, but it was quite possible. Some of these birds which have been ringed in New Zealand have been found in South America only thirty days later, having covered five thousand miles at an average of 160 miles per day.

Albatrosses mate every two years and usually only one egg is laid. It is reputed that, like swans, they mate with the same partner for life, but observations of the royal albatross at Tairoa Head in New Zealand indicate that this may not necessarily be the case. They live to the age of thirty if some calamity does not intervene, and the survival rate amongst the young is high. They do settle on the surface of the sea to rest and sleep, and when sitting there look rather like pictures of the dodo. Despite Coleridge's *Rime of the Ancient Mariner* not all seamen considered the albatross to embody the soul of a dead mariner, and they used to be caught and killed by the crews of sailing ships who found that once a bird had been pulled onto the deck it could be set free as the deck was not long enough for an albatross to take off. It is nice to think that catching these beautiful, graceful birds, second in size only to the condor, is a thing of the past, and that they have no other natural enemy apart from the elements.

Now and again we saw seals. Usually the birds showed us where they were because they clustered over anything in the water. Only twice did we see whales, and fortunately not too close. There seem to have been many more instances of yachts being struck by whales in recent years, but no one seems to have come up with a sensible reason for it, and I cannot believe that the whole genus have taken it into their heads to become more aggressive towards yachts. Maybe it is just that there are more yachts about now, and therefore the opportunity occurs more often. I wonder whether the use of lighter coloured anti-fouling paint has not got something to do with it. All fish are lighter underneath so that a predator looking up is less likely to see them against a lighter background. It is possible that a surfacing whale is less likely to see a boat with a white bottom, than one with the more traditional dark red or blue bottom which would show up better against the surface of the sea. Although I have had whales surface very close to me, I have never been struck by one. On the other hand I have avoided too much noise and movement on board when they have been close.

We would all have liked to have seen more whales, and I was surprised that we only had two sightings. There are still far too many being caught by the Russians and Japanese, and this is difficult to justify when everything that is produced from a whale can be produced by alternative means these days. Why these two nations should continue to hunt whales, and take them in such vast quantities that the largest mammal on Earth is threatened with extinction, at a time when all civilised countries are aware of the need to preserve as much as we can of our natural environment, is an international disgrace. It reflects no credit at all on the Russians and Japanese, and very little on anyone else because they do not make enough fuss about it.

On 7th November, having sailed 2,817 miles in nearly thirteen days, we reached fifty-five degrees south in longitude, seventy-eight degrees east. We had been averaging nearly seven degrees of longitude a day for some time but although we would have covered the distance quicker further south, by this time we knew that the pack ice was at fifty-seven degrees south and I did not want to race too close to that. The seawater temperature was down to just over one degree Celsius, and the air temperature fell below freezing every night, but did at least rise to about two degrees during the day. All the aluminium coaming was painful to touch, and a thin film of ice covered the mast and boom. We had to take the mainsail down that afternoon in a snowstorm to re-fasten the two top slides, and we found that it too was iced up. Normally this would not cause much difficulty, as a sail usually moves a bit and this would dislodge any ice on it, but we had been on one tack for fourteen hours and the sail had not been panting so ice had formed. Paul as usual did the repair, his fingers becoming almost useless in the process, and when he came to start feeding the sliders back into their track, I felt he had suffered enough and it was time to lead by example. I soon regretted my decision. The slides were absolutely frozen, and holding them quickly drew all the warmth out of one's fingers, so that after the third or fourth one I was guiding my disembodied fingers which were feeding no sensations back at all. The worst part was after all the slides were back and circulation began to return to my hands. It hurt like hell, and I stayed on deck until it was over to make the change more gradual. The temperature inside the boat varied between two and three degrees, three when we had the galley in use, but it felt a lot warmer down below because one was out of the wind. People who had just come off deck were easily identified by their steaming hands!

That evening we had another gale which lasted right through the next day, and as the glass fell twenty-two millibars in eight hours we undersailed the boat for a while until things settled a bit. Visibility was down to just over a boat's length in the snow and I wondered whether I had not come too close to the ice. In that sort of visibility one does not feel over happy at running at ten or more knots, as even if we saw something ahead we would not have been able to alter course fast enough to avoid it. Nevertheless lookouts were posted up in the pulpit, and relieved, half frozen, every half hour. I was thankful that the nights in that latitude lasted only about five hours.

The gale eased on the 8th, the sky began to clear, and we saw some beautiful contrasts in colours on the sea. One moment it was leaden, and the breaking crests were dull; the next, a shaft of sunlight would hit the surface, transforming the sea to a beautiful blue colour speckled with wave crests glistening with incredible brightness. The trouble with turning back to look at the waves was that spray, picked up by the winds, hit you in the face, and although the seawater felt warmer than the air, it soon felt intolerably cold as the wind cooled it down.

We did our only serious broach that afternoon, which buried one side of the boat in the water, and yet again proved the excellence of the ventilation system which allowed water to pour below. If the designer had been there at that moment fifteen very angry men would have held him under one of those waterfalls, which were, ostensibly, sealed up. The heavy spinnaker wrapped itself around the forestay, despite the net that was set up to prevent this, and had to be brought down. We had had quite a bit of trouble with spinnaker nets and Golf Charlie offered to produce one that would prevent the spinnaker wrapping itself round. It took five days, and when completed, with special boards to which it could be tied when taken down to avoid a tangle, it looked most impressive. Unfortunately, it took about ten minutes to set up, and on one occasion nearly three-quarters of an hour to take down. Numerous modifications were made, but it never really got better, and it became a standing joke on board, whenever Golf Charlie strode purposefully forward with an assistant trailing his tail of ropes and labels. Still it performed its primary function all right; it did prevent the spinnaker from wrapping around the forestay.

Unfortunately the spinnaker was torn when it wrapped, and we found ourselves yet again without a suitable spinnaker to set, so we boomed out a yankee to weather and hoisted the reacher to leeward and the boat loved it. She romped along and became very easy to steer.

The sudden easing of the boat's motion, and the relaxation of some tension as people realised that we had no other spinnaker to hoist, and were, in any case, going as fast as if we had one set anyway, brought on a sudden burst of high spirits. The Major at the helm asked for his gloves but found he could not put them on as Paul had stitched them up halfway in. This apple pie glove prompted some most un-Sandhurst-like language. Then Les Best decided to jettison our by now leaking galley waste bucket and replace it with a new one. Unfortunately he did not tell Golf Charlie that he had found a spare, and the horrified commissar saw Les throw overside what he thought to be our last gash bucket. 'You Kiwi vandal,' yelled Golf Charlie, and then, turning apoplectically on Herman, who had popped his head up to support his catering partner, bawled 'You . . . You . . . Visigoth.' The crew were rolling around nearly crying with laughter. However, a sobering fact about throwing the bucket over was that we lost sight of it within five seconds, not a pleasant thought for anyone going overside, as Peter commented.

For some time I had been having great difficulty making contact with Cape Town on the radio, and even the boats only twenty degrees or seven hundred miles astern of us, like *ADC Accutrac*, could not hear us, and I could not hear them. Under the race rules we were supposed to report in twice a week, but this we just could not do, despite our theoretical four hundred watts output. Fortunately the service's entry *Adventure* was still getting through to the UK, and reported nearly all the boats each time. The spectacular Aurora Australis which was brilliantly illuminating the sky during darkness was not helping radio transmissions either.

The Auroras are a dawnlike glow seen towards the poles in both the northern and southern hemispheres. It is caused by the collision of electrical particles emitted by the sun and atmospheric gases at a height of sixty miles or more above the Earth's surface. These electrical particles are drawn towards the north and south magnetic poles as they approach the Earth, which is why the usual Aurora is rarely seen nearer the Equator except in times of great sunspot activity, when a great

Aurora can occur outside the polar areas. The fact that we could see the Southern Aurora, at fifty-five degrees south, indicated a greater than usual emission of electrical particles by the sun, and it undoubtedly affected our radio transmissions.

On 10th November, we crossed the meridian of one hundred degrees east, which put us over halfway to the finishing line. The day did not start at all auspiciously; while doing Peter's watch for him during the morning, I decided we could set a spinnaker but the halyard jammed when the sail was half hoisted. It would neither go up nor come down, and while I was pondering the problem its bag fell and it broke out. The weight of wind in the sail was sufficient to pull the halyard out a bit, but it also allowed the sail to swing about and it eventually caught round the main boom and tore, causing a wail of anguish from Paul. We hauled in the remains and lashed it as best we could to the mast whilst we set another headsail to keep the boat moving. There was no alternative to sending someone aloft to unclip the halyard and then go on up to the masthead and change the spinnaker and masthead block.

I used to enjoy going aloft in those sort of conditions, and will still do so if I have to. But ever since I was halfway between the spreaders and masthead on *Frigate* in the 1973 Admiral's Cup when she broached, I have been happy to let someone else volunteer if they want to. In this case, Peter volunteered, and having organised what the deck party was to do, I went aft and took the helm to hold the boat as steady as possible. Peter was hoisted aloft and we hauled up a new block and rove a new halyard. Despite all I could do, we still took the occasional roll and I estimated that Peter was being swung through about eighty feet at times when he was at the masthead. He did the job, however, and I watched thankfully as he was lowered back down onto the deck looking decidedly green. He said that he had been nearly sick whilst aloft and I believed him, but whether you would call it seasickness or airsickness I do not know. One counts oneself lucky to have a seaman like Peter in one's crew.

At noon that day we talked to *Great Britain II* and *King's Legend*, the only boats in radio range, and both reported icebergs to the north of them. They were both about twenty miles north of us and one hundred and two hundred miles astern of us respectively, which meant we had passed to the south of their bergs. According to *Adventure*, the US Navy had reported a remote possibility of bergs north of fifty-five degrees south, but these bergs appeared to be at about fifty-four degrees, the equivalent latitude of Leeds in the northern hemisphere.

It is not often realised just how vast is the area of ice over Antarctica. The area of the Earth's surface below latitude sixty degrees south is over ten million square miles, nearly all of which is covered by a thick surface of ice, all moving slowly outwards at a rate of about three cables a year. At this rate over three thousand square miles of ice is cast loose each year into the Southern Ocean in the form of icebergs.

The coast of Antarctica is bordered by pack ice, made up of glacier ice from the glaciers flowing northward from the continent, and sea ice that is formed by the sea freezing into ice at a temperature of below minus two degrees Celsius. The pack joins together during the winter when its depth is increased due to snow falls, but breaks off quite suddenly from late August onwards. Initially the pack ice drifts westwards, due to the west-going current south of about sixty degrees south, but it has a slight northerly coefficient, and once it has reached this latitude, tends to be swept into the great eastward movement of water in the Southern Ocean. The density of the ice forming an iceberg is about 0.9000, but varies depending upon the amount of salt in it. With most of its mass below water, an iceberg is only slightly affected by the wind, and its movement is almost entirely controlled by the ocean currents. The extreme limit of icebergs, which usually occurs in December, is as much as forty degrees south in places. We had had reports that the border of the pack ice lay at about fifty-eight degrees south, and John Ridgeway, in *Debenhams*, had run into it at about that latitude a few days earlier, so we should not have been oversurprised at reports of icebergs at fifty-four degrees south.

I had never seen an iceberg, my time at sea being largely spent in the Tropics, and I was quite keen to see one close to. At the same time, we were in a race, and could hardly take time off to go looking at a berg if we did see one, and anyway I had hoped that the bergs would stay well south of us, as the thought of running into a large lump of ice while pushing a boat flat out with a spinnaker up is not conducive to good sleeping below.

But unless we ran into a large cluster of bergs I decided that we would press on and hope that our lookout would see a berg in sufficient time for us to take avoiding action.

Later that afternoon, at about 17.00, we saw our first berg some four to six miles away to the north. It was difficult to assess its size properly because it was over the horizon, but I estimated from sextant angles that if it was four miles away it was at least seven hundred feet long and 150 feet high and if further away was larger. To leeward of the berg we ran into a lot of quite large lumps of ice, or growlers, and these really did worry me as, although quite large, they were seldom more than a few feet high and difficult to see as the waves washed over them. I decided, in view of this, not to sail under spinnaker after dark, as the boat could be manoeuvred much more safely and quickly under twin headsails. We did see quite a few more bergs, and glanced off a small growler one night, fortunately without damage—in fact no one below even knew it had happened—but I am glad that icebergs are not a normal hazard at sea.

The Major and I had been discussing giving everyone a treat at the halfway mark, and had decided that we would make a curry for dinner. The date had to be chosen in advance so as not to upset the normal cooking schedule, and also because it gave us longer to enjoy the planning stage.

To make a curry properly one ought to make it the day before it is going to be served as this gives it time to mature. We could not do this as we did not have enough saucepans and also one does not like leaving a pan of runny food lying about in a boat which is rolling and lurching the whole time. We started immediately after breakfast by frying six large sliced onions in a saucepan in two ounces of butter and a cup of cooking oil. When these were brown we stirred in a whole 200-gramme tin of curry powder and 100 grammes of paprika. Immediately the smell of curry began to permeate the whole boat. Once the mix was well fried, we added eight pounds of chicken pieces and kept stirring it for about ten minutes before adding two cups of salt water, a tin of tomatoes, and four garlic cloves well chopped up. We left the concoction boiling for a while and then let it simmer for a couple of hours before we tasted it. A few improvements seemed necessary so we added a couple of chicken stock cubes and a whole bottle of tabasco sauce to give it a bit more heat. The curry matured all afternoon and was turned out with rice for dinner. Two of the crew said they didn't like curry but came back for seconds and the whole lot disappeared. I had hoped to have a bit over to make mulligatawny soup, but no such luck. Still, a satisfied clientele is always rewarding for a cook.

The curry obviously kept the crew alert as we hit no ice all night, although a berg came into view to the north again at daybreak. November 11–12th gave us our best day's run, of 298 miles in twenty-four hours, much of this due, we felt, to the fact that the wind came round to south-west by south and we had the reacher up for much of the time. For some reason the stern did not dig in as much when reaching as it did when running, and the boat went faster. It was harder work for the helmsman though it kept us warm, and it also meant that we took more water over the deck which inevitably found its way below. A front during the night gave us snow, sleet, hail and rain, and I allowed each watch, apart from the lookout, helmsman and one in the cockpit, to stay below when not required for working the boat, as there was no point in freezing everyone. But at daybreak we went back to having the whole watch on deck when on duty, as once the cooks were up there was too much noise to allow the off-duty watch to sleep.

We had now travelled 4,068 miles, at an average speed of 9.55 knots. I still hoped to make the trip in thirty days which meant that we had to average 230 miles a day but we were trying to push our average speed up to ten knots. As things were, however, if we kept up our average of over 250 miles a day which we had been making for the last ten days, we were going to have no trouble. We still had the Tasman Sea to cope with, though, and if we met calms that would slow us down badly. Still, we had pulled out on the rest of the fleet, and the nearest boat to us, *Great Britain II*, was 190 miles astern, so we had every encouragement to morale to keep pushing.

Australia was almost north of us now and I got out the next chart, the fourth to be used since leaving Cape Town. We also began to run down the Earth's Variation at last. At one time we had had sixty-one degrees of Westerly Variation, which meant that if we wanted to make a true course of 090 degrees, we had to steer 151 degrees on the compass to compensate. I had explained this to those of the crew who did not navigate as I did not want them to think I was setting a course for the South Pole and misleading them as to our whereabouts. We felt that this rather extreme variation might have been the cause of our Dead Reckonings being slightly out because, although we knew from the charts how much Variation to apply, we thought that the angle of dip might be quite steep and therefore the horizontal directive force of the Earth's lines of magnetic force, which control the compass, might be weak, and the compass would swing more easily as a result. I had been checking the compass, by taking bearings of the sun and stars with it and then calculating the true bearings, but it had never exceeded six degrees off what we expected. It was when I transferred our position onto the next chart and compared the lines of Variation that we realised what was wrong. The lines of Variation did not agree. Our next chart was a later publication so we used what it told us, but it is time the Admiralty re-published the chart for that part of the Southern Ocean. Although it had been corrected it needed a major revision. I do not suppose there is much demand for it, though, apart from crazy yachtsmen every few years.

Whilst thinking about the compass error, it occurred to me that perhaps our compass had heeling correction magnets in it, but we had no literature on board so I could not check it. If it had—as we had done nothing about them in Cape Town, and as far as I knew Les had not reversed them when he crossed the Equator—we now had a compass set up to be accurate when heeled in the northern hemisphere, and here we were well into the southern hemisphere. As our errors when heeled were not that much, certainly less than a helmsman's normal error, it did not matter too much, but it is something that I should have thought of, and checked, when I joined the boat in Cape Town.

I have never liked the 13th day of the month, although I tell myself that being a rational human being I am not superstitious. Nevertheless the 13th always worries me a little, and I am very cautious on Friday 13th of any month. In November the 13th was a Sunday, which should have been all right, but in fact it gave us our worst experience of the whole leg.

Just after noon, we had gybed and were tidying up afterwards, the spinnaker filled and the lazy guy tautened up under Bill who was leaning overside setting the main boom guy. It happened so quickly that he did not have time to pull himself back and he was flung into the air and fell back into the sea. Fortunately, the accident was seen, and someone yelled 'man overboard' immediately. We had the spinnaker and full main up at the time and were making about ten knots in a force five following wind and rather lumpy sea, which had been easing slowly since the last gale half a day before. I was standing in the cockpit and jumped to the port rail to see Bill's startled face pass beneath me. Julian tried to throw a line but it tangled, and the Major, who was aft, grabbed a lifebuoy and threw it to him. It landed about five feet away from him, and he swam towards it and pulled it beneath him to provide support.

Bill's first reaction was one of surprise, then he tried to grab the hull, but there was nothing to grip. He does not remember grabbing the lifebuoy, but as the boat sailed away, he could at least console himself with the thought that he had been seen. Back on board we were letting fly the spinnaker sheet and guy and trying to bring the boat round into the wind whilst the crew poured on deck and began to heave down the spinnaker. I posted three lookouts whose sole task was to watch Bill who was by now about a cable astern. Although he was disappearing behind the swell waves, he was visible when on top of them, his yellow oilskins showing up particularly well. Peter, who was on the helm, had started the engine, and was trying to motor us round but the boat's head would not come up through the wind, and the spinnaker had come back against the mast and was helping to hold us back. We swung off to clear the spinnaker and when it flew out astern we hauled it in aft, but the boat would still not come round. Eventually we realised that although the engine was running in gear the propeller was not turning. Julian leaped down to check the gear box, and I got a party organised to get a headsail up so that we could sail back if necessary. A yell from Peter stopped us—the propeller shaft was turning. 'Oh Christ,' I thought, 'we've lost the propeller.' Bill had been in the water for about five minutes by now, and I was beginning to worry that if we did not get to him soon, the cold would kill him. We had drifted further from him, and he was not so easy to pick out two to three cables away, but we knew his general whereabouts because the seabirds had gathered over him, the same way they had collected over an injured seal a few days before.

We were working feverishly to get the yankee set, when Peter called out to us again. He had us motoring at last. What must have happened was that the propeller, which is of the folding type, had seized closed through lack of use since leaving Cape Town, but by revving the engine up Peter had created enough centrifugal force to open it up. We headed back towards Bill at full throttle, rolling alarmingly in the sea until we got the mainsail organised, and as we got closer, I was relieved to see that Bill was still conscious. I conned Peter up to weather of Bill, and we stopped a yard clear of him and three of us leant over the side and hauled him up. Desperation must have lent strength to us, because Bill is very solidly built and weighs fifteen stone, and normally we could never have done it, even if his clothes had not been waterlogged.

As we hustled Bill below to the doctor, I told Peter to get us back on course, and get the spinnaker ready to hoist again. The Doc stripped off Bill's clothing, and he was vigorously towelled, whilst his hand, which was cut when he went in, was bandaged up. Apart from being very cold, and the cut hand, he was none the worse for his experience. We had been incredibly lucky. On the previous race, three men had fallen overside in the Southern Ocean and all three had drowned. I said a very heartfelt prayer of gratitude, and thanked my lucky stars that I was sailing with a good crew, because their response had been magnificent. I have never lost a man at sea, although this was the second time I had had one go overside, and it was one record I was determined to maintain.

Once I had seen that Bill was OK, I went back on deck to find us still lying head to wind. Peter was fiddling with the engine controls, and the engine stopped suddenly on us. We soon found the reason. When we had stopped to pick Bill up, a rope staysail sheet had gone overside and was now firmly caught round the propeller. There is only one way of dealing with this sort of problem: someone has to go into the water with a knife, and cut the rope clear. I looked around desperately for a volunteer, anyone who might save me from having to go into that freezing water, but everyone was suddenly doing something vital. The previous time I had had to dive in the Southern Ocean I had gone in naked to repair the rudder on *Suhaili.* The moment I had jumped in, the cold had taken my breath away, and I had realised that my breathing was getting faster and shallower and I was not going to last very long. This time I put on a wet suit, and socks on my feet, and then gently lowered myself into the water. It was freezing. How Bill had survived ten minutes I could not think, and he reckoned that he could have lasted about twenty minutes more. I duck-dived under the hull and had a look. The sheet was twisted round and round the propeller, and it took two attempts to unravel the end. I then went under again and tried to pull the jam clear, but the rope was held firmly between the propeller box and the 'P' bracket. I had hoped to save the sheet, but as it was so tightly jammed it had to be cut, and Julian passed me down a knife. By this time I could not really feel my hands, but they grasped the handle and seemed to have the knife firm. It took two attempts to get the rope clear and check that the propeller was OK and then I was hauled on board. Someone was very kindly waiting on deck with a large glass of brandy, which made me feel better. My body was OK where the wet suit had protected it, but my face, hands and feet were completely numb.

Once I was back on board, Peter, who had been holding the boat hove-to whilst I fiddled around underneath, paid off, and got us back on course, and reset the spinnaker. Once we were under way again we took stock of the situation. Bill was off deck for a while with a cut hand, but was otherwise fine. David Alan-Williams had been thrown into the whip aerial by the spinnaker guy which had bruised him and put him on light duties for a couple of days, but it broke the whip aerial. We had a shortened staysail sheet, too short for use, so we rove another, and a couple of stanchions had been bent. Later, on the slipway in Auckland, we also discovered that the 'P' bracket was bent out of true about five inches, but we did not realise it at the time. All in all we had come out of it all very lightly, and I think we were incredibly lucky.

The inevitable question was whether Bill would have gone in if he had had his safety harness clipped on. The answer is probably that he would not have, but I think he would have been very badly injured. The spinnaker exerts a great deal of pull, and the guy, having tightened up, would have lifted him until his harness took the weight, and then slipped up the front of his body and onto his neck and face. As it happens, we probably had less to worry about because he had gone in, than if he had been harnessed on board. Whether he should have been harnessed is a matter of opinion. We did wear harnesses and used them a lot of the time, and in particular when it was blowing up. Had the wind been stronger and the seas higher, Bill would have been clipped on, but would probably have done the job in a different way anyway.

I think in retrospect, that there was a lot we could have done differently to get him back sooner. Firstly, the spinnaker, sheets, guys and halyards should have been let go completely, so that the sail blew clear of the boat and left us unencumbered. If it had floated we could have picked it up later, but if not it would just have had to be sacrificed. Secondly, if we had had some sort of a line coiled on each quarter that could be thrown overside to a man in the water, there is a chance he would catch it and be much closer to the boat once we stopped. It is almost impossible to pull oneself up a line onto a boat if the boat is travelling at more than five knots, but if there was a bowline in the end of the line, at least the person could hang on. It does not take all that long to luff the boat up into the wind and bring her to a halt; it is turning round that takes the time. Thirdly, I think that boats with folding propellers should run them briefly twice a week to prevent them sticking. Our propeller refusing to open cost us more time than anything else. If the weather conditions had been worse, it would have taken a lot longer to get the boat under control and stop her, and having thrown one lifebuoy out, we would have had to throw another over shortly afterwards so that we had something else to follow back to the man in the water. But we only had two lifebuoys.

I had had a four-man liferaft put just behind the helmsman for just this sort of emergency, but in the event no one thought to throw it over. Neither did we throw over the marker buoy because with all its clutter of lights, drogues, dye markers and so on, it just could not be cleared away quickly enough. For the right reasons, yacht safety equipment has been made too complicated, and this negates its effectiveness. The simplest safety item to throw over was a lifebuoy, and it worked. Other safety equipment wants to be as easy to release and throw.

One aspect of the day's events was that I had now two of the crew unfit to work in their watches. It made matters somewhat easier that Bill and David were in different watches, but we could not run a watch with only five people. To get over the problem, we cancelled the cook's schedule, and David and Bill became full-time cooks until they were fit to work again. It was a bit unfair on them, but the boat had to be sailed. Neither liked it very much, and after two days David was passed fit and Bill said that he was OK as well. I gave Bill a rope to hold, took the other end myself, and told him to pull. He tried, and attempted to hold back his wince, but it was obvious that his hand needed a bit longer to recover, and he had to cook for another day before he could pull on a rope safely!

That afternoon we tuned in on the yacht 'chatter net' and discovered that we were not the only ones who had had a dramatic day. On *Great Britain II*, the spinnaker had gone overside, and the guy holding it had wrapped itself round the waist of a crew member and round the skipper's leg. The crewman had passed out, and was in considerable pain, and Bob James could not use his leg. They asked us for medical advice and I put David Dickson on the radio. He asked a number of questions, and in between waiting for answers I got him to explain to me what he thought the trouble could be. He prescribed morphine to keep the crewman quiet, but his main concern was that there might be internal damage and bleeding. I wanted to know how long he would need to tell, and how urgent medical attention was. The nearest boat with a doctor on board was us, about two hundred miles ahead. Apart from us *ADC* had a doctor but they were seven hundred miles behind *Great Britain II* and would take at least three and a half days to get to them, whereas if we turned round and headed back, and *Great Britain II* carried on, we could probably have put David on board within twelve hours. Obviously I did not want to effectively pull out of the race, which is what this would have meant, but the race was very secondary to possibly saving a life. David decided that there was very little he could do for the time being, as he would have to wait a few hours to see how things developed, and we arranged a schedule for four hours away. In the meantime *Great Britain II* altered course slightly, and headed for Hobart in Tasmania.

I did mention that we had a man overboard, but refused to name the person for the time being. If we had said that Bill Abram had done over, by the time the message got back it could well have been so distorted that it would not have included the information that we had recovered him safe and sound, and could have caused unnecessary suffering to his family. We waited until it was possible for Bill to speak to home personally and tell them what had happened before we named him. That way it did not matter how distorted things were. His family had spoken to him and knew that he was alive and well.

As if the 13th had not given us enough trouble, the wind rose during the evening, and by midnight we were reaching in a full northerly gale, accompanied by snow as usual. The snow settled, and the following morning we had to be careful up forward as quite large lumps of ice kept falling from the mast.

Great Britain II did not come up for two of the four-hourly schedules. When we next spoke on the 'chatter net' they said they had been busy or asleep, but their patient was feeling better anyway. I thought this was rather inconsiderate, as our doctor had spent a great deal of time sitting by the radio trying to get through, and had lost quite a lot of sleep as a result.

On 15th November, having reached 135 degrees east, or roughly due south of Adelaide, we altered course to the north-east for the North Cape of New Zealand. The distance was about the same to Auckland whether we went up the east or west coasts. Both Peter and Les said that the winds were not as strong or reliable on the east coast as they were in the Tasman, so we opted for a straight run up the Tasman, round North Cape and then down the east coast to Auckland.

The Tasman Sea, the area of water between Australia and New Zealand, has a reputation of producing some fairly unpleasant weather. It is largely dominated by the Southern Ocean, but the presence of Australia, and its upsetting effect upon the normal oceanic weather patterns, means that the Tasman gets its fair share of warm and cold fronts. We had to hope that a high pressure system would not develop while we were sailing through the sea as this would give light winds, slowing us up, and enabling the rest of the fleet, who would still be in the Southern Ocean, to close the gap we had developed between us and them. Not that there was anything we could do about it. If a high appeared we would be slowed up, if it appeared after we had rounded North Cape it would slow up the others. On these long races, where the boats get into separate weather patterns, you have little choice in the weather you have got, and the least skilful crew a few hundred miles from a more skilful one will appear to be doing better because they have a more favourable wind at that time.

Psychologically, everyone seemed to get a lift from heading up north to a warmer climate. We had all grown accustomed to living in damp clothing in a wet boat, but the thought of getting into warmer weather bucked everyone up, and a form of Channel fever set in although we still had over two thousand miles to go. The Major produced a sweepstake on our finishing time—the person who chose the nearest half hour won the lot. It cost one pound each, participation was compulsory, and the winner bought drinks for everyone else.

So far, we had been remarkably lucky with the breakages on this trip. The spinnaker guys, which were wire at their ends so they could slip through the ends of the spinnaker poles more easily, had had a lot of wear, and we had had to re-splice them quite often. The main trouble with them was that the thimbles in the eyes wore through with the constant movement, and when I re-spliced the ends we put stainless steel thimbles in instead of the galvanised mild steel ones to make them last longer. Apart from this, we had only needed a regular winch maintenance routine, when each winch was stripped down, greased, and reassembled, and the main engine run a couple of times a week to oil its insides. All in all we had been most fortunate with our gear. For some time, however, we had been troubled by peculiar noises coming from the rudder. Our investigations showed us that the noise was external, and it appeared to be the rudder scraping against the hull as it passed through amidships. There was nothing we could do about it at sea; the scraping noise did not sound loud enough to warrant heaving to and taking the rudder out, a fairly major task anyway, so we just had to put up with it. In trying to find the noise we had noticed quite a lot of movement in the rudder stock, about a quarter of an inch at times, and this was transmitted back to one of the right angle gear boxes which altered the direction of the rods which transmitted steering wheel movement to the rudder. This box was moving about quite a lot and at speed, when we applied a lot of helm, the after bulkhead, to which it was fastened, moved alarmingly. We tried to tom off the after bulkhead to check the movement, but this was only partially successful, and in any case caused the other fastenings holding the gear box to take more load, so eventually they too began to give way. We did not want to slow down, so we rigged up the electric drill from the generator, and our two Kiwis disappeared into the lazarette armed with drills, bolts, clamps and spanners. At odd intervals they yelled up for no movement, and then as soon as he could, the helmsman put the helm amidships and left it so until the boat began to yaw badly then he would yell out, count to five, and move the wheel to bring the boat back on course. Peter and Les had those five seconds to remove the drill and get their fingers clear. It did not take them all that long to do the job. The box had been held by brass screws to the stringer, and we were amazed that they had lasted this long. We drilled through the stringer and refastened the box with bolts, which stabilised the whole system a good deal. A further check to the steering showed that one of the connecting rods was moving slowly. It had 'walked' about three-quarters of an inch and was left with about a quarter of an inch holding. This was rather more difficult to fix, as we could not get a grip on the rod, which did not seem to want to 'walk' the other way. We got it back a quarter of an inch but that was all we could manage, so we kept checking it the rest of the trip.

Heading north-east brought us round on to a reach, and we had two very good days' runs of 278 and 276 miles. The 278 miles was a 23-hour day as we advanced our clocks an hour during the day to compensate for our easterly movement, and to keep ship's time as close as we could to local time. In all we had to advance our clocks by eleven hours during the trip as we travelled through nearly 160 degrees of longitude, nearly halfway round the Earth. If we had not altered the clocks, the sun would have risen earlier each day until we would have had sunrise at five o'clock in the evening when we reached New Zealand. By changing the clocks an hour at a time, we kept the change down to small chunks which did not affect anyone, and we kept the ship's time close to astronomical time and to the local time of countries in our longitude. I used to make the changes quite arbitrarily, but tried to keep real noon, the time when the sun passed overhead, as close as possible to twelve o'clock midday ship's time. When we did advance clocks we did it at 14.00 hours which instantly became 15.00, and the watches changed at 13.30 so that each watch had half an hour less to do in their long six-hour watch.

We were close enough to New Zealand by now to be picking up Wellington Radio, which was putting out calls to the yachts twice daily. On the first occasion we heard them I tried to put a link call through to the United Kingdom, but came up against a system that was designed to make this almost impossible. Having made contact with the station, and passed on who we were and what we wanted, we were switched through to Wellington Traffic, who wanted to know who we were, what we wanted, and if it was a link call, who was calling whom and how it would be paid. By giving a boat's signal letters and issuer of those letters, that is GPO London, we usually were allowed to transmit and were eventually billed by London, but Wellington would not let us do this so we had to call collect which cost more. Having got all the required information through, Wellington Traffic put us through to the International exchange of Wellington GPO who promptly asked us for the same information again. All this took time and, where the circuit was poor and words had to be spelled out, we came up against a further problem in that the New Zealand GPO do not use the international phonetic alphabet. By the time we had got all the information through so that all the forms could be filled up, which took as much as an hour on one occasion, we were getting very low on battery power, and the frequency we were using probably needed changing as well as conditions change rapidly morning and evening. Although all the operators tried very hard to help us, the system beat us time after time and I only got through to the UK twice, and both times one side or the other was unintelligible. Part of the trouble lay in our radio set, which was running the batteries down very quickly, but the Radio Telephone system was set up for large ships with plenty of power, not yachts where, however good the radio installation, power had to be generated well in advance.

By Saturday 19th November we were east of Tasmania and about halfway between it and New Zealand. The sea was noticeably flatter, the big rolling swells were missing, and the weather was much warmer. A front in the morning had given us a full gale during which we surfed for a while and once Peter exceeded thirty knots for ten seconds. We had covered 102 miles in eight hours as a result, but as the wind eased in the afternoon our speed dropped slowly. We sighted a large whale in the morning, quite what sort we could not decide, there being three very firm opinions to choose from, but it had a tail fluke five feet wide. In the evening, an exhausted shag landed on deck, and it stayed with us on and off for a number of days. It had trouble deciding where to land, as having selected one of the mast spreaders, it glided in but was thrown off by the accelerating wind in the slot between the main and the headsail. Later it landed on the boom which was very photogenic but obviously uncomfortable, and it eventually settled on deck. We tried to avoid disturbing it whilst it recovered strength and ate the food we laid out for it.

The sea was sloppy after the front, and we waited a while for it to settle before hoisting a spinnaker. As usual Golf Charlie went forward first to hoist his spinnaker net and ran into difficulties almost at once. It took him forty minutes and four assistants to get the job done, accompanied by a fair amount of leg pulling. As he came aft he told me that he had not been tangling it deliberately. I told him that was what worried me about the system. If he had tangled it deliberately, I could excuse the time lost, but when an intelligent person like him took so long the time had come to find a new system.

The doctor and Barry were on galley duty, the doctor spending most of the day making up a liver pâté which turned out a bit lumpy but had tremendous flavour and was enjoyed by everyone except Bill who had gone on a diet which did not allow him to eat anything that rich, but seemed to allow him to eat double his usual ration of chocolate and sweets.

The wind left us completely during the night and our speed dropped down to 2½ knots at one stage and then came up from the north-east, so we had our first taste of beating for nearly four weeks. The wind was a light force two to three once it came up which put our speed up to about eight knots, but we still had our third worst day's run of 181 miles. We listened to the chatter net hoping that the others were getting light winds as well, but no such luck; they all seemed to have closed up between forty and sixty miles. We appeared to have got behind a high pressure system which was gradually moving eastwards, and flattening everything as it went. Unfortunately, to the south-east of us where the rest of the fleet was things were better.

All the boats had been swapping their weather positions, but this time *King's Legend* decided that they would not give theirs. *Great Britain II* was particularly concerned as they had missed the canal broadcast from Sydney, and they offered to swap their current condition report for it with *King's Legend.* I came in at that point and offered to do a swap. The next moment Cornelius, the owner/skipper of *Flyer*, came up and asked if he could join in the negotiations! Radio reception was much improved by this time and we were picking up most of the other boats once more.

For the next three days we averaged just under ten knots, but it was hard work with the constant changes in wind direction and force, varying from north-easterly force two to south-westerly force eight in a few hours, and every rise or fall in the wind or slight change in direction requiring a change in sail to gain the best results. Behind us, the wind seemed steadily better, and *Great Britain II* closed up from 250 to 130 miles within three days.

On Wednesday, 23rd November we were only 180 miles from Cape Reinga, the north-westernmost point of North Cape, when I took a star sight in the morning, and with anything like decent winds should have sighted the lighthouse there at dusk, but the wind went very light and for much of the day we were down to six knots. We got the floater out at one stage, a very light sail used when there is next to no wind, but the moment it was on deck the wind got up, and we held off hoisting it in case we had a further misunderstanding of sailmaker's technology and gave Paul some more work. In the middle of our discussions, Ronnie appeared on deck dressed for the south pole commenting that he was going to scare hell out of the wind!

Still, it was a nice warm sunny day, and each watch was sailing the boat as hard as they could, so I allowed everyone a bucket of fresh water for washing as we still had our tanks more than half full. Nearly everyone took advantage of the opportunity, encouraged by Bill and I who were able to point out that we were the only two to have had a wash in four weeks.

It was amazing how easily we washed off the hard weather-beaten tans we all thought we had picked up in the Southern Ocean! But, as it was a nice day, most of us were soon wearing shorts and began to put some of it back on properly. We also took the opportunity to scrub some clothing as one likes to look one's best on arrival in port.

Making a landfall is always an interesting time for a navigator as he wants to be as accurate as he can, not just for his own pride, but also because, if he is wrong in his position, the boat might lose time working up to the point on an unnecessary tack. On Wednesday evening I took a star sight and from it calculated that we ought to steer 040 degrees and we would sight Cape Reinga just after 03.00 on Thursday morning. The Admiralty Pilot says that there is a current running up the coast, but as we had not had any effect from it so far, I decided to ignore it. I was called on deck at 03.35 when we picked up the light bearing 033 degrees at about thirty miles range, so we were in fact 3½ miles south-east of where I had hoped we would be. The wind was blowing from the north-west, which had probably given us a bit of leeway, so we hardened up. As the day came we could see the low outline of the land to the east. 'Aotearoa,' said Peter confidently, explaining this was the Maori name for New Zealand, which means land of the long white cloud, and thereby put to rest the crew's fears that the skipper might have found the wrong land.

It was a slow beat to Cape Reinga, a rocky promontory off the end of miles of sandhills, and when we at last drew abeam, we found the current was strongly against us, so it was not until 10.40 that we eventually rounded North Cape and set course south-east for Auckland, 216 miles away. There was a fair amount of traffic off the Cape, and a considerable number of fishing boats in the vicinity picking up cray fish.

We sailed steadily south-south-east, being buzzed three times by aircraft, two of which came in really close. Meanwhile behind us, the wind improved, and we heard that *Great Britain II* was due at Cape Reinga at 21.00, some thirteen hours behind us—not that it mattered too much as she had to come in seven hours before us to win—but if she was getting better winds, the chances were that the others were too, and we needed quite a bit of time to beat them on handicap.

At 20.00, having just passed Cape Brett, and whilst we were having a huge meal to eat up some of the fresh food still on board, we started to get a series of flashes from the lighthouse. We got out our Aldis and received 'Condor welcome' in morse which was a very nice gesture, but, as we were soon to learn, typical of the warm openness of the New Zealanders.

After dinner, as few people wanted to sleep, we had a major clean up below, and then held a census to see what we carried in the way of clothing so that we could all dress the same on arrival. Some people laugh at this habit of having a crew uniform but a person's individuality is only disguised, and the boat looks a lot smarter if the crew dress alike. Normally in a race, it is not always practical, and certainly we had not bothered what we wore at sea. But coming into port, especially when there is a welcome laid on, it does give a good impression.

At daybreak on Friday 25th November, we had Rangitoto Island in sight, and were beating slowly southwards across a rippled sea. Our thirty days had been up at 01.30 that morning, so we had missed our target there. Still, it left something behind to do for another time.

A dozen or so yachts came out as we closed in on Auckland, and as we passed Rangitoto, the whole of Auckland Bay opened up before us. More yachts were waiting, and the shoreline was packed with people. Peter had told us that the people here were enthusiastic sailors, but we had not realised how enthusiastic. We crossed the finish line at 09.33 and 21 seconds. I had intended to drop sails, but there were so many people about that we sailed up the harbour and only took them down when we were just off our berth at Marsden Wharf. As we sailed up harbour, all the ships in port sounded their sirens. It was altogether an unforgettable welcome.

We had sailed 7,037 miles in thirty days, nine hours and $3\frac{1}{2}$ minutes, an average speed of 9.65 knots, on the direct day's runs, which did not take into account the tacks necessary to make good the course. For about 160 hours, or nearly a quarter of the course, we had winds of force seven or above, and fifty-eight hours when the wind was force two or less. We had sufficient food and water left on board to go on sailing for nearly another month, and the boat herself was capable of being sailed on, just as hard, as all her equipment was intact.

4. AUCKLAND TO RIO

All times G.M.T.
P A C I F I C
O C E A N
Rio de Janeiro
arr Jan 28 (1510)
Auckland
dept Dec 25 (2200)
Jan 1
Jan 8
Jan 15
Jan 22

Our reception in Auckland was tremendous, and we found people warm and hospitable. Quite a lot of organisation had gone on before we arrived, and small but important items, such as our washing, were speedily taken care of. In our case, members of the Devonport Yacht Club had volunteered, and each of us had our washing taken away by a different family and returned a few days later smelling decidedly better than when they left us! We also found that many people were prepared to take us back to their homes for a good meal and a stable night's rest. Although the boats were moored in the centre of the commercial port at Marsden Wharf, we soon found our way to the Royal New Zealand Yacht Squadron which had made all competitors honorary members during their stay.

Auckland is the largest city in New Zealand, although Wellington is the capital, and the people are sailing mad. Not very surprising when one sees the interesting cruising grounds they have close to hand, and the pleasant climate. At least it was warm and sunny during our first week, but we were told that there was usually more rain about than this early in December. Those of the crew who had not had a surfeit of sailing found that there were plenty of berths available on local yachts if they wanted to race. The Takapuna boating club even laid on twelve Laser dinghies so that *ADC Accutrac*, *Great Britain II* and ourselves could have a form of team race. Peter's local knowledge helped us to a narrow victory! We also met up with the pop group Fleetwood Mac, who were giving an open air concert outside the city. Free tickets got us on stage for the concert, the first such event I had ever attended, although the younger members of the crew seemed to understand the performance perfectly. In return we took part of the group out sailing, taking advantage of the occasion to sail up the harbour and back, under spinnaker, beneath the new Auckland Harbour Bridge with its Nippon Clipon. This title had puzzled me at first until a local had explained that a Japanese company had built the bridge, and halfway through the Council had decided that it was not going to be wide enough, so they asked the contractors to add an extra two lanes each side. They looked like an afterthought—hence the title.

Knowing that Les would be out to relieve me within a week,

I arranged the de-storing of the boat and a thorough clean out, and booked the Harbour Board slipway for a clean off and repaint. Whilst we waited for our turn on the slipway, people went off to see the country, and I took the opportunity of going down to Dunedin to see the people who stood by me when I went aground there in *Suhaili* nine years before. We had a wonderful reunion, lasting only twenty-seven hours of which I slept for three, but I was shown over the area, with its attractive hilly countryside, and promised to return for a longer stay.

Meanwhile the other boats were finishing the second leg, *Great Britain II* nearly a day after us and then *King's Legend* and *Flyer*. On Monday after our arrival Otto Steiner, the Chairman of the Race Committee, told me that *King's Legend* had put in a protest against both the Committee and ourselves. I was livid at the news as, apart from the fact that it would have been courteous for the skipper of *King's Legend* to have told me in advance that he was going to protest, and indeed the Racing Rules demand this, I have never been protested in a race before.

Their protest, which amounted to three rambling pages, was basically that we should not have had our rating reduced by the Mast Correction Factor, or the penalty for having a mast made of GRP and carbon fibre, before the second leg commenced. It was a perfectly reasonable point to make, but had Clancy, the American skipper of the boat, bothered to obey the Rules and tell me in advance, I could have pointed out why our rating had been reduced and saved everyone, including the Protest Committee drawn from members of the Royal New Zealand Yacht Club, from a lot of unnecessary effort.

The Committee met on the Tuesday after our arrival, and I started by pointing out that the Protest was invalid as it had not been put in within twenty-four hours of *King's Legend*'s arrival as required by the Race Rules, and at no time had I been advised that a Protest was going to be made. I was informed that *King's Legend* had told us at the start of the leg, but as we were opposite ends of the start line, I did not see how they thought I would hear them half a mile away. In any case we had been regularly in contact on the radio, so why had it not been mentioned then, or since they arrived in Auckland? Otto now asked me nevertheless to allow the Protest to be heard, as he wanted the whole matter thrashed out, and I agreed.

Otto then explained that although the race was taking place in 1977–78, as a great deal of preparation was necessary by competitors, it was decided to fix the rules well in advance, and in fact the race was being run under 1973 rules. As there was no penalty for using exotic materials in 1973, he was absolutely right to allow us to have this deducted from our rating and in fact we should not have had this addition to our rating from the start of the race.

The Committee asked Clancy if he had any comment, and in reply he withdrew his protest. There was nothing more to discuss, but it was suggested that we protest the Committee to have the exotic penalty removed from the start of the race. I discussed doing this with Otto, but he said that as we had broken our mast and lost twelve days anyway in the first leg, it was not going to make much difference if we did have our rating reduced by two feet, and it would save having to rework all the results if I did not protest, and I agreed.

It seems that once protests start, there is a tendency for them to continue. The next problem arose when Eric Tarbarly appeared to join in for the last two legs of the race in his *Pen Duik IV*. *Pen Duik* had come straight from the USA where she had been refused entry in races because of her uranium keel, a material heavier than lead and as such banned by the International Offshore Committee for racing boats. We knew about the uranium keel, but were not aware that it was totally banned; we thought it was an exotic material like our GRP carbon fibre mast, and should have been treated as such—although, because of the Protest Committee's decision, no actual penalty would now be applied.

By the time Tarbarly appeared in Auckland, I had returned home and Les had taken over the boat. Although he knew about the results of *King's Legend*'s protest against us, he was amazed to see in the results of the second leg our rating reported as 68.8, a rating that included our three per cent exotic penalty. Alarmed by this, he contacted Otto Steiner, pointing out that we had an exotic penalty, whereas *Pen Duik*, with an exotic keel, had none, and *Pen Duik* also had an age allowance of a further one foot in rating, although age allowances had not been introduced in 1973. The result was an absurd difference of eight feet in rating between boats of three feet difference in length, which was giving the race away. To gain some measure of equality, Les asked if we could re-enter the race with a slightly different name and thus come in with our real rating which was now 65.8 feet. This was refused by the Race Committee. Believing that we were carrying an exotic penalty for a mast we no longer carried, whereas Eric Tarbarly had no penalty for what was quite definitely an exotic keel, and confused by the reference to 1973 rules, which, if properly applied did not allow for exotic penalties or age allowances, Les wrote to Otto Steiner putting his case, but was told in reply that if he did not like things the way they were he ought to put in a Protest. Les was left with no alternative as he was unable to get things sorted out any other way, and as a result put the Protest against the Race Committee. His Protest was that the Rating Rules were not clear and appeared to unfairly handicap *Heath's Condor*. On the evidence from the Race Committee that the race was being run under 1973 rules, Les's Protest was dismissed, but it was indicated that all boats would have their ratings readjusted to levels that pertained to 1973. As this meant that our exotic penalty was again confirmed as withdrawn, and no age allowance would apply, Les felt that his Protest had achieved its purpose and was perfectly satisfied with the result. Although we would rate at something under 66.8 he felt that a fair decision had been reached, and the race would benefit as a result. For some reason, however, before the race restarted from Auckland, it was announced that *Pen Duik*'s entry had only been accepted provisionally, which was difficult to understand in view of the decision of the Committee to run the race under 1973 rules.

It was with considerable surprise, and alarm, that during the third leg, on 6th January to be precise, Les intercepted a message passed on from *ADC Accutrac* to *Pen Duik VI* saying that *Pen Duik* had been disqualified by the Race Committee on *Heath's Condor*'s Protest. Les was dumbfounded, and even more so when he discovered that *Heath's Condor*'s exotic penalty had been reinstated at the same time. It appears that the Committee had had a complete change of mind after the third leg had started, and discovering uranium was now banned by the IOC, had decided to forget altogether their own decision to run the race under 1973 rules. One could not refute the logic of replacing our exotic penalty if this was the case, but utter confusion reigned as a result. The race card for the leg stated that 1973 rules applied, but now it appeared they only applied to certain points and no one knew which ones. The French not unnaturally were furious at this cavalier treatment of their sailing hero, one French magazine even going so far as to claim that the Committee only disqualified *Pen Duik* because she was in the lead! But owing to the way the message had been worded everyone assumed that Les was responsible, whereas in fact he was as confused as anyone, as he knew he had not put in a Protest against *Pen Duik*.

The French magazine's claim was of course quite absurd but the whole affair could have been handled better. Everyone wanted Eric Tarbarly to be in the race, and had the Protest Committee's decision after Les's Protest been carried out, he would have been. It was the sudden change of mind that confused everyone, and this points out the need for consistency in applying the rules of a race once they have been published. In effect, there ought to be no waivers or alterations for special cases once a race has started, and in this race there had been a number, admittedly many of them affecting us, such as the business of the radio receiver on the first leg, and removing the exotic penalty for leg two. But before one condemns the Committee for allowing these alterations it should be remembered that this Round the World Race is unique as the distance of any single leg is more than twice the length of any other race, and the Committee were not very willing to impose restrictions on competitors who might have spent nearly four years and over a quarter of a million pounds to take part. Considerations of safety in a race where the yachts are sometimes two thousand miles from the nearest port must and did take priority with the Committee, and I feel that they found themselves on this, their second race, involved much more in a real race than the first event, which in comparison was closer to a cruise in company. Inevitably, when racing gets serious, the rules are watched more closely, and the Committee, having had no protest in the first race, were unprepared for the ones that appeared in the second. One thing is certain: the seriousness of the racing will not be lessened in the third race, and one hopes the lessons learned from the whole unfortunate business of the protests in Auckland will be applied by the Race Committee for that race.

Meanwhile, in Auckland, preparations for the third leg to Rio around Cape Horn were proceeding. *Heath's Condor* was hauled out and repainted. It was while she was on the slipway that we discovered that the propeller shaft's 'P' bracket had been bent five inches out of true. Many wise men were consulted as to how a bronze casting could be straightened, and all advised caution. The problem was solved by a friend of Peter's coming along with a long lever, attaching it to the casting, and heaving it straight!

We had fewer crew changes in Auckland than in Cape Town. Ronnie Roos returned to South Africa, but Barry Buchannan decided to stay on to do the next leg. Bill Abrams and I returned home to be replaced by Roddy Coleman and Les Williams, and Peter Visick joined from Cornwall. Les thought it would be better to carry one extra on the third leg, because if we tore sails, Paul was effectively off watch; he took on another New Zealander, Allan Prior, who fitted in immediately. An accountant by profession, Allan was an experienced ocean racer, and stayed with us to the end of the race.

David Alan-Williams was elected commissar for the leg and spent a lot of time running around arranging the stores for the voyage. The only disappointment, for a country that exports meat, was the quality of the meat delivered on board. Better New Zealand lamb could be bought in the UK. An error had been made somewhere in the ordering as well, for all the meat arrived ready frozen. Yachts have limited freezer capacity, and in order to get all the meat required for a leg into a rather small freezer, it needs to be unfrozen so that it will stow tightly. The meat was put into the freezer, but nearly one hundred pounds of it just would not fit. None of the other boats could take the surplus, even temporarily, so a local hotel was inveigled into accepting it, and Roddy set off across town to find three polystyrene chilli-bins. These measure about four feet by two feet, and Roddy had to stagger back through Christmas Eve shopping crowds with them on his head, shoulder and under his arm!

The race was planned to re-start on Boxing Day, which gave everyone a good chance of setting out with a hangover, and the odds of this happening increased when Whitbread laid on a barbeque for Christmas Day.

The start was chaotic. There was no control over the mass of spectator craft, and *Pen Duik* and *Great Britain* were both over the line when the gun went. The first mark, two miles from the line, was a small buoy which was completely hidden by spectator craft, and when it was finally sighted it was straight downwind, so a spinnaker was hoisted to cover the two hundred yards to the buoy. While it was marvellous to have such a send-off, once the start gun goes one no longer thinks about anything but racing, and spectator craft, although they showed the interest of the Aucklanders, were suddenly a bloody nuisance.

Heath's Condor slowly overtook *Great Britain* and *Pen Duik*, but the moment more open sea was met—after clearing Hauraki Bay and getting in to the Bay of Plenty—a strong force seven headwind was encountered and *Pen Duik* sailed faster and pointed closer to the wind. There is nothing worse for a racing crew than to discover that one's competitor is both fast and points better close hauled; in these conditions one's skill, and the skill of the designer, really show up—somehow downwind performance does not seem quite so important. But if your boat will not point as high without stopping there is nothing one can do about it. *Pen Duik* was proving to be a better windward boat in strong headwinds, so we had failed in this respect to produce a better boat. Still, she could not expect strong headwinds all the way, and it remained to be seen how well we would do against her once we got the following winds in the roaring forties.

At nightfall, as the wind slowly eased, the nearest boats astern were hull down, and *Pen Duik* was three miles ahead. By daybreak on the 27th, White Island, an active volcano, was close by, belching out sulphurous smoke and steam.

Like most New Zealand place names, White Island has a Maori name as well, Whakaari Island. Unlike most other countries populated by Europeans, the New Zealanders have continued to use many of the Maori names rather than impose new ones. The Maoris were not the first settlers of the country. When the first Maori discovered New Zealand about AD 950—according to legend a man from Tahiti called Kupe was the captain of the canoe—they found people already living there. These earlier settlers were most likely of Polynesian extraction as well, but tradition does not relate when they arrived. Their life must have been pretty idyllic, with the giant moas to hunt, and fish easily caught in the rivers and around the coast. Kupe is supposed to have made a landfall close to North Cape, but he must have been an adventurous type, because he almost immediately set off to explore further south. He went through Cook Strait and up the west coast as far as Porirua, where he left his anchor stone and took on board a new one to prove he had found new land. His original anchor, a large stone with a hole drilled through it to take a warp, now rests in the Dominion Museum. He then turned south again and sailed down the west coast of South Island, finding the famous greenstone on the way. This stone is greatly valued by the Maoris, for it is beautiful as an ornament and can be easily shaped to make an axe or war club. Kupe circumnavigated South Island, and then, according to legend, sailed back to Tahiti via Rarotonga and Rangiatea, although there is some doubt today as to whether this return journey was really possible. Nevertheless the Polynesians seem to have been aware of the Aotearoa, and they can hardly have known about it if someone had not got back and reported its existence.

The main Maori migration commenced during the eleventh century, most of the new colonialists, according to the story, sailing there deliberately to avoid overcrowding or wars elsewhere in Polynesia. Kupe's sailing directions, which, like nearly all Maori information, were passed on as a chant from generation to generation, must have helped these later arrivals, who crossed many miles of sea in canoes hollowed out of solid trees, with a wash strake sewn on top to give a little bit more freeboard. But one cannot help wondering how many perished in this great migration, when space was limited for supplies which consisted of dried shellfish, coconuts, fruit and perhaps a few live animals.

By the sixteenth century, the main migration was over, and the Maoris had organised themselves into the nearly fifty different tribes that existed when Cook arrived. They were a warlike lot, and their intertribal battles were ferocious, the losers usually ending up being eaten by the victors. When the white man first arrived he was known as 'long pig', for the obvious reason that those unfortunate enough to be caught were cooked underground like pig in the traditional Maori *hangi.*

By the time White Island had dropped astern, both *Great Britain* and *Flyer* were astern but *Pen Duik* was about five miles ahead. There was only East Cape to round before setting course for Cape Horn, and all day the boats sailed in sight of each other. *Pen Duik* was about six miles ahead at nightfall when the wind eased, and became variable. *Heath's Condor* tacked out to the Ranfurly Bank to get the maximum advantage from the tidal streams setting south. Tacking to each wind shift, but keeping in the current, by 04.00 the next morning she was east of East Cape when an unlit yacht was sighted, which at daybreak was identified as *Pen Duik.* A hard night's work had paid off.

There is nothing like having competition close by to keep everyone on their toes, and the closeness of *Pen Duik* acted as a great incentive to everyone. The wind steadied to an east-north-east fifteen to twenty knots, and with sheets eased, *Heath's Condor* slowly opened up a lead, sailing about half a knot faster. So although *Pen Duik* was faster to windward in these conditions, we were faster off the wind, which was encouraging.

The International Date Line was crossed that night, the evening of 28th December, so at midnight the boat sailed into another 28th December. The time on the boat, instead of being twelve hours ahead of Greenwich Mean Time, became instantly twelve hours behind GMT; midday in Britain on a certain day, instead of being twelve hours after our noon, was now twelve hours before ours. This changing of a day causes enough difficulties for the navigator, for whom it is vital to be correct, but to a lot of the crew it was totally baffling. The first people to be baffled by it were the survivors of Magellan's expedition, who found that everyone was a day in front of them when they got back to Spain after circumnavigating the world from East to West, the opposite way to us. If we had not had two days the same date, we would have found the UK a day behind us when we got home. The crew did not of course get an extra day in their lives, as we had had a number of twenty-three-hour days all the way across the Southern Ocean, and there would be more to come before the boat got home, adding up to a total of twenty-four hours by the time the circumnavigation was completed.

It has always seemed to me very clever of the British to have somehow arranged it that the International Date Line is as far away from themselves as possible, so that they very rarely get headaches having to work out whether to add or subtract a day. New Zealand and Hawaii, although only a few hours apart, are on different days—imagine the confusion if Britain and France were on different days. The Date Line does not in fact slavishly follow the meridian of 180 degrees east and west, it detours around land masses and groups of islands so that no single group has some islands on one day and others on another, although they are only a couple of miles apart.

It was now just after midsummer in the southern hemisphere and the whole weather system had moved further south, so Les decided to take as near a Great Circle course as he could, which would take him nearly ten degrees further south than had been possible in the second leg of the race. Provided he could get reasonably good weather forecasts, he should be able to keep north of the lows. It meant going close to the ice, but it also meant that he would sail the shortest distance to Cape Horn. This course also put the Chatham Islands, a small group of islands 360 miles to the east of New Zealand but a part of that country, right in his path.

With winds from the north east, the boat was sailing fast, with slightly eased sheets, and the course was laid to pass to the north east of the islands. Once committed to this course a wind change could prove most unfortunate, because if the wind veered towards the east, the boat would have to beat to clear the islands or, even worse, head right off to pass them to the south-west and lose time.

Two large pinnacles of rock showed on the horizon at daybreak on 29th December. The visibility was remarkably good, and at first Les thought the rocks were quite close and must be the Sisters Rocks which lie north of Chatham Island. This was bad news as it meant that the boat would have to beat to clear the islands. However, Peter Blake was hoisted to the masthead and from that height was able to see that the pinnacles were in fact distant peaks on the islands, so it was possible to maintain course.

The Chatham Islands are not well surveyed, and vessels are warned to keep at least three miles off unless they have local knowledge. Chatham and Pitt are the main islands, Pitt being about twelve miles south of Chatham. Both are inhabited, and the Maoris record people living there when they first arrived in New Zealand. The Admiralty Pilot, with its usual brevity, manages to make Chatham Island sound like a very desirable place to visit: 'Chatham Island, or Whare-kauri, is of irregular shape, its eastern and western coasts being indented by Hanson and Petre bays, respectively. The general aspect is that of beautiful rolling downs covered with grass and patches of fern, intersected by belts of forest scrub, with very little undergrowth. There are several lakes on the island; the largest, Te Whanga lagoon, is salt, and covers about 72 square miles.' Who could resist that? The five hundred or so inhabitants have to be envied, if the description is anywhere near accurate; and to add to that, the waters abound with shellfish and blue cod.

By 11.00 on 29th December the island had passed to the south, and looking astern it was possible to make out *Pen Duik*, which had been to leeward, being forced to navigate carefully through the off-lying reefs. Of the rest of the fleet only *Flyer* went north of the Chatham Islands and as a result a large gap had developed between these three boats and the rest.

Up until this time, the centre of a high pressure system had been moving along just to the south of the boat and at almost the same speed. This was the cause of the unexpected easterly winds which had forced the leading boats to beat all the way from East Cape in New Zealand. At mid-morning the wind suddenly died and then switched round to the north-west, giving a force two following wind. *Pen Duik*, who minutes before had been faced with tacking out of the reefs, suddenly had a stronger free wind and was able to spinnaker-reach clear, and close the gap between the boats. Within a short time, another sail appeared on the horizon, heeled over with the wind, and *Flyer* came up rapidly, stopping only when she reached the calm patch with *Pen Duik* and *Heath's Condor*. A good lead that had been contested for days had been wiped out in a few hours by a quirk in the wind, and effectively the race might just as well have started again from that point. *Heath's Condor* was becalmed for eight hours, the others about six and three hours respectively, when at last at nightfall a light wind arose, and she was able to fine reach away. But not for long as the centre of the high moved over again, and *Heath's Condor* and *Flyer* were becalmed together once more; *Pen Duik*, having used the short spell of wind to sail more to windward, was out of sight to the north. In this sort of situation the only thing to do is to sail away from the path of the high pressure centre and try to find better winds to north or south. *Pen Duik* had gone north where she could expect headwinds from the high, but perhaps she had advance warning of a low pressure system to the north-west off New Zealand which was moving south-east at eighteen knots. *Heath's Condor* was to the south of this low's path, the wrong place to be, but the information did not come in time to allow her to sail north of the path. Having sat on the wrong side of a high pressure system for days, praying for a low, the first low pressure system to emerge was going to offer nothing but more and stronger headwinds.

The weather to the east of New Zealand in the Southern Ocean should, in theory, be the same as that found between Cape Town and Auckland: a series of high presure systems going across towards South America in the northern part, and a series of low pressure systems going the same way on the edge of Antarctica. The idea is to keep between the two and have good strong following winds. However, for some reason there is a tendency for these systems to stray from their usual paths, and a very careful watch has to be kept if one is going to stay with westerly winds, and not be faced with easterlies. When I sailed this route on my own, I had experienced five weeks of easterly winds between New Zealand and Cape Horn in about latitude forty-five degrees south. As at that time I had been unable to receive weather forecasts, my only guide had been a not too reliable barometer, but it had shown that I was north of the highs. A more southerly course, say in latitude fifty to fifty-five, would probably have given me an easier and faster run.

Reading the weather correctly plays a vital part in ocean racing, and weather forecasts are like gold, especially in areas like the South Pacific, where there are large gaps in the reporting systems. Golf Charlie had managed to get the New Zealand forecast, giving the position and track of the low, but there was not time to take advantage of it. *Pen Duik*, having headed further north, was north of the path and, when the low arrived, was to get westerlies, whilst *Heath's Condor* got easterlies and further problems. The third leg was about to be decided by how much notice of the weather the boats received, and how the crews reacted to the information: a fairly normal situation in any race, only instead of it making a few miles difference as it would in a race across the English Channel, in a race around the world it could make a difference of hundreds of miles.

All the yachts were keeping in touch on the radio telephones, and most had agreed to celebrate the New Year when New Zealand did. The radios were switched on at 23.30, and the sounds of revelry from the boats flooded the frequencies. It is not easy to hold a party at sea on a boat, as the boat still has to be sailed, but by switching people around it can be done and everyone gets a turn at enjoying themselves. Of course you have a slightly noisy watch coming on deck at midnight, but by 04.00 when the watches change, they are usually as quiet as those coming on deck after their fours hours' 'sleeping it off'. We on *Heath's Condor* decided that our party would take place the following night, but when the time came it was literally washed out, as the boat was under storm staysail and four reefed main beating to windward in an easterly gale. The low had passed to the north. Obviously there was a Jonah on board, and it was decided to sacrifice a pot plant that Justin had bought in New Zealand. The barometer rose at once. A coincidence like this gives one a nasty feeling that maybe there is a large unpleasant sea god out there, and one wishes one had not made a joke of making a sacrifice—except the glass was rising.

There is more than a suspicion that any excuse would have been used sooner or later to dump Justin's pot plant. He had been given it in New Zealand and had suspended it above his bunk with an assortment of bits of string so that it swung around dangerously in the tiny cabin just at head level. More than one person got a bruised head from it, and on one occasion it tipped over, depositing a load of earth in Justin's sleeping bag. In cleaning up, he managed to spread the earth fairly generously, and from that moment on, his plant's life was under constant threat. A pot plant has as much place in a boat as vegetables would in a window box at Buckingham Palace.

No one else tried to grow plants on the boat during the race, but some peculiar decorations did appear around the bunks. Golf Charlie, who apart from having a complicated tacking arrangement on his bunk so that he was more or less level regardless of the angle of heel, had masses of netting into which he placed clothing and cameras. He added some plastic grapes to this tangle in Auckland and it was difficult to see whether his bunk was occupied or not.

Beating to windward in a storm is the most unpleasant form of sailing there is. You have the feeling, as the boat bucks and jumps in the waves, that you are not getting anywhere; the bow rises up as a wave comes in and falls with a sickening thud once the wave has gone, shaking the whole boat. Sleeping in these conditions is very difficult, and one is almost glad to be on watch. In *Heath's Condor*, water poured in through any small gaps it could find, dripping on people and gear. Socks, sweaters, curtains, towels—almost anything—were jammed into the ventilators, but they still dripped, though the crew hardly noticed it with the boat sealed up and condensation everywhere. The biggest leak was by the mast, where the water was coming in by the gallon, and Paul made a special water catcher there so that it could be collected in a container and dumped overside. Three people were kept constantly baling out the bilges, as the water there was running up the inside of the boat almost to the deckhead—we were paying for not having a sump in the boat and a relatively flat bottom.

Flatter bottoms are all right for the out and out racer which is going to be at sea for a couple of days at the most, but no good on a longer race, as water rushing up the inside of the boat every time she rolls, soaking people, gear and stores, is most depressing. The only solution would be a multi-suction pipe bilge pumping system, but even then the water has to be trapped somewhere so that you can get at it.

The first day of the new year passed miserably and by evening the wind was gusting force nine to ten, and the boat was down to a staysail only as a secondary depression came across. Justin's pot plant had obviously not appeased the sea-god, who was whipping up a very steep easterly sea in a westerly swell. It might have been better to have sacrificed his porridge. Justin has many excellent attributes: he is a first-class

11. Some of the yachts greeting *Heath's Condor* on her arrival in Auckland

12. The bow wave when the boat is moving at about 20-plus knots

13. A spinnaker being hoisted inside a special zippered bag that could be quickly pulled open to release the sail

14. The deck from the masthead

15. A large iceberg to leeward in the Southern Ocean. At times there were two or three of this size about

16. Rounding Cape Horn, with Roddy Coleman on the helm

17. Cleaning up after Crossing the Line

18. The author trying out a new all-weather ventilated hat

19. Hauling in the blooper prior to a gybe

20. Back with my family

sailor, always in the thick of things, but as a cook he is a one man gastronomic disaster. When it was his turn to share the cooking, we always knew that the menu would be unusual, and his porridge was typical. You either drank it as a gruel out of a cup or you almost needed a hammer and chisel to cut it into chewable chunks. On one occasion someone stuck the spoon in the mixture, and then held the saucepan upside down. Nothing moved! On this occasion it was the hard variety that appeared, which was perhaps just as well as the boat was bouncing off the waves heavily and anything loose in a plate was likely to go flying, as did the tin of treacle. The tin was retrieved before too much came out, but quite a lot oozed onto the galley work top. Justin was serving up at the time, and a couple of bowls had gone flying across the saloon a moment before. He placed these recovered bowls firmly into the puddle of treacle with the remark that that should hold them! Standards are, of course, relative to what you are used to and the environment you find yourself in. In a wet boat that has been pounding for over a day, treacle and porridge everywhere does not appear to be half the disaster it would be in a house.

When the gale force headwinds first struck, the boat had been able to stand up to the winds with a jib, staysail and reefed mainsail set. But it was soon obvious to everyone that although a good speed was being maintained, the mast was bending far too much for safety; and so the jib was taken off and the mainsail reefed down until its head was level with the upper spreaders. This effectively meant that the top third of the mast was not being used, and it reduced the bending considerably. On *Heath's Condor*'s mast the two running backstays came in to the mast at this point, so it was possible to give plenty of support there. Inevitably, though, this safety measure meant sacrificing speed, which came down from ten knots to six knots. Les was faced with the racing man's greatest dilemma: to push on and risk breaking the mast, or ease up to reduce the risk to the mast but know that you are not racing as hard as you possibly could. I think he took the right course of action. No race has ever been won by a mastless boat – as we had learned to our cost on the first leg – and in addition, if the mast had gone in the middle of the Southern Ocean, the nearest land was at least 1,500 miles away to windward. (That was, of course, if

New Zealand could be called to windward when an easterly was blowing, but in theory it was to windward.) Though if the mast had gone you could bet your last farthing the wind would have changed anyway. A jury rig would have been essential as the boat carried only enough fuel to motor three hundred miles, and a jury rig would have depended upon how much of the mast remained on board. Les was all too aware of the dangers when a mast broke, for we still had a fibre glass patch in the hull where one of the mast fittings on the GRP carbon fibre mast had knocked a hole in the side before it had been dragged on board after breaking. And, of course, there was always the risk of injury to the crew to consider. Against this, he knew the other boats, which were getting somewhat similar conditions, would probably press on and build up a lead, and by reefing down this was a penalty he had to be prepared to pay. And so it proved to be, for at the next chatter hour, *Flyer, Great Britain* and *Pen Duik* all reported their positions well ahead.

It is terrible feeling in a race when you discover that the competition is getting away from you, especially competition like *Flyer*, which you should be well ahead of to do well on handicap. Crew morale inevitably takes a tumble and conditions on board did not help. Damage to the boat in these appalling conditions was surprisingly light, but the covers on the forward hatches were swept away, making the hatches less watertight, and no one regretted the extra work in Auckland that had been put into re-bolting and sealing them to the deck. It is the continuous stream of minor repairs that take their toll. For instance, the port cockpit drain jammed and had to be stripped out to clear it. The blockage turned out to be a piece of anti-chafe material that had come off the spreaders. The calor gas locker drain also jammed as a grape had got into it. This was discovered when water started to come through the watertight inspection hatch in the chartroom and soaked the charts. The regulator fell off the generator. This was just one day's mishaps, all of which had to be put right in dreadful conditions.

Of course, far from land and with no services available, there is a much greater sense of urgency about carrying out repairs and doing maintenance that would usually be handled by specialists in port. The fact that you know no one can assist you alters your whole mental approach to problems that would seem insurmountable in everyday life. You do not approach a problem by thinking that it would have to wait until an expert ashore can deal with it. Instead, you start by saying to yourself 'Now who or what have we got to deal with this?' The generator was a classic example, when it began to give trouble—emitting sparks and making peculiar noises. Upon opening it up it was discovered that the brushes on the commutator had worn away completely, damaging the commutator in the process. We carried no spares at all, but Julian and Peter Visick, working all day, removed the brushes from the electric drill complete with holders, and modified them so that they would fit. There was a standby system, in that the main engine could be used to charge the ten batteries underneath the saloon seat, but a great deal more fuel was required for this, and there was not enough diesel oil on board to cater for regular charging and leave sufficient for motoring in an emergency. The generator was made to function again, and the risk of running out of electricity avoided.

It may seem a bit ridiculous to be worrying about power in the boat's batteries when only seventy years before full-rigged ships had sailed these waters without any electrical power at all, but we are all creatures of our times. Apart from the need to keep radio communications going, *Heath's Condor* is totally dependent upon electricity for lighting and instruments, and although torches could be used to illuminate the compass in an emergency, a modern yacht deprived of her instruments for showing speed, wind direction and wind force is at a severe disadvantage with her competitors. It could be done—our forefathers managed—but our race was in a different period of time. Frankly, had instruments been available to the seamen who sailed in the ships and barques at the turn of the century to give them the sort of information that is available to the modern sailor, they would have been fitted. The sailors of that time may have preferred sail to steam, but they were not slow to adopt new ideas and techniques that assisted them.

As if to mock man's puny efforts, the wind suddenly eased after three days on 4th January, but not of course, before a panel in the mainsail had been ripped and the whole sail unbent and taken below for repair. The storm mainsail was bent on in its place but it was only two-thirds of the size. So ironically, the moment it was possible to set full sail, they were unable to take advantage of the situation, and Paul was once again off watches until repairs were complete. At least in the lighter winds the boat was reasonably upright, but manoeuvring the heavy 1,000-square-foot mainsail around the sewing machine took nearly all the saloon space, and almost eighteen hours.

A light headwind slowly became a westerly wind at last, and under spinnaker *Heath's Condor* began to eat into the lead of the boats ahead. By this time she was already fifty-seven degrees south, further south than she had been on the second leg, and an ice lookout was posted although the ice limit during the Southern summer is considerably further south in these longitudes—about 130 degrees west. The weather clagged in, reducing visibility to less than one hundred yards in a light drizzle. The fact that it was not snowing was encouraging, as it meant that the warmth of the air might extend over a large area and this would hasten the melting of icebergs—hopefully before they strayed into the course of the boat. In fact, icebergs were around—the other boats reported them—but none was seen by *Heath's Condor* until 8th January.

January 6th brought the unwelcome news of *Pen Duik*'s disqualification. The chatter net fairly buzzed with indignant French voices. The suggestion was put forward that the competitors should decide on a handicap for *Pen Duik* and inform the Race Committee of a joint proposal. Everyone agreed except *Flyer*—and, subsequently, *Great Britain II* changed her mind. This emotive appeal by the competitors would probably not have been accepted by the Race Committee anyway, but it needed to have one hundred per cent support to have a hope.

The same day brought a small finwhale in close to the bow where it played at being a dolphin for a while. Whales of various types were seen quite frequently thereafter, and always brought a crowd on deck armed with cameras eager to try and catch one spouting. The trouble is that they spout immediately they surface and so one can never have the camera ready and pointing in the right direction. It is as hard to record this with a camera as it is to catch a porpoise or dolphin close-up completely out of the water. Numerous pictures exist of the tails of dolphins out of the water, but very few of the whole animal.

On the 8th, at sixty-one degrees south, the first iceberg was sighted. The sky cleared, and brilliant sunshine appeared as the boat sailed past about four hundred yards away from it. It was quite a large berg, about half a mile radius and 130 feet high. As the boat went past, a large lump fell off with a tremendous splash and roar to join the other four large growlers in the berg's lee. The next morning at daybreak, if such a thing can really be said to occur this far south where twilight takes the place of night in summer, a large berg appeared right ahead. The rising sun illuminated it in the most spectacular way and everyone had plenty of time to view it as there was next to no wind. This berg was three miles long and the boat coasted along its southern "shore" about two hundred yards off.

Icebergs were regularly sighted over the next week as the boat sailed east just south of the sixty-second parallel of latitude. Sometimes as many as five would be in sight at one time, and it was always a question of avoiding the leeward side as that was where the growlers lay. Many were breaking up quite quickly like the second one sighted, and lumps falling off became quite a common sight. Whilst the wind remained light and westerly the icebergs provided a pleasant attraction, but the moment the wind got up and visibility was reduced by driving rain or snow, they became a real hazard. A hundred yards of warning is very little in which to gybe or alter course radically to avoid a big berg, and one never knows which part of the berg you have in front of you, so it is a gamble as to which way to go, usually decided by the tack you are on at the time. Generally, one hardened up because it was easier and safer.

The pack ice was reported to lie at about sixty-three degrees south, so that when the wind turned easterly again, Les was forced to head north and away from the great circle track he was trying to follow. One hates heading away from the rhumb line track, especially as, had the ice pack not been in the way, the south easterly course would have been a closer course. But pack ice is no place for a thinly skinned yacht. However, the westerlies were at last beginning to predominate, and the great circle course could be laid most of the time.

The next week provided an interesting contrast of strong westerlies accompanied by rain and snow, the occasional easterly, and periods of comparatively light winds. The temperature fell to one degree centigrade for both air and sea, and in rain and snow goggles became essential. Accidentally looking into the driving rain in a gale left one temporarily blinded for nearly a minute unless one's eyes were protected. With the boat moving along better, morale rose, started almost inevitably by the Major getting loose with the booze locker and mixing up an explosive cocktail one evening which had the effect of perking everyone up—once they had got over the initial gulp. It was too cold for Golf Charlie to strum his guitar properly, but the tape machine blasted out a mixture of punk rock and Mozart depending who got at it first. I am afraid that I cannot bring myself to appreciate punk rock; my generation grew up with Elvis Presley and the style engendered by his music in the 1960s, and I find this more recent stuff in no way compares. A sign of age I suppose, but it meant that if I got close to the cassette player when I was on board, punk rock was quickly ejected and Mozart replaced it. There was not all that much in between apart from Fleetwood Mac, and after meeting them in Auckland they were universally popular on board.

A sign of the rising morale was that when almost three inches of snow fell on deck one evening, nearly everyone was on deck for a ferocious snowball fight. The exceptions were the helmsman and the two cooks who happened to have dinner ready at that point and were complaining bitterly that it would be ruined by the time the rest of the crew went below to eat. It was no use making excuses for the food on board: when cooking you were judged entirely on how good the meal was when a person got it in front of them. A more sympathetic attitude might have prevailed had we carried a special cook who had nothing else to do, but as everyone had to take a turn in the galley, the criticism was merciless when a meal was not quite right.

Sailing along day after day with just the occasional iceberg to brighten an otherwise deserted horizon might seem monotonous, but the sea is always changing, and one's attention is usually focused on the boat and the ever-changing waves in the immediate vicinity. One has to be at sea for a longish period to really appreciate the attraction of the waves about you; their constantly changing patterns almost mesmerise you, and you can sit contentedly for long periods of time just watching them. Of course the regular maintenance of items like winches, and checking running gear for chafe, helps pass the time as well, and occasionally something more serious occurs which provides interest of a different sort.

The mast had been a constant source of worry to everyone when sailing hard on the wind, and every wave the boat pounded on caused it to shudder alarmingly. It is these sudden forces that weaken or break gear and rigging, and on 14th January the half-inch-thick stainless steel 'V' bolt on the masthead crane that supported the spinnaker halyard head block just parted. The spinnaker immediately pulled out ahead and its wire halyard began to saw through the mast at the point where it came out from inside the mast. Every effort was made to lower the halyard, but it was too firmly gripped in the crack it had sawn and would not free. It would not haul up either, which meant that the head of the spinnaker was some eight feet out forward from the mast. The only thing to do was transfer the spinnaker onto the other halyard, and Peter Blake, who seemed to be developing a liking for going aloft, went up in a bosun's chair to do this. Even Peter, at six foot four inches by far the tallest member of the crew, could not reach out far enough from the mast to reach the spinnaker, and the only hope of getting the head in so that he could reach it lay in collapsing the sail—not an attractive proposition when you have a man at the masthead. Les ordered the reacher set, and then ran off wind so that the spinnaker could collapse behind the reacher and be less likely to fill again, and the boat would be more steady. Peter was lowered down the mast about twelve feet, and as the spinnaker collapsed was just able to grab the head for long enough to clip on the other halyard. Once this was done, the weight of the spinnaker was taken up on the other halyard, so that he had a relatively easy job to unclip the jammed halyard and rescue its head block which was flying all over the place and threatening to injure him.

There was nothing that could be done about the broken 'V' bolt—there was no spare on board—so that damaged halyard was coaxed into the mast and the boat just had to make do with one spinnaker halyard for a few days until an alternative system of holding the headblock to the masthead could be worked out. This was not as disadvantageous as it may seem. In short ocean races it is usual to hoist a fresh spinnaker before taking in the existing one, and this requires two spinnaker halyards, but we found that with even the full crew of fifteen or so on deck, we just could not manage this operation quickly enough, and we lost less time by taking down the existing spinnaker and then hoisting a fresh one which used the same halyard.

The boats within a couple of hundred miles of *Heath's Condor* seemed to be getting roughly the same sort of winds at this time, so that *Heath's Condor* was slowly improving her position on nearly all of them. The exception was *Pen Duik* which, sailing about two hundred miles further north, seemed to be getting a better wind and fairly hurtling towards Cape Horn, gaining a little on all the other boats each day. Whatever *Pen Duik*'s official position as far as the race was concerned, she was certainly proving to be a flyer, and from Eric Tarbarly's point of view there was no better way of cocking a snoot at his disqualification than by reaching Rio first. Somehow, by staying a couple of hundred miles north—and, incidentally, thereby sailing a greater distance—Tarbarly had managed to get more than two hundred miles ahead of the fleet, a pretty impressive performance. But it is competitors like this, who leave little to chance and sail hard, who provide the most interesting competition.

Pen Duik rounded Cape Horn on 15th January, about 440 miles ahead of *Heath's Condor*, which still lay behind *Great Britain II* and *Flyer*. For many of the crews, rounding Cape Horn under sail was one of the main reasons for coming on the race, and the actual event was looked forward to with a mixture of excitement and apprehension: excitement because they could then say they had rounded the world's most famous maritime landmark, and apprehension because it achieved its fame through the appalling weather that can prevail around it.

Through most of its passage around the world, the Southern Ocean is unrestricted in breadth and depth, averaging between 12,000 and 1,500 miles in width and 2,000 fathoms or two miles deep. Abruptly, as this huge river of water approaches South America, it is faced with a gap of only six hundred miles between Cape Horn at the southernmost tip of South America and the northern end of Graham Land, a peninsula protruding out from Antarctica. This gap is called Drake's Passage as Sir Francis Drake was the first man to sail through it during his circumnavigation of 1582–85. He chose this way to avoid the Spanish outposts in Magellan's Strait, the route used by Magellan, which lies among the islands north of Cape Horn. The southernmost land mass happens to coincide with the northernmost point of Antarctica, and in addition the water shallows to less than a hundred fathoms at the same place. The water mass in the Southern Ocean suddenly finds that it has to squeeze through a gap one-twentieth of its size, and so of course it accelerates. Whenever a wave from deep water runs into a shallower patch it becomes compressed and its crests move closer to each other with the result that the waves get steeper. This is exactly what happens at Cape Horn, and one could expect unpleasant seas in that area on these grounds alone. But the Horn lies at fifty-six degrees south, so that stronger winds up to storm or hurricane force can also prevail, and this makes matters even worse.

The Horn has such a tradition in our maritime history because, until the opening of the Panama Canal in 1913 it provided the last route by which sailing ships could compete economically with steamers. A steamship's engines just could not be governed sufficiently to cope with the change in loads caused by the propeller being in the water one minute, and turning in air the next, as the ship pitched in rough seas. The result was that until 1913, a sailing ship could, by rounding the Horn, travel as quickly as a steamer between Australia and Europe or the east and west coasts of the United States. Nearly everyone who went to sea in ocean-going sailing ships up to the First World War could expect to round the Horn, and some sailing ships were still doing it in the 1930s. Even though sailing ships would sail as soon as they were loaded, they would prefer to round the Cape during the summer months from November to March, thus avoiding the appalling winter storms from April to October. Beating around the Horn from east to west against the prevailing winds in winter time was a hazardous venture, and in 1905, of some 130 vessels that sailed from Europe to the American west coast, only fifty-two reached their destination without any trouble. Four were definitely wrecked and a further forty-nine were still unaccounted for four months after they should have arrived, although most of them struggled in eventually.

The passage from west to east is easier, as you are usually running before the winds, and this was the route taken by the race. Even so, following seas can build up to extreme heights, and yachts have been rolled end over end by larger than normal waves. Of course it can also, on rare occasions, be calm. In 1969 I lay becalmed about six miles off the Cape in *Suhaili* for seven hours. When I got home that time I mentioned this to an octogenarian master mariner and member of the Cape Horners' Club, who looked at me with piercing blue eyes from under large white bushy eyebrows and said, 'Don't you go telling people that, you'll ruin our image!'

Heath's Condor, however, got strong following winds two days from the Horn, and for the first time on the third leg the crew were able to enjoy the fast exciting downwind sailing which had been such a feature of the second leg. *Flyer* was not far ahead and a six-hour schedule was set up so that the boats could swop progress reports regularly. The *Endurance*, a Royal Navy ice patrol ship, was in the vicinity at the time and was listening out on 4 megahertz. Les got through to her during the evening of the 16th, but reception was too poor for a conversation.

January 17th, coincidentally the ninth anniversary of my rounding of the Horn in *Suhaili*, began with light northerly winds which slowed things down a bit. Twenty miles to the north *Flyer* was sailing well in variable winds. *Great Britain II* had rounded early that morning, 140 miles ahead. The wind died during the morning watch, and then came up from the south-east, force two to three, before slowly veering so that by 08.00 a spinnaker could be set. The Diego Ramirez Islands were sighted at 10.00 spot on track. This group of islands lying fifty-six miles west-south-west of the Horn are a good safe landfall, as there is plenty of clear water either side of them. The islands and rocks around Cape Horn are littered with wrecks of vessels which would have been safe if they had kept further out to sea. Surprisingly, the Diego Ramirez Islands are sometimes inhabited during the summer.

For some time the only birds seen had been the occasional

petrel, but as the islands were approached, bird life suddenly re-appeared in abundance, albatross and cape pigeons in particular. It may be that few albatrosses were seen up to then as it was their breeding season, and those suddenly sighted in such numbers off the Horn were part of breeding pairs hunting for food for their partners and chicks.

Isla Gonzalo, the southernmost island in the group, was passed to the north at 12.30. *Flyer* had passed north of it at 10.30, so she seemed about sixteen miles ahead. The swell was now enormous, but, despite the south-east wind, the waves were not breaking, and the boat was roaring down the huge hill-sized waves, and then climbing ponderously up out of the valley the other side. The spinnaker, full on the downward swoop, tried to stay filled as the boat started to climb, but each time was held back by the boat and collapsed on itself. The sea changed in colour from an almost Mediterranean blue to a dark green as a sixty-foot shallow patch was crossed and provided extra excitement for everyone on board. None of the crew, apart from Julian, had rounded the Horn before, and were looking forward to seeing the famous Cape.

The snow-capped peaks of the Groupo Hermite Islands were soon in sight—snow-capped although the highest peak in the group is only 1,690 feet and this was midsummer. The Hermite group or, as they are sometimes called, the Islas del Cabo de Hornos, consists of four islands: Deceit, Herschel, Hermite and Horn Islands. Horn Island is obviously the southernmost island, and the Cape reaches a height of 1,330 feet. The feature from which the island gets its name lies two miles west-north-westward of the Cape, and consists of two towers of rock, which were thought to resemble horns, hence the name. In Spanish, the Cape is known as Cabo de Hornos, indicating more than one horn which is correct, though in English we just call it Cape Horn. The cliffs behind the shore at the Cape are almost black in colour and, despite the strong winds, covered with rich green vegetation.

Les took *Heath's Condor* to within two miles of the Cape, making about twelve knots in the force six winds. Of course everyone wanted to be photographed steering past the Horn, so Golf Charlie was appointed official photographer, and patiently photographed everyone in turn at the wheel, in the slightly bored manner of a seaside photographer with a busload of holiday-makers. A special party parcel had been put on board in Auckland just for this occasion and was discovered to contain paper hats, masks and balloons. This was opened as a celebratory drink was being constructed, and the resulting party was a great success. An escaping balloon caused considerable interest to the albatrosses, especially as it kept being suddenly lifted into the air in gusts, and they pursued it until it disappeared from view in a snow squall. No doubt there is still an albatross flying around wondering what on earth that funny thing was that, when pecked, gave a loud pop and disappeared.

The Horn bore west at 17.45 when it suddenly disappeared in a snow storm. The course was set for Le Mairie Strait across the entrance to Beagle Channel, a distance of about seventy miles. By now the boat was in the lee of the westerly swell for the first time since clearing New Zealand, and she was really moving in the flat sea. There was a lot of leeway to catch up. *Flyer* was not yet in sight, and *Great Britain* was nearly twenty hours ahead. *Pen Duik*, although out of the race, was still a moral force to be reckoned with, but she seemed too far ahead to catch in two weeks.

Heath's Condor had been quite lucky passing the Horn, for even in summer more than thirty per cent of the time the wind blows at over force seven, but once past to the East, the percentage of winds of this strength drops dramatically. However, williwaws—wild sudden gusts from nearly any direction—suddenly strike from the land, and across the wide entrances to the several wide channels very strong steady winds can be experienced. Further north, the dreaded pamperos blow out to sea reaching hurricane strength and arrive with next to no warning. In 1901, the 5,900-ton barque *France*, one of the largest sailing ships ever built, was struck by a pampero that heeled her right over and caused her cargo to shift. Despite a heroic effort by her crew, they were unable to keep the water out, and she subsequently foundered. A yacht has the advantage that she has no cargo to shift, and provided not too much water gets in the deadweight of the keel will bring her back upright, but very serious damage can still be sustained. On *Heath's Condor* we were terrified of a knockdown of this sort, because if the wind pressure held the boat over for any length of time, the faulty ventilation system would let in more water than we could bale out.

During the night of the 17th it blew sixty knots with a mixture of rain, hail and snow. When the first squall hit, the spinnaker was let go and recovered, but the spinnaker staysail's head blew out at the same time and, although the sail was recovered, a halyard was left up the mast to be recovered later. Temporarily under reefed main only, the boat was still doing fourteen knots.

According to Dead Reckoning, the light at the entrance of Marie Strait should have been sighted at about midnight. But nothing was seen, although in the occasional clear patches there was an impression of land on the port bow. Sometime later a light that seemed to be flashing twice in every fifteen seconds was sighted, but the light at the southern entrance to the strait has a characteristic of flashing twice every fifty seconds, and there was another halfway up the strait flashing twice every ten seconds according to the light list. So although it was more likely that the light sighted was the one halfway through the channel, it would not have been prudent to count on it. A running fix was taken, and a course set to clear land whichever of the lights was actually in view, and the running sail was taken in so that speed was reduced until a more definite fix could be made. Quite strong currents flow through the Marie Strait, reaching up to eight knots in certain points, but only running at three knots in the centre of the channel. In the darkness it was difficult to tell which way the current was going, but as the sky lightened early in the morning it appeared to be going northwards so it looked as if the boat had got into the strait about five hours before high water when the tidal stream turns northerly. At the northern entrance the boat sat on a wave with deep troughs before and behind for quite a few minutes doing a steady nine knots, although this did not mean that the water was travelling that fast, just that the wave was moving along at that speed. At least during her passage, *Heath's Condor* missed all of the tide rips and overfalls, except for a large wave at the end, fortunately going the same way.

At dawn, *Heath's Condor* cleared the strait, and in the increasing light suddenly saw *Flyer* about five miles ahead. Both boats set spinnakers, Les getting the large working one up on *Heath's Condor*, despite the imminence of squalls, before handing over to Peter Blake at 05.00 after nearly thirty hours on the go. At noon when he awoke, he found the boat had been gybed as the wind had come round to the south-west, and *Flyer* was noticeably closer, although not yet abeam. Shortly after the chat show at 14.00, *Endurance* appeared on the horizon led by her helicopter which did quite a bit of filming. As if to give the cameraman an even better shot, *Heath's Condor* was hit by a squall in the middle of it all and heeled right over, necessitating a reduction in sail. It must have been a thrilling sight for *Endurance* to see two large yachts racing flat out in very boisterous conditions in one of the more deserted parts of the world. Slowly but surely *Heath's Condor* was overtaking *Flyer*, as indeed she should have, being the larger boat, but everyone was impressed with how well *Flyer* was sailing. It was not until 18.30 that she was on the beam, so she was sailing only one-third of a knot slower, a remarkable performance. Once *Heath's Condor* got ahead, however, *Flyer* seemed to drop astern quite quickly, although the following morning as Steeple Jason, a large pinnacle of rock, came into sight she could still be seen astern. Of course, the nights were still short, but noticeably getting longer each night as the boat drove north. *Flyer* was out of sight by noon, when on the chat show it was learned that *Great Britain II* was thirty miles nearer, a double reason for celebration and a great morale booster.

The next twenty-four hours were amongst the most exciting of the whole voyage. Encouraged by passing *Flyer* and gaining on *Great Britain II*, the boat was really pushed to the limit under storm spinnaker, staysail and varying amounts of mainsail, and a record day's run of 309 miles was achieved. Not without incident however, as just after midnight a sudden gust hit the boat and heeled her right over. At the same moment, the bow dug into the back of the wave in front, and the whole boat was stopped dead, pivoted round and heeled hard over. The sheet and guy were let go but jammed. The siren went for all hands on deck just as the boat lurched. Roddy was sitting on the end of his bunk as it happened, and was thrown right across the saloon about seventeen feet, finishing up in a corner with most of the loose items from the galley. Somewhat shaken, he got up, still in his sleeping bag, and staggered back to the cabin to get into his oilskins. As he reached the entrance, Justin rushed out and bumped in to him. 'Don't hang about, Roddy,' said Justin, 'it's an emergency, hurry up and get on deck!'

Eventually the guy was released and the sail was hauled in, luckily undamaged. The main boom guy was broken during the chaos, but the boat was lucky to get away with such little damage from such a potentially dangerous situation.

The wind stayed at gale force, although boats astern were reporting more variable winds, and at the end of the next twenty-four hours another three hundred miles had been covered. *Great Britain II* was now less than a hundred miles ahead, although she reported a three-hundred-mile run as well, which was disappointing. Any hopes of continuing the mad rush up the west coast of South America to Rio were dashed when Golf Charlie managed to pick up the morse canal weather forecast on the 21st. The isobars showed up in almost the exact pattern shown in the Admiralty Pilot for January, except that in their centre there was a high pressure instead of a low. The high's centre was directly in *Heath's Condor*'s path, while *Great Britain II* should have been experiencing light following winds, and *Pen Duik* was probably clear to the north or might be held up. In one way, this high opened everything up again as, depending upon where the centre moved, some boats could be stopped and others still moving. As *Heath's Condor* had been a hundred miles behind *Great Britain II* when the high appeared this should have worked to her advantage. Les decided to alter course to the north, rather than the north-east, and try to creep round to the west of the high. It meant that light headwinds could be expected, but the boat's movement through the air would make these winds fresh from a relative point of view, and *Heath's Condor* should have been able to keep up a good speed, better than if she had had a light following wind.

In fact the wind died away completely for over eight hours during the next twenty-four, before coming up from the north-north-east and backing slowly round to the north-west. *Great Britain II* held a light following wind and did eighty miles more in the same time, but at chat hour was becalmed. It all now depended upon the high sitting on top of *Great Britain II* until *Heath's Condor*, with a good force three north-westerly, could catch up. There was a risk to keeping inshore on this final stretch, but the risk seemed worth while as one thing of course is always certain: if you take the exact course of a boat in front of you, provided the boats' speeds are roughly the same, you will never overtake her!

For the next three days, the weather played up, giving northerlies of up to force nine, which meant pulling nearly all the sail off the boat to avoid slamming and breaking the mast. In the middle of it all, the boat suddenly felt as if she grounded twice and then a large whale surfaced alongside. Fortunately the whale did not seem too upset by being disturbed, but the bump put the log out of action so from then on Les could only guess at his days' runs.

When a patch of lighter weather came on the 25th, the mast problem was to a certain extent improved by taking the baby stay, the innermost of the three forestays, forward and fastening it to the base of the intermediate stay. This gave it a better, more shallow angle, and thus increased its holding power, and made it possible to tighten up the shrouds to the lower spreaders and hold the mast firmly at that point. This done, all the after shrouds were tightened to give greater support and, hopefully, stop some of the mast movement. Unfortunately, whilst this steadied the lowest section, the upper sections took on an alarming bend from the lower spreaders, and the lower shrouds had to be slackened off a bit to try and keep the mast straight. The problem of tuning a mast is always a difficult one. Personally I like the standing rigging good and tight so that there is a minimum of slackness on the lee side when heeled. But the whole objective is to keep the mast straight on either tack. Any bending should be in the fore and aft plane to help flatten or fill the mainsail, and this is controlled by the backstays and running backstays and, in *Heath's Condor*'s case, the three forestays.

A very interesting tactical situation had now developed. *Heath's Condor* was west of *Great Britain II* and about fifty miles north of her on the 27th, but lying further inshore, not in the most favourable position. It all depended upon what the wind did. If *Heath's Condor* got a north-easterly wind, *Great Britain II* was home and dry; if the wind stayed north-westerly, she could just lose out.

The wind decided to veer round to east by north during the night which was bad enough, but obviously someone had upset Neptune because that night:

(a) A mainsail leach line parted.
(b) A batten fell out of the mainsail.
(c) The main halyard parted and was replaced by the main boom topping lift.
(d) The spinnaker halyard used as an emergency topping lift parted.
(e) The mainsail headboard came adrift from its slides.

With only a hundred miles to go to Rio, the wind freshened to force five. But at dawn *Great Britain II* was in sight to the east just ahead of the beam. So the tactic of going inshore had paid off, and now we would find out if it would pay off enough. It all depended again upon what the wind did. If it backed to the west *Heath's Condor* stood a good chance. If it veered to the east, *Great Britain II* was sure to win. In fact it veered and *Heath's Condor* was able to lay the finish line close hauled, but *Great Britain II* was able to have a freer run under a spinnaker set shy, and she made the line first by thirty-five minutes. Still, that's ocean racing, and to have caught up over two hundred miles in the last ten days on a slightly larger boat was no mean feat.

5. RIO TO PORTSMOUTH

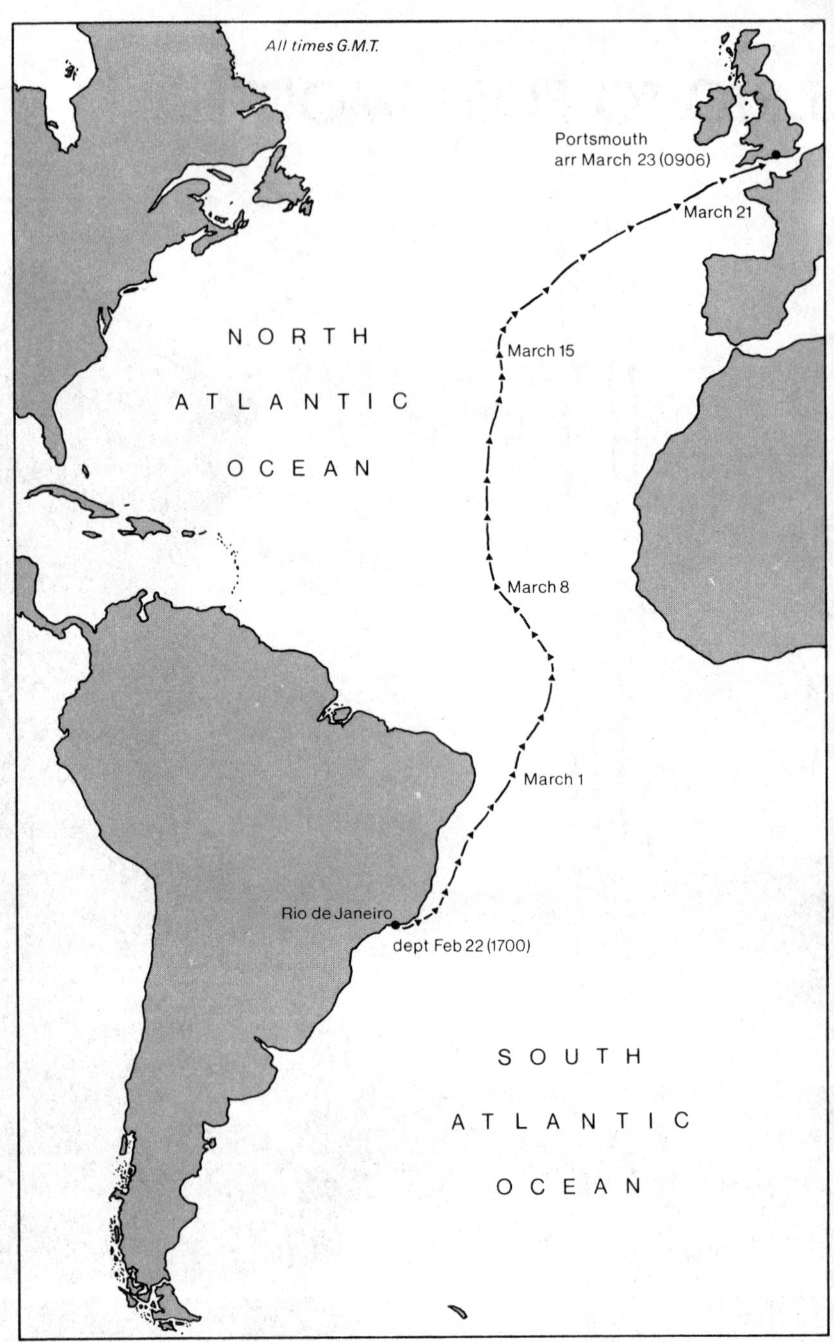
All times G.M.T.
Portsmouth
arr March 23 (0906)
March 21
NORTH
ATLANTIC
OCEAN
March 15
March 8
March 1
Rio de Janeiro
dept Feb 22 (1700)
SOUTH
ATLANTIC
OCEAN

Brazil is a rapidly developing country, and Rio de Janeiro, a city spread over and around exfoliated mountains surrounding Guanabara Bay, is its largest city with a population of eight million people. Rio has a fantastic reputation. Copacabana beach and Sugar Loaf Mountain are world famous, and as the city is set just off the Tropic of Capricorn, the climate is usually warm. Too much so at times, because it can become very humid in the smaller bays around the city and sleeping on board a confined boat in those conditions is very uncomfortable.

As the yachts came in, they were moored up Mediterranean fashion, that is, an anchor out from one end and the other end held to the harbour wall by ropes. The exclusive Iate Clube de Rio was acting as hosts to the fleet, as they had done before. This is Brazil's most exclusive club. Membership costs ten thousand pounds for a share, and there are annual dues on top of that. Membership is limited to four thousand, I believe, but the club probably has only a hundred or so boats. It does have a magnificent swimming pool and a long veranda covering a bar. I am never quite sure whether the members appreciate having about 150 yachtsmen suddenly descending upon them and sharing their facilities. For the most part they put up with it graciously enough, but any crew member who thought he was going to be treated as a hero because he had just rounded the Horn was in for a disappointment, as people just were not interested.

The main attraction for everyone was Mardi Gras, the annual carnival that lasts for four days up to and including Ash Wednesday. Each year the different districts prepare their floats and sambas for the competition, and tremendous prestige is gained by the winners. The costumes worn by the dancers are incredibly extravagant for people who may live on the breadline for most of the year, but this is typical of the contradictions found all the time in Rio. For the four days the Carnival lasts, people live in a dream world in which everyone sambas and the all-pervading sound of samba music continues day and night. It is a crazy four days, but not an experience anyone would wish to miss, and for the crews of the boats it probably ranked next in importance to rounding the Horn as a reason for doing the voyage.

The Yacht Club throws its own carnival party, the tickets for which cost forty-five pounds, so few crew members could afford to go officially. In fact, it soon became obvious that, provided you were dressed for the part, no one cared. This party, which takes place around the swimming pool, is an all-night affair, and as one samba band collapses they are hauled off and another replaces them. If anyone felt hot, they fell, or were pushed, into the pool, and climbed out to carry on dancing.

A separate party was thrown for the race prize giving at which, for some reason, no relay of bands was laid on. The result was inevitable. As soon as the band walked away at 23.00 just as the party was warming up, people made their own music out of anything they could find—tables, chairs, plates—anything. The catering manager grew so alarmed that he called in the riot police who arrived fully armed with shields, machine guns and tear gas! But the appearance of four hundred fearsome-looking police did little to quell the party. A few riot police fell into the pool to join others already there and then the tear gas grenades began to go off. Most of the crews had never come across tear gas before, and the first thing to occur to them, as their eyes were watering, was that the booze must have been particularly good. When it was realised what was happening, people got out fast. In retrospect, it is lucky that the police were restrained as it only wanted one to start shooting and a totally unnecessary tragedy would have taken place. The Club's commodore was furious at the breaking-up of what was, by Rio standards, a perfectly normal party, and he sacked the catering manager on the spot.

While the Carnival was in progress no one could do anything to get the boats ready, and in any case permission to use the Naval Dockyard's slipways had not come through, as Admiral Schiech, who commanded the base, was not asked early enough. The Dockyard was perfectly willing to allow their slipway to be used, and when the Admiral heard what was required, he gave his permission immediately. The result was a bit of a scramble to get all the boats slipped in time, but it was all right on the day. On *Heath's Condor* Les had been so worried about the mast that we decided to see whether it would be possible to have some stiffeners fitted. We were lucky to meet up with Hubert Reece, a retired US Navy Engineer Captain who was working as a specialist aluminium adviser to the

Brazilian Navy. He informed us that not only could the Dockyard do the work, but the Admiral had said they would. This was excellent news, as the mast had really worried Les in the strong head winds of the third leg, and none of us was happy about sailing the boat hard in the north-east Trades in the final leg unless the mast was strengthened. There was only one problem: aluminium rivets for the job were available in Brazil, but we doubted whether these were strong enough. What was required were monel rivets, and these could only be imported. Fortunately, when it was discovered that we needed them, I was still in the UK and Les was able to phone me and give me time to get them, as well as a couple of dozen urgently required spares, and take them all out with me.

In the meantime, the Dockyard got on with the work of preparing some stiffeners, and the boat motored round to have the mast removed. Although the mast has only to be lifted nine feet to be clear of the boat, it requires a tall crane to do the job as the centre of gravity of the mast is about fifty feet above sea level. The large dockyard crane was more than big enough, and all seemed to be going well when suddenly, with the heel of the mast resting on a wooden chock ashore and everyone waiting for the crane driver to gently lower away, work stopped. There was no explanation for over ten minutes as to why work stopped; it just did, and the men sat down as if they were having a statutory break. Eventually a message came through that unless the crew of the yacht dressed properly no more work would be carried out! Dressing properly meant wearing a shirt, shorts and shoes, not just bathing trunks which was what most had on at the time. The crew were incredulous. From what they had seen of Rio so far, no one bothered too much about what they wore at any time, and during the Carnival some of the costumes had been exceedingly skimpy. However, the boat was now in the Naval Dockyard, and no matter what went on outside the gates, inside was run as a military establishment. The moment everyone was 'properly dressed' the mast was carefully lowered, and work commenced.

My plan was to fly out on 14th February. I would have gone out earlier, but at the beginning of January I had contracted shingles, and I was giving myself as much time to cure it as I could before going out to a hot climate. Even so, when I went I could hardly use my left eye and found it necessary to take pain killers about four times a day. Whereas I was mentally fit, I was far from physically so, and no one could tell me how long it would last, or whether it would get worse. Nothing was going to keep me from doing the last leg, but I had to face up to the fact that, apart from navigating and making tactical decisions, I was not going to be much use. In the circumstances it seemed advisable for the boat to have someone else available to take my share of the physical work, and also to act as cover for me as far as tactics and navigation were concerned. Peter was more than qualified, but as mate of the boat he had enough to do, and one did not want him to cease pushing his watch when they were on duty. Les was due to go home, but agreed to sail the last leg as a watch leader just in case I collapsed. Julian agreed to give up his watch and serve under Les. I think it says a lot for the personalities involved that three experienced yacht skippers could so readily accept the situation, and much more that it did not lead to any difficulties on the way home. We all worked as a team concentrating upon our objective, but I suppose we were helped by the fact that we had known each other for years. I was, not unnaturally, delighted that Les agreed to come along. This gave us tremendous experience in depth, and meant we were fielding our 'first fifteen' for the last leg.

We had fewer crew changes in Rio than in the other ports along the way. Barry Buchannan returned to South Africa, and Roddy Coleman, David Alan-Williams and Peter Visick returned to the UK. To replace them we kept Les on board, and Ianto Jones, a fisherman and diver, joined us from Scotland. The crew was two less than on the previous leg, but we could see fewer problems on the last leg, and it meant a weight saving of at least a third of a ton by the time you had added up the weight of two men, their personal gear and the weight of food and water they would consume in a month. The heavier we were the slower we would go, so any weight saving was going to help, and we felt confident of managing the boat efficiently with fourteen men—or, more honestly, thirteen and a half as I only counted for a half.

I staggered into Rio airport with 120 kilos of excess baggage and a radio technician flown out to sort out our and *King's*

Legend's radios, both of which were still giving trouble. My five large bags on a trolley attracted the immediate interest of the Customs, and I was told to open them all up. My personal clothing was allowed—and a large new experimental radar reflector I wanted to try out—but my cameras, sextant and all the vital spares, including the rivets, were not. The Customs Officer did not speak English and I have no Portuguese, so an interpreter working for the airline did his best. It was explained that the cameras and sextant were personal property, and after ten minutes of argument this was reluctantly accepted, but there was no way the spares were going to be allowed. There is a Brazilian law which prohibits the importation of anything that Brazil itself manufactures, and although I pointed out that the bulk of the spares were for a British yacht and could be put aboard under bond, I was told this was not acceptable. I had some two-inch stainless steel split pins which were made in Brazil so my bag was impounded. I took a receipt and headed for the yacht club, a drive of three quarters of an hour, and found Les. We went to the Race Control Office and were told that a local customs officer could help, but in the end he was unable to arrange things for us. With only a few days to go to the start, we were getting desperate. Then we were told that we had to go, as far as I can understand it, to a government-appointed fixer who would arrange the amount of bribe to be paid so that my bag could be released. If I had known it was a question of a bribe whilst I was at the airport I would have paid it then, much as I dislike the practice, but this had not been made clear, and indeed perhaps the Customs like to be bribed officially. The fixer was most pleasant and did not charge his usual fee, which was generous, but it took until the day before we sailed to get the bag cleared. I had one attempt, but after a full morning in the city and then an hour and a half in an un-air-conditioned Customs' office which was unventilated and unbearably hot, I began to feel really ill and gave up. The fixer's substitute failed on his own. Bob Bell did it in the end, but it took him a full working day and a hundred and fifty dollars to achieve it. The rivets were put in the evening before the race started, from bosun's chairs as the mast was back up by then, held by fifty rivets we had begged from other yachts.

As far as I can gather there is no way around this problem of getting spares out to a yacht in Rio. The only thing to do is ensure that you require nothing there, and take aboard anything you might need before you reach Brazil. One thousand rivets is rather a large number to carry around just in case, and of course we had no idea in Auckland that we were going to need them or we would have bought them there.

Work progressed well on the boat for we were receiving tremendous assistance from the Navy, and each day the boat motored round from the yacht club to the dockyard so that we could overhaul the mast whilst it was ashore. It is a pleasant and interesting trip. The channel out of the yacht club is tortuous, but once clear of it is an easy run in hot sunshine round past the Nautical College and Old Imperial palace, which is now the headquarters of the Brazilian Hydrographic Department, into the dockyard. The Imperial Palace looks as out of place in its setting as does the Brighton Pavilion, which in some ways, and in particular its colour scheme, it resembles. It was here, at the end of the last century, that Brazil's last king was sent into exile. The Brazilians did not dislike him or they would have shot him, but they just decided they wanted to be a republic so he was taken from the palace, where a party was in progress, put on a ship and sent away.

Before leaving the UK I had sent a message to Eric Tarbarly suggesting that we have a private bet of a case of champagne for who got back into Portsmouth first. It was not quite clear that he would not be allowed in the race officially for the last leg, and I felt that, having come this far, this would give him something to go for. It would also make the last leg that little bit more interesting for us. We had both spoken on a French TV programme about this, but he had not committed himself. Once I got to Rio I sought him out and asked whether he would accept. I was quite surprised when he said he would not, his reason being that we were a longer boat, which by three feet or so we were, but he had a proven flyer and well worked up crew, and in his position I would have agreed just for the hell of it. His crew seemed to bear us a certain amount of animosity, due I suspect to the rumour still going around that we had protested them in Auckland—despite the fact that anyone could have checked up and discovered this was not the case—and they avoided us whenever possible. This was unnecessary, but when one of them asked us for our mail for England so that he could post it for us when they arrived—indicating they would be there well before us—I suffered a sense of humour failure. They were not prepared, as a Cockney would put it, to put their money, in the form of a case of champagne, where their mouth was, but they were prepared to needle us.

Tarbarly's unofficial presence in the race presented us with a tactical difficulty. Whilst we were delighted to hear that the Race Committee had invited him to join in the last leg, it did present us with something of a headache. If he got home first everyone would say he had won, so we had to cover him, but at the same time, from the race point of view, we had to cover *Great Britain II* and try to beat her as well. This would be fine as long as the boats stayed reasonably close, but if *Great Britain II* and *Pen Duik* took different routes we could only cover one of them and if the other got away we lost the race physically or morally. Of course, had *Pen Duik* been in the race, we would still have had to cover two boats, but she would have been under pressure to cover as well. As it was she could do as she wished, cover us and *Great Britain II* if she liked, but if she did not or began to get the worst of it, she could always do something different or even just head straight for France and not cross the finish line at all, in which case all our efforts could be wasted on the wrong boat. However, we decided we would just have to play it by ear as the race progressed.

For some reason it had been decided that two of the crew were required to sort the food out for the last leg, and Graham and the doctor elected to do it. The job must have been exhausting as it appeared to require frequent stops at the club bar for rest and refreshment. In all it took them close to two weeks to make up the lists, check what remained on board, find out where to buy things, and actually get them. Admittedly, there had been no language difficulties in our other ports of call, but I got the distinct impression that while it was found necessary to visit certain tourist attractions to decide on our food requirement, the whole job could have been done much more quickly using the well-stocked supermarkets.

While these two got on with the food, the rest of the crew worked all day on the boat. On the weekend of the 18th and 19th we went across the harbour to Niteroi where the Rio

Sailing Club had its base. This was a much smaller club, less formal and more sailing orientated, and it made a pleasant change from the constant bustle of the yacht club. Also it seemed to get a cooling breeze. This breeze had not favoured the yacht club, making sleeping on board a difficult business and far from refreshing on account of the humidity. Bob, in his usual ebullient form, arranged a party for us at the sailing club the night before the beginning of the last leg. It poured with rain to start with, but once it cleared things really got moving. Unfortunately I was unable to drink alcohol so I went back to the boat early and turned in. The only cure for shingles appears to be plenty of rest, and I wanted to be as fresh as possible for the start.

Before the race we had the usual skippers' briefing where any last-minute alterations to the rules or regulations are given out. Otto Steiner confirmed the situation regarding *Pen Duik VI*, and said that the French Racing Authority had been ordered to withdraw her rating certificate. He also announced all the yachts' ratings, and I noticed that we were up once again to 68.8 feet. We seemed to be being deliberately baited but there seemed little point in raising the matter at the meeting and in any case we were allowed up to twenty-four hours after arrival to protest if we wanted to, so I did not say anything at the time.

Wednesday, 22nd February at 14.00 hours was the start time, and as before we intended to get to the vicinity of the start line, off the Nautical College in the Middle of Guanabara Bay, well in time so that we could get a measure of the wind and tide on the line. At 10.00 when we were loading last-minute supplies, I received a message to report to the yacht club office. A couple of days before, when we were anchored off the club, we had swung round and just touched the elaborate but shaky pulpit of a power boat. Its crew had been on board at the time but had done nothing, and we had re-fastened the four screws that held the pulpit into its platform, three of which had been missing anyway. I was now told that we must pay for the damage we had caused this boat. What made it more galling was that I was told that if we did not pay, a writ would be served on *Heath's Condor* and we would miss the race. It was pure blackmail, and made me as mad as hell, but we had to go and we could not afford the time-consuming complications of a possible lawsuit. We paid the skipper of the power boat seventeen pounds and got away. Rio may be a delightful place for crews, but it provides its fair share of problems for a skipper.

We just had time for one trial run at the start line before the five-minute gun went, so we hastily gybed round to get a favourable position as far to windward as we could. With two minutes to go we tacked on to the starboard tack and went straight for the line. Most of the boats were roughly in the middle of the line so it became a little crowded for a while, but by being on starboard we at least had right of way as boats flashed past on either side. Just before the start gun went, *Great Britain II* crossed close in front of us on port tack, a risky manoeuvre as I could have gone closer to the wind and forced them to tack. Then the gun went—we were off. I found that steering with one eye was a bit of a strain, but in the excitement of the moment I never even noticed it as my attention was entirely on the sails with Peter and Les letting me know who was where. As soon as we had clear water we tacked to head towards the yacht club and a more favourable current. Rob James brought *Great Britain II* about on top of us as if we both were sailing dinghies. But confident that I had the faster boat, I luffed him just a little so that his ketch rig became less efficient than our sloop, and we were soon clear ahead out of his lee. I almost tacked on him in turn for the fun of it when he went about again, but we wanted to get closer inshore to where the tide suited us better. After we passed Laje Island, which lies at the middle of the entrance to Guanabara Bay, we went east while most of the other boats went west. They were right and we tacked back, cutting across *Debenhams*'s stern as we went. John Ridgeway shouted something about getting a photo of us astern of him, and we gave him a cheer in return.

The strong wind that had made the start so exciting eased as we cleared the harbour entrance. Looking around we could see some light ripples out to sea, so we sailed out to try and keep some wind, and this paid off. Inshore we could see *Pen Duik* and half a dozen others barely moving as we rounded Isla do Pai in company with *Treaty of Rome* and *Disque D'Or*. We now had very light headwinds, which veered slowly and came in puffs, which made the rest of the day's progress a lottery. It paid to be offshore, though.

Having divided up the watches, and eaten an excellent steak dinner prepared by the Major and Graham, we settled down for the night. Some rather interesting vegetables had been procured in Rio, and Graham produced a potpourri of them which was very good. After the second sitting he found he had some over and was going around banging his saucepan asking if there was 'anyone else for exotic veg'.

We light drifted all night and at daybreak found *Flyer* about a mile ahead of us. She seemed to be the lead boat. *Pen Duik* was slightly astern and inshore, and *ADC* directly astern of us. There were other sails astern of *ADC* but they were difficult to identify. It looked as if no one had made a breakout.

We rounded Cabo Frio just after 09.00 and headed out to the point at which the Brazilian coast turns north-east. There is a choice at this point: whether to head out into the South Atlantic or to try and run north-east up the coast. The weather in the South Atlantic is dominated by the South Atlantic high which usually hovers just east of the centre of the ocean. This causes the winds to revolve in an anti-clockwise direction around the South Atlantic, and this in turn generates surface currents that follow the same direction, one running north up the west African coast as the cold Benguella current. Off Recife, South America's most eastern point, the south Equatorial current splits up. Part of it turns north-westwards along Brazil's northern coast and flows into the Caribbean; the other part, the Brazil current, flows south-westerly down the Brazilian coast. Thus for a strip of about three hundred miles off the Brazilian coast there is an adverse strip of current flowing at between one to one and a half knots. Close inshore there is next to no current or a slight favourable counter current. The winds close in to the coast tend to follow the Brazil current, and blow from the north-east or east at best, but to count on this is a slight gamble as the high pressure centre has only to move slightly south-east and then the low over central Brazil shifts east, creating a northerly wind. The most steady and consistent winds in this area are the south-east Trade winds, and in *Suhaili* I had picked them up at this time of the year at about latitude twenty-three degrees south and longitude twenty-eight degrees west. So the choice was to run up inshore with the favourable current and possibly variable winds, or head out across an unfavourable current but pick up the good steady Trade winds. We decided on the latter course because it also meant we would cross the Equator further east, and I have a theory that in March at about twenty-seven degrees east the Doldrums do not extend to any great extent north or south. This theory is based entirely upon two fairly quick transits of the Doldrums from south to north in *Suhaili* at about this time of year in 1967 and 1969, but it was more recent information than the pilot could provide. I should point out, however, that as I was not further east or west of our own present position on those two occasions, I have no idea what the weather was like elsewhere, and it could well have been better in some other longitude. Certainly it would not pay to go too far east, and to be right over on the Brazilian coast would run the risk of local factors making the Doldrums wider.

The fleet split up at Cabo Frio. *Pen Duik, ADC* and *King's Legend* all went inshore; *Adventure* and *Treaty of Rome* did the same for a while but then came out, and the rest headed out roughly east of north-east to meet the Trade winds. Of course the moment we had made our decision to head out the inshore boats started to do better, but I had the feeling it was not going to pay them in the long term, particularly if we could find the Trades quickly.

For the first three days we had yachts in sight which was depressing, and to add to our problems Les went down with what the doctor described as a salmonella infection, a form of typhus, which scared the living daylights out of me. Any infectious disease is dangerous in a small crowded yacht, but typhus was really alarming. I told everyone to be particularly careful about their personal hygiene, and we used hot water instead of our usual cold seawater for washing up. Les was isolated in his bunk which fortunately was separate, and everyone told to keep clear of him. We also kept his eating utensils separate. The doctor dosed him and he went to sleep for nearly a day, awakening much better, but feeling weak. We left him off watches for two days until he felt strong enough, and in the meantime Julian went back to leading his watch and I transferred Golf Charlie from Peter's watch to balance things.

This scare served to remind everyone of the importance of keeping clean on board, and Les lost some of his paunch which did him no harm.

The inshore boats were out of sight on the 24th, and we had got nicely into the lead of the boats heading out to sea. Inshore, all the three larger boats were north of our latitude, and obviously finding a better current, but as we were sailing along the hypotenuse of a triangle and they were going up one of the other sides, latitude was not a fair method of comparing positions. *King's Legend* was the closest inshore by nearly twenty miles and she was fourteen miles north of anyone else which seemed to prove the point about the north going counter current. For a while we had an east-south-east wind blowing force four and we began to hope that we might have picked up the Trade winds at 39½ degrees west, but a succession of line squalls, each backing the wind a trifle, proved we had not. In the late afternoon we sighted a sail ahead and immediately began to discuss which of our competitors it might be, a worrying thought as we should have been going faster. It turned out to be a thirty-five-foot ketch bound for Rio. We passed about seventy-five yards apart, but as we were racing and doing about ten knots at the time, we did not stop to have a chat.

Whether it was my lecture on hygiene or just the heat, I do not know, but everyone started taking seawater baths in the afternoon. We used salt water soap which does not lather very well, and washing-up detergent was a much better alternative. Unfortunately we did not carry sufficient detergent for washing dishes and ourselves, so we had to go back to rubbing harder with salt water soap. However much you rinse after using the soap, you still feel a little greasy. There are detergents specially made for salt water, like tepol, and provided no one's skin is allergic to it, it is probably the most sensible thing to carry. Salt water is good to wash in as when you have dried off the salt tends to keep your skin quite fresh; but nothing can beat a rainwater shower, and as the rain is usually cool it feels luxurious. Before deciding to soap yourself, though, it is advisable to check the rain cloud to make sure the rain will last long enough for a rinse as well. I have been caught on a number of occasions beautifully covered in soap just as the rain stopped, and I know I am not alone in this. You have no choice then but to rinse off quickly with salt water as otherwise the soap will quickly dry on your body. Whether there is any truth in it I do not know, but when I was in the Merchant Navy we used to shower under a scupper whenever we got a heavy rainfall as we believed it helped get rid of prickly heat. It was not a rare occurrence in Bombay as the south-west monsoon began to break—and between rain squalls the atmosphere was very humid—to see a crowd of naked ship's officers rushing out to take advantage of every rain squall. We believed in it enough to ignore worrying about exposing ourselves anyway!

The gradual veering of the wind and light patches between squalls slowed us up a bit, and by the 25th the Swiss entry, *Disque D'Or*, was giving a DR position only six miles astern of us and said she had *Pen Duik* four miles ahead of her. We had nothing in sight at all, but as most of the boats had not been able to see the sun or stars, a certain divergence of positions was inevitable. I am inclined to err on the cautious side in these circumstances, and it could have been that we were a bit further ahead, but when *Pen Duik* came up with a position twenty-three miles ahead of us I just did not believe it. This would have put *Disque D'Or* ahead of us as well, and although our day's run was only 150 miles, I did not see how she could have averaged nearly two knots faster than us in roughly the same conditions. It was, however, interesting to notice that Tarbarly had quickly given up the inside course and had headed out to join those of us trying to get to the Trade winds.

The next morning my fears were put to rest when we sighted *Pen Duik* on the horizon astern of us, so either I had been unduly pessimistic the previous day or Tarbarly had been over optimistic. He tacked away to the east very soon after we saw him, which was a pity as we always seemed to do our best with opposition in sight. He dropped back a bit on us by chatter hour, which also showed that the inshore boats had run into calms and we had now got to the north of them, so their tactic was not paying off after all.

The wind was at last showing signs of steadying from the east, but rather contradictorily, for whenever we got a squall it backed nearly four points and increased to twenty-four knots. We did not bother to tack in these squalls, but kept on the starboard tack sailing freed off for speed. The constant variation in wind strength meant continuous work changing sails, but the crew were fit and keen and seemed almost to relish the work.

As in any collection of people, there are always those who will rush to do any job, and those who will hesitate a moment to see if someone else is going to do it. It was noticeable that taken as a group, the three Kiwis in the crew very much fell into the former category. In fact as individuals they were just the sort of people one likes to sail with as they were always cheerful and had easy-going natures, but never held back from working. Justin, who had come under Peter's influence early on, seemed to be following his example, and if there was ever a job to be done you would usually find these four tackling it.

February 27th was a bad day, partly because *Great Britain II* got ahead of us—though this we felt could be put right—but also it was the day we discovered that all the egg boxes were riddled with maggots. Graham, who was checking the food, discovered them, and was in the process of throwing all the eggs overside when I found out what was happening. I stopped him at once because I could not see how the maggots could be affecting eggs that were undamaged, and eggs are a useful part of one's diet. Instead of throwing them all away, we put all the eggs into buckets of salt water and threw away their containers. This did not get rid of all the maggots, however, and as we had nothing else to fumigate with, I decided to try burning polystyrene as the fumes given off are poisonous. The result was a most satisfactory cloud of noxious fumes, but an unfortunate side effect was that the after cabin became blackened as the fumes were thick and sooty. Julian took the blackening of his bunk and clothes very well, all things considered, but he decided to live elsewhere for the rest of the trip! Although the fumes seemed noxious enough, they were not sufficiently so to kill the maggots, which slowly extended their empire as the voyage progressed. The answer to this sort of problem is always to carry something that can be used for fumigating at sea if necessary, although I have never had this particular problem in a yacht before. We discovered afterwards that other boats had experienced the same problem with eggs shipped in Rio. The answer seems to be to check each egg when it arrives, throw away any that are broken or cracked, and wash each one before putting them on board in something that will not harm them but will kill the maggot eggs. As it is not really practical to wash the polystyrene boxes the eggs are delivered in, these are best dumped and some other means of storing them found.

While the food was being checked we also worked out that our fresh water consumption so far averaged eight gallons a day, or just over half a gallon each. As we were not rationing water for drinking purposes this was quite good, and meant that we would have more than enough to last the voyage provided nothing dramatic occurred. We had picked up some concentrated fruit juices in Rio to which water was added before serving. A couple of jugs of juice were always kept in the freezer, so that a cold drink was always available to anyone who wanted one. It meant a load on the batteries, which in turn meant running the generator longer, but we had plenty of fuel on board for that and one luxury was not going to spoil the crew.

At daybreak on the 28th *Pen Duik* was in sight two and a half miles to the west. She must have sailed harder on the wind than us to come that far west, but she had drawn level again. Although we slowly dropped her on our port quarter, her presence indicated that she was a very fast boat indeed, and we could not afford to relax at all. We debated going west with *Pen Duik* so that we could keep her in sight, but at that moment *Great Britain II* was ahead and obviously our first priority must be to overtake her again as quickly as possible. The wind was now a fairly steady easterly force four, and we were fine reaching, not our best point of sailing. We had hoped to catch up *Great Britain II* and then move further ahead, but in fact *Great Britain II* was opening up on us.

We were almost right under the sun by this time and down below the heat was most uncomfortable. One way of alleviating this was to leave all the hatches open and keep pouring water onto the deck as its evaporation cooled the boat down a little. I found the heat gave me very bad headaches and my eyes swelled up so I took a couple of pills and went to sleep throughout that day. The result was that I could not get to sleep that night, so I sat up on two sail bags which had been arranged to form a settee. It was cool and pleasant, and gave me a good opportunity to revise my star identification. I found everyone interested in the stars and before long we had the tables out and were calculating the whereabouts of even quite insignificant ones. The evening saw the awakening of interest in navigation by quite a few of the crew, and four of them settled down to learn how to use a sextant and work out a sight. By the end of the voyage three of them were able to do it with considerable accuracy. However I cannot take credit for this as they worked most of it out for themselves.

We passed beneath the sun just before noon on 1st March, which made taking a meridian altitude interesting as the sun shot round in azimuth very quickly over a long arc. With the sudden interest in navigation, I had someone to check my readings using the yacht's sextant. Much to my surprise there was a difference of fifteen minutes, or fifteen miles. Initially I put it down to inexperience on the part of the observer, Les Best, but as the sun's reading got greater and he continued to give roughly the same difference, I decided to check the sextant. I found it had an index error of fourteen minutes off the arc, and was thus reading low and would have put us north of our true position. I could not help wondering how long the sextant had been like this, as not everyone checks the index error every time they use their sextant—though it only takes a few seconds and at least ensures the accuracy of one's readings. Anyway it gave Les Best and me a happy hour while I corrected all the errors in the sextant until we finally agreed that everything was at zero.

Our latitude at noon was seven degrees thirty-two minutes south, and according to my calculations we were beginning to feel the effect of a strong west-going Equatorial current. The wind was also a little variable, and once again we began to get squalls which either indicated we were rapidly approaching the Doldrums or, at longitude thirty degrees west, we were still not fully into the south-east Trades. There were compensations, however. At chatter hour we learnt we were on the same latitude as *Great Britain II* but more favourably placed as we were thirty miles east and both of us were ahead of *Pen Duik*. The boats that had chosen to go close to the Brazilian coast, among them *King's Legend* and *ADC Accutrac*, were some 120 miles further south, and we could not understand why they had not come out. They were 250 miles west of the leading group and obviously not getting as much wind, a fact they must have realised as they were both quite a lot east the next day.

During the afternoon a sudden loud double bang was heard which brought us all on deck wondering what had happened. The answer was—nothing. Concorde had just gone overhead faster than sound. We were to hear this distinctive double bang quite often while we were on the flight path to Rio, and then we heard it again as we came up the English Channel when we were south of Plymouth.

As we were getting near to the Equator, we began to prepare for Crossing the Line, but this time there were only three novices: Les Best, Allan Prior and Ianto Jones. I posted a proclamation warning everyone to be ready to greet His Majesty on Saturday 4th March, and appointed Golf Charlie as prosecutor and Justin as defence. The Major agreed to act as chamberlain and Peter as the lord chief justice. We actually crossed the Equator in the evening of the 3rd, but King Neptune was busy elsewhere at the time. At the appointed hour, however, the Court, appropriately dressed, came streaming on deck and the three initiates were quickly overpowered and tied to the mast. Then the trials began. Allan Prior was first. There were two charges: one of offering his sister to the crew for which his defence counsel said there was no defence, it was quite disgusting, and the second of going on a debauch in Rio. Allan yelled that this was not true but was told to be quiet as he had no say in the matter. Justin challenged the charge, but the chief justice silenced him by saying the charge was certainly true as he had been there. Everyone cried guilty, and Allan was anointed with a hideous mixture. Ianto was next and was accused of having a fishing licence. Justin said that was true. 'No, it can't be,' said the chief justice, 'as we have not had any fish.'

'Ah,' said Justin. 'But his licence is only valid for the northern hemisphere, and in any case the chief mate stopped him fishing as he calculated that trailing the line would cost us an hour in 5,500 miles.'

'Objection,' said Golf Charlie. 'The defence is irrelevant and impertinent.'

'Sustained,' said the chief justice, democratically.

At this point it was felt necessary to point out to Justin that he had only recently crossed the line himself and he was talking too much. 'The defendant pleads guilty,' he yelled immediately and Ianto was anointed. Les Best came next and was accused of being small: no defence. He was also accused of spending a whole month in Auckland overhauling one of the loos and it still did not work. The defence tried to say that he had also overhauled the steering gear but was ruled out of order by the chief justice who impartially said that all he had overhauled in Auckland was his girlfriend and little else, to which everyone shouted guilty, and sentence was carried out. It took a couple of hours to clear the decks of the mess.

To round the day off, the three Kiwis, or 'Trevs' as they were called, decided to throw a party to which everyone was invited provided they wore gumboots and were prepared to listen to an hour-long tape of Fred Dagg (a New Zealand comedian). I think by this time the non-Kiwis in the crew knew more Fred Dagg stories than the Kiwis but it was a good party.

The wind went light during the afternoon after the Crossing the Line ceremony, and as we were three degrees north of the Equator it looked as though we might have found the Doldrums. But seven hours later, at 22.00, we picked up a light northerly wind which, after swinging around slightly, became fairly steady the next morning. We had got through the Doldrums remarkably quickly and felt that we should have opened up a bit on the other boats as a result. No such luck. At daybreak on the 5th *Great Britain II* was in sight about six miles south-west, and later on, at chatter time, *Pen Duik* reported being 120 miles ahead. As she had been slightly behind two days before, she must have had a particularly lucky run through the Doldrums, and had obviously kept a better wind which is possible enough even though she was only some 150 miles to the east of *Great Britain II* and ourselves. So my theory that it was quite easy to get through the Doldrums at about twenty-seven degrees west was not far out. It just seemed that on this occasion 29½ degrees west, where *Pen Duik* crossed, would have been better. One hundred and twenty miles is an awful lot to catch up, even in a long race, and it was bad luck for *Great Britain II* and ourselves that this had happened. It also took a lot of the excitement out of the race, for when we had been reasonably close we had had plenty of chance sightings of each other which added to the interest. Now we had a hard slog to try and pull back about six miles a day between the Equator and home—not an easy task. We needed some good luck of our own.

Once into the north-east Trades, the wind is more northerly to the east, and swings round to be more north-easterly the further west you go. To start with, however, it is usually northerly and we headed north-west still on the starboard tack, sailing slightly freed to gain speed.

By coming quite far over to the east, we had given ourselves sea-room to sail free once we got into these northerly winds and this meant that we should not be driven as far west as the old sailing ship route. A modern yacht can in any case sail at least twenty degrees closer to the wind, but the straighter our course north, the quicker we would get up to the Azores. On the two previous occasions I had sailed this zone in *Suhaili*, not the best of performers to windward, I had ended up about forty degrees west which meant I sailed quite a lot further. On this occasion, we only reached thirty-four degrees west and so missed the Sargasso Sea which is one of the most interesting phenomena in the north-east Trades. It is a large area of the central Atlantic Ocean in which fronds of Sargasso weed, which are broken off the shores of the Caribbean and carried out into the Atlantic by currents such as the Gulf Stream, congregate and grow, although it is doubtful if the weed reproduces itself at sea. The old sailors were convinced that the small patches of saffron-coloured weed they saw were just the fringe on an enormous area that would trap their ships and keep them held fast until they starved. In fact the weed comes in very small patches, perhaps an acre in extent is the largest I have seen; on that occasion I put *Suhaili* straight through the middle to see what happened. The result was a clear track of blue water in my wake where the weed was pushed aside.

It is often forgotten that a large boat has a theoretical top speed that is probably twice that of the average family cruiser, and this leads to problems when you want a lot of seawater for personal or deck washing. Bucket handles that will take the strain on a bucket thrown overside at six knots will not take many throws at eleven or twelve knots, and ours were no exception. On 5th March our last bucket was lost, and a massive bucket making session commenced. Paul completed the first one which would have held about four gallons, but no one, not even the maker, was prepared to risk throwing it overside as the risk of being dragged after it would have been tremendous. Julian produced a more handy sized one made from terylene instead of canvas, but the tiny holes made by the needle used to sew up the seams let water through instead of swelling up and closing, and we had to be quick to get it across the deck if we wanted water below. Julian made the handle an integral part of the whole construction, so there was no risk of it breaking off, and in fact it survived the voyage with credit.

Now we were through the Doldrums it was time to start concentrating on the real obstacle in the last leg, the Azores high, the large area of high pressure set between the westerlies that prevail around the British Isles to the north, and the north-east Trades to the south. Although it centres itself over the Azores, it moves around quite a lot, and of course the clockwise circulation of winds around it move with it. To go to the east of it, between the Azores and Spain, meant head winds, but this was the most direct route for Portsmouth. To go to the west of the Azores meant following winds and a greater distance to be sailed but led one into the westerlies of the North Atlantic sooner. On the whole, if winds are light, it is preferable for them to be head winds as their speed is added to the boat's speed to give a stronger wind over the deck. If there is a light following wind, the boat's speed has to be subtracted from the wind speed, and this means less wind power to propel the boat. Thus, if the Azores high was over the Azores, it would pay us to go inside and sail with headwinds. If it was east of the Azores it would pay to go west. The trouble is it cannot be relied upon to remain static, and one can commit oneself to one course of action and then find that the movement of the high has made this the wrong move. Before leaving the UK I had had a long conversation with David Houghton at the Bracknell Weather Centre, and although it was asking a lot to get an idea of the weather one month ahead, he told me that the indications were that, if anything, the high would be to the south-west of its usual location. If that was the case we would go inside it and hope everyone else would go into it. In fact the high was south-west of the Azores for the first week of March.

This is where it becomes invaluable having someone on

board to concentrate on the shipping forecasts and plot them regularly. By tuning in and recording the forecast, which comes over in morse code, and then waiting whilst Golf Charlie translated and decoded it, we were able to plot the whole north Atlantic weather pattern every six to twelve hours and, by making comparisons, look for trends. In fact we took weather information from three sources: Portishead, Portugal, and Portsmouth in Virginia. The first two covered the same area, and occasionally differed slightly, but the American forecast concentrated on the western Atlantic and gave us an indication of what was on the way.

There were snags to all this. In order to get the weather the navigatorium had to be used, and there was not enough room in it for someone to record and plot the weather and for me to sleep. After moving around the boat with my sleeping bag every time this occurred for a couple of nights, I decided it would be simpler if I just took Golf Charlie's bunk, and he slept in the navigatorium. This was not very successful either as others wanted to use it as well, for log writing and so on; I finally decided that the best thing was for me to use Les Williams's bunk, and he and Peter could use Peter's bunk on the hot bunk principle. Not particularly fair, but I was beginning to feel less pain from my shingles and my left eye was becoming far more usable, and if I managed a good ten to twelve hours' solid sleep somewhere in each twenty-four hours, I felt a noticeable decrease in the itching. In fact by 7th March, after a fortnight at sea, I had improved to the point where I ceased having to take pain killers every four to six hours, and was down to one or two a day. Having lived with shingles for ten weeks, this marked improvement was most encouraging.

For the next three days, until 10th March, we pressed on heading as nearly north as possible, but keeping the boat slightly freed, both to gain speed and avoid banging into the waves. We steadily increased our lead over *Great Britain II* by seven or eight miles a day, but *Pen Duik* increased her lead over us by about six to seven miles a day, and seemed to be getting a slightly more easterly wind. She was even able to sail closer to the wind than us and still gain distance, which was infuriating. From being two degrees west of us at the Equator, by 10th March she was two degrees east of us and obviously planning to go to the east of the Azores high, which on that day had moved over to Spain making even going east of the Azores a sure bet for south-westerly winds. However, we had noticed that the high seemed to move across and spend a couple of days over Spain, then it would disappear and a new high formed over the Azores. The pattern so far indicated a four- to five-day cycle for this, so it was a question of timing one's arrival in the area in a longitude that gave one the most favourable conditions. Tarbarly obviously felt that it was right for him to go east, and *Great Britain II* seemed to be doing the same thing although she was astern of us. Every racing man knows that you cover your opponent, but I felt it was too early yet to be sure that they were doing the right thing. If the cycle of movements of the high remained the same, these boats could well find themselves beneath it as it crossed to Spain. As it usually formed a ridge during this process they could be stopped dead, whereas a boat going west would get light, becoming stronger, south-westerlies. So we maintained a northerly course although the decision was giving me ulcers!

Stronger north-easterly winds now came up and we found it necessary to reduce sail although the speed did not suffer. We had been solidly on the starboard tack since leaving Rio, and were getting accustomed to the constant heel to port. These stronger winds heeled us over further though, and bilge water started to slosh up level with the lower outboard bunks. We again cursed the fact that the boat had no well, so that we could get rid of some of this water, made more unpleasant because some of our tins of food had blown, and the smell of rotten food accompanied the bilge water everywhere.

But despite the discomfort, morale remained high. The Major decided to make a bucket which leaked less than Julian's. Justin was rechristened 'Trev Smart' because he was always with the Kiwis, and I found a T-shirt in the chart table left on board for me by friends in New Zealand which had a picture of a Kiwi on it and underneath the legend 'Pluck me gently' which, according to someone writing in the log book, made me very happy. I certainly flaunted it in front of the Trevs, which produced some mutterings. The T-shirt must have been put on board as a response to one I had made for our arrival in Auckland which said 'Have a good day, pluck a Kiwi' and was a direct response to those produced out there for the British Lions tour which had on them 'Bash a Pom a day'.

Three days of heavy progress, and we had ceased to lose out to *Pen Duik* so much but were not gaining anything either. On the other hand we had got fifty miles clear of *Great Britain II*. We were past thirty degrees north and I was more than ever convinced that the high was going to be east of the Azores, or just about to move east by the time we got to it, so we continued our northerly course where possible, although at times we found ourselves steering north-west because the wind had backed. This was agonising, because if I was wrong about the high, then when we were forced round onto a north-westerly course, we ought really to have tacked and gone north-east which was nearly straight for Portsmouth. It is not a very comfortable feeling to be deliberately sailing at right angles to the course for the finish line, but the Azores high is not a normal sailing hazard.

Still, if I was wrong, the crew seemed happy enough, even when later in the day the wind died on us and our speed fell to four knots. The log has the following comments:

'Bad news, poor course.'

'The good news—we didn't go very far.'

'You never can tell with highs, said Pooh.'

And later on: 'T. Smart has designed a new 720 degree compass.'

On another occasion the log was again used for the wrong purpose—the right purpose being to note purely navigational information and sightings of interest—this time when we got the news from home that the crew account was one thousand pounds overdrawn. This fact was noted in the log and underneath someone put, 'Are we going the right way?'

We did have slight cause for concern that day when we discovered that our two aftermost water tanks had developed a leak, and we had lost one-third of our total water capacity and half of that left. A quick calculation indicated that with 140 gallons remaining we still had enough to see us home at half a gallon a day per man, but we would have to be careful in case it took longer than expected to get through the Azores high.

We took the opportunity of reasonably calm weather to carry out a few repairs. Peter and his Trevs went aft to shore up the aft bulkhead which was now de-laminating. We had tried everything to beef this bulkhead up as it just was not strong enough to take the strains exerted on it by the steering gear, but to the end it gave trouble. At the same time Les decided that we could not go on with just the one WC and he would repair the after one. He was seen disappearing aft with a large hammer in his hand, and a succession of gigantic thumps reverberated around the boat. This worried me as Les is not the luckiest of people with WCs. In 1972 just before the start of the Round the Island (Wight) Race, he had pumped out a WC muttering that it was very stiff. A particularly hard pump was too much for the mechanism, and it blew back covering him with the contents. We had passed the Needles before he was fit to come on deck! This time he reappeared saying that he had fixed it. About an hour later he asked Ianto if he would go down and clean out the aft bilge as he thought some rotten food was in it. Ianto them discovered how Les had cleared the aft WC!

The 13th was also the day—why is it always on the 13th that things like this happen?—that we discovered the maggots were extending their empire, and had reached as far as the oilskin locker, which being next to the galley was frequently used for storing food canisters, some of which had spilled. It also held seven spare halyards, and was in fact hardly ever used for storing oilies, which went on hooks in the passageway. The co-inventors of the maggots, as Herman described David and Graham, commissars for the trip, came in for some criticism but it was not really their fault. Anyway the Trevs tackled the problem with their customary zeal, and cleared the whole area out and disinfected it. This kept the maggots at bay for the rest of the voyage.

Pen Duik did not report that day, nor the next two, so we had no idea whether she was suffering the same conditions as us. When *Great Britain II* came up on 14th March she had closed right up on us and had also become becalmed, but nearly four degrees to the east. We had now reached the stage where *Pen Duik, Great Britain II* and ourselves were committed to our choices of course round or through the Azores high. We were going west, the other two east and the centre was right over the islands, which favoured us, as the high's next move was almost certain to be to the east again, giving us a run through while stopping the other two. If this happened, all Golf Charlie's hard work decoding the weather would have paid off and we stood a good chance of making up our lost lead on *Pen Duik* and getting home first. What was also obvious to me was that if our plan paid off, the other twelve boats in the race, the nearest of which was *Flyer* three hundred miles astern, could see which of us was right and get home more quickly. As this was a handicap race, I did not feel like giving away vital tactical information, which we would be doing if we gave even our position each day on the chatter net. I decided therefore to stop reporting in on the chatter hour and just keep quiet. In retrospect I think was wrong. All the boats in the race reported their positions and weather to each other each day, and although the reports from boats astern of us could not help us, and ours could help them, I think we should have still reported even if only to say we were all right, and I would certainly do this in a future race. The trouble was Tarbarly did not always report in, and I felt that if he could keep quiet as to his progress we could do the same.

The chartroom was rapidly being taken over by the embryonic navigators, and on more than one occasion I had to fight my way through to plot our noon position. While I had no wish to discourage this enthusiasm, I found it a bit much when tables and navigation books were borrowed but not put back. On one occasion I spent nearly an hour looking for Norie's Nautical Tables, deliberately creating a lot of fuss because I had already asked three or four times for things to be put away after the borrower had finished with them. They were eventually found in the loo. I know now just how frustrating it must be to be a librarian.

The 14th saw me feeling well enough to do a watch again, and I was up at midnight to do Peter's watch for him. The wind was so light that we found ourselves steering either 310 degrees or 120 degrees. I could not bear the thought of going south of east even though it was nearer the course for home, so we hung on at 310, knowing that if nothing else, we were heading straight for the south-westerly wind belt. Bracknell did its best to discourage us, as Portishead came up with a forecast that the high was going to extend into a ridge between Newfoundland

and the Azores, which if it happened meant I had made entirely the wrong decision. To start with, this forecast looked like being horribly accurate, as apart from diurnal variation, the barometer remained rock steady.

Sitting steering for a while, and then just watching the course and sails can be a most relaxing pastime, but I quickly found I was becoming bored with the inactivity, and as it was quite cool decided to make some soup. Naturally all our soups were powdered, and as such have exactly the flavour that the manufacturer thinks will suit his market best, and I can never resist the temptation of adding one or two extra ingredients just to alter the flavour a little. This time I used oxtail as a base and added onions and tabasco sauce with a spoonful of Bovril. I thought the result pleasing, but others found it only interesting, so I was able to have more than my fair share of the result, although I was disappointed in the reaction. I felt that the crew on a Round the World Yacht Race should have shown a greater sense of adventure, but when I mentioned this they muttered something about surviving which I could not quite hear.

I handed over to Les at 04.00, and by breakfast the wind had freed us onto a course of north. As this rather indicated that the high was west of us and moving north, we were none too happy, but at least we were moving northwards.

We alternated between flat, glassy calms in which every star was clearly reflected in the sea, and light ripples which indicated puffs of wind. The sunsets were tremendous, the sunrises equally dramatic. It was warm by day, but pleasantly cool at night, and there was plenty of sea life to look at. Portuguese men-of-war made an appearance, and it was interesting to see what they had caught in their long trailing tentacles which give a very nasty sting.

Their stingers are in fact small harpoons which, when fired at a target, remain attached to the parent body so that the target can be hauled in and eaten. Sailors who have come into contact with tentacles wound round ropes do not quickly forget the very intense burning pain—and paralysis or even death can result if too many of the harpoons hit the body. With fish, perhaps only one or two harpoons will strike to start with, and these in themselves are insufficient to kill, but the struggles of the fish inevitably bring it into contact with other tentacles and more harpoons are fired until the fish is dead and can be eaten. Portuguese men-of-war propel themselves by means of a sail which is set at an angle to the body on top. This sail will flip over into the water at intervals so that it is kept moist. For years it was thought that the angle of the sail on these jelly fish in the northern hemisphere was the mirror image of the angle of the sail of those in the southern hemisphere, but recent research has proved this not to be the case, and both types have been found in the Canaries. If a steady wind is blowing, the different types will move apart at an angle of about ninety degrees. We saw a small turtle, apparently trapped in the tentacles of a Portuguese man-of-war, but it may have been eating it; the Hawksbill turtle is known to eat them, but keeps its eyes closed to avoid the harpoons. We saw quite a few turtles just south of the islands, none close enough to catch or photograph properly, and of course the inevitable shoal of dolphins appeared. The largest came one evening when we were all sitting out on deck having one of the Major's concoctions and listening to Golf Charlie playing his guitar. This shoal was visible from about two miles away, leaping in groups of four or five, up to five or six feet above the water. They came towards us, but as we were not moving very fast we did not provide much amusement for them and they were soon on their way.

The next two days would be critical. The race was now a lottery, and the movement of the high pressure centre would effectively decide who was going to win. As the boats astern rushed north, each in turn was stopped at about thirty-one degrees north, so the whole fleet was closing up. If the wind suddenly came up now the race would virtually restart again with only just over a thousand miles to go, which would have given the race to the smaller boats. As it happened, the ridge to Newfoundland did not appear and the centre of the high moved very slowly eastwards, and we moved very slowly northwards until, on the 17th, the wind ceased to have a westerly coefficient but became easterly again, and then veered quite quickly to the south-west. It was very light at first, and we could only just gather way, but slowly it increased and we began to move. Our happiness was enhanced by the thought of the others three hundred miles to the east, who were now over a hundred miles south and therefore roughly under the centre of the high. The calculated gamble of going west looked like paying off.

We saw the peaks on Fayal Island early in the afternoon of the 17th, showing quite clearly although they were a good forty miles away. Almost at the same time we spoke to RRS *Discovery* which passed quite close doing some research work. By this time we had a spinnaker and blooper up and were heading 050 degrees. Although the course for home was further round to the east, I decided to keep quite a bit of north in our course so we would get into the stronger winds earlier. I laid a course for the south-west tip of Ireland to start with, which kept us north of the rhumb line, but not far off the great circle course.

Shortly after sighting the *Discovery* we went close by a killer whale, which we watched cautiously as many attacks on yachts have been attributed to them. However, this one left us alone; perhaps we were too large, or it just was not hungry. I suppose they attack yachts for the same reason that they hit ice floes to knock penguins off—in the hope that something edible will fall off.

By the 18th we were moving well, and had got closer to the finish line than *Great Britain II* which was still moving at an average of only four knots. We did not know where *Pen Duik* was as she did not report, but on the 17th *Great Britain* had her in sight just off the easternmost islands in the archipelago, so we might well have got ahead of her too. On the 19th *Pen Duik* did report and she was seventeen miles behind us, so the race was still wide open, but our tactics around the Azores had enabled us to take the lead from being nearly 150 miles behind.

I knew that I could not keep our position from the other boats indefinitely as we were bound by the race rules to report in at least twice a week. However the Race Committee had a habit of reporting the latest positions received and giving out results based on these, rather than waiting until they had all the reports in for all the boats at one time, and then finding out what was really going on. Tarbarly obviously thought he was in the lead, indeed the French press had already said that he was winning—as usual. I wanted him to continue to think that was so, but not break the rules. The way I got round it was to put a call through to Sue, my wife, tell her to subtract the date of her birthday from each of the four sets of figures that made up our position in latitude and longitude, and then give it to Race Control a day and a half later. We were thus plotted well astern of Tarbarly, and anyone of the competitors phoning in for information would have difficulty working out where everyone had been at the date time of our last report. This had the added advantage that our friends ashore knew what our true position was. Again this may not seem particularly sporting, but I do not know Tarbarly and I was not going to have him pulling into France instead of crossing the finish line so that the French press could say 'he would have won if he had finished'. It was important therefore for him to think he was in the lead. In fact I think I misjudged the man: I now think he will pull any advantage he can out of the rules— fair game provided you get away with it—but I do not believe he would have been unsporting enough not to finish.

One good thing came out of all this. One of the other yachts picked up my message to Sue, so everybody else knew we were all right (not that any of them had been too worried). But of course they did not know where we were, and most of those behind us were piling into the centre of the high and slowing right down. The high had only to move north-east and we would be the only boat home for a week.

A series of cold fronts was sweeping across the North Atlantic and we ran into our first on the 19th March. We hung everything up and went for our lives. Inevitably we did a wipe out, fortunately letting go the weather sheet and guy on the spinnaker before we got completely out of control. We set the storm spinnaker instead, but Les, who was on the helm, did not like it and we swapped it for a running headsail which was much more comfortable and just as fast. Some of the younger members of the crew, the embryonic dedicated ocean racers, objected and said we were not trying hard enough, but I pointed out that we older folk of the 'baggy wrinkle and Breton red trouser brigade' knew a thing or two, and although we might not seem to be going so fast because the boat was steadier, we would cover more miles in the right direction. The log proved the ancient mariners correct. There is nothing wrong with cruising techniques in the right situation, and this was the right situation. If we had pressed on under spinnaker, we would have had a wipe out at best and broken something at worst. As it was we sailed on comfortably at 11½ knots with no risk of breakages.

Our main concern now was to maintain our lead on Tarbarly who had proved in the past that *Pen Duik* was faster than us, and I was worried that even though we were pressing the boat as hard as I thought safe, *Pen Duik* might still be gaining on us. Fortunately Tarbarly was now reporting in on the chatter net and we were able to get his position each evening. On the 19th he was 119 miles south and sixty-four miles east of us, but although he was east, we were closer to the finish line by about seventeen miles. But there were still over a thousand miles to go, and he had jumped us before. By the 20th he was fifty-eight miles south and twenty miles west and we found that far from losing distance on him we were getting away, which was a tremendous boost. The nearer we got to the finish line the better our chance of beating him to it. We had set a 'Bristol rig' at dawn on the 20th. This is one head sail boomed out to weather and another set loose luffed to leeward. I do not like putting two headsails up a forestay together, or both hanked on, as in an emergency you have to get both down before you can sort the problems out, and two headsails coming down together is asking for trouble. The great advantage of the Bristol rig is that you can put up as much sail as a spinnaker would give you, but the cloth is heavier, and having a sail set out on each side forward steadies the helm, as does a blooper with a spinnaker. Later in the day the wind eased and veered so we set up for reaching, but when it backed again we set a spinnaker anyway. Our day's run was 256 miles—not bad, but then it is never as good as you would like.

The heavy weather had put a strain on the after bulkhead again, so Peter and the Trevs went aft to fix it. We were rapidly running out of materials for tomming off the bulkhead, and beginning to consider what could be sacrificed if necessary. The saloon settee was an obvious choice, and then we could rip out lockers. Les's bunk, by far the most comfortable on board, was also high on the list, but I did not like to tell him that. If we had had to have it he would have been the first to agree.

We were at last within range of Land's End radio, and once we got through found that there was a flood of people wanting to talk to us. It was difficult to give a good interview while constantly dodging the question as to exactly where we were, and where Tarbarly was in relation to *Heath's Condor*. It was even more complicated when we were told that a Nimrod aircraft would be out to see us on the 21st and could I give a position for a rendezvous. I did not like the idea of giving a false position to the Air Force, so I gave as accurate an estimate as I could of where I thought we would be, and just hoped no one would put two and two together.

We crossed into 'soundings' during the night. This is the old term used to describe any area of water where the sea bottom is less than a hundred fathoms from the surface, and thus in range of a deep sea lead line. I have only once used a deep sea lead and it was an incredible business stationing a crew member right forward with the 35-pound lead, and then the others all along the gunwale with coils of ropes in their hands. The officer stationed himself roughly where he thought the length of line let out was equal to the depth of water, and then at a given signal the lead was tossed overside. As it went its thrower yelled 'Watch there watch', a cry repeated by each man in turn as he threw his coil of rope overside. When the lead hits the bottom it noticeably stops, but you have to be quick or you will miss the sudden slackening of the lead line. The boat's way through the water soon drags out more line, and if you measured it late you would get a false reading. Once the sounding has been taken everyone lays on the line to haul it all inboard, by far the hardest part of the operation, particularly when the boat is moving at ten knots.

The European Continental shelf, like many others around the world, for some reason drops off quite suddenly at one hundred fathoms. To get an accurate idea of where you are in relation to land is quite easy if you find the hundred-fathom line. We had no intention of stopping to take a sounding, nor were we even equipped with a deep sea sounding lead, and our echo sounder was not effective at that depth. There are other ways of telling when you have crossed into soundings, however, because the ocean bottom suddenly rises as it meets the slope leading down from the Continental shelf, which slightly compresses the ocean waves. On the sea's surface this shows as a shortening of the wave length, and a steepening of the wave fronts. While you do not suddenly go from long easy waves to short steep ones, within an hour or so the alteration is noticeable. Indeed it is quite distinctive if you are watching for it in the boat's motion, as once you cross into soundings you start to get thrown about more.

By the 21st we had covered another 243 miles, the wind had eased a little, and this and the more choppy seas made us lose speed. *Pen Duik* was forty-eight miles further from the finish line and we only had 411 miles to go. *Great Britain II* had had a bad day. She had been becalmed for six hours and broken her main boom; this cost her over a hundred miles, and put her out of the running.

Morale was high and Channel fever, the infectious happy feeling that comes towards the end of a voyage, began to set in. It showed in a number of ways, the most obvious being that people started to collect their gear together ready to leave. This led to some interesting discoveries, in particular some rather unwelcome wet and stale ones underneath the water tanks. In most cases they were thrown overside, if not quickly by the owner then pretty shortly by someone else. It is unfortunate that it was only at this late stage in the voyage that some crew members suddenly began to realise the importance of being tidy in their habits and with their gear. Surplus worn-out clothing was also given the heave-ho, as it was soon realised that there was no point in keeping the garments any longer. Another way Channel fever can show itself is in a more careless attitude towards the boat and her gear. The 'she will get a refit when she gets home, and the sails are worn anyway' type of thinking is not to be encouraged, particularly on a race, and when our lead was only a precious four hours. We had two sail tears on the Tuesday; the big yellow spinnaker blew out—but that was mainly because of the heavy sloppy seas which threw the boat about. The mainsail also ripped right along the foot, but in this case old age, or rather a hard short life, was to blame. We put the flattening reef in and carried on.

The RAF Nimrod found us during the afternoon and buzzed around for about twenty-five minutes to allow cameramen on board to shoot film. We were in fact well ahead of the rendezvous I had given them, but she was only a few minutes late so it had not taken her long to find us. It made a number of dramatic low passes, none of which worried us—we were far more concerned that she keep low and lessen the chance of anyone else seeing her and guessing we were close-by!

Another front came through on Tuesday evening, giving us very strong westerly winds, gusting over fifty knots across the deck. Once again we swopped the spinnaker for the boomed out running sail. As the wind increased, so did our speed, and soon we began to surf. We averaged close to twelve knots all night, once again loosening off the steering box which was now being examined as a matter of routine every hour, and a hammer was kept ready to knock the shores back in more firmly every couple of hours. All of us caught what sleep we could fully clothed in oilskins in case everyone was needed. The motion of the boat was reminiscent of the Southern Ocean again, and with the wet gear and falling temperature it was beginning to feel just like it, too. None of us slept well and were all relieved when a cold grey dawn came along. I think as much as to have something to do as any urge to go faster, we set the gale spinnaker at 06.00 and changed up to the No. 2 spinnaker an hour later when the wind eased a little.

Towards midday we passed south of the Scillies, and we put a call through to Race Control giving them an ETA for the following morning between 10.00 and 12.00. With less than two hundred miles to go, we could now decide whether we would go inside the Solent or out round the Isle of Wight. We rang through and warned people who were coming out to meet us that we would pass the Needles at between 06.00 and 08.00 and run down the Solent with a favourable tide.

A big effort was made to get the boat smartened up and we ran the engine for a while just to check that it was in running order. People disappeared for up to an hour at a time to shave and clean themselves, and fighting almost broke out to get into the WC every time some gleaming clean-shaven almost unrecognisable figure emerged. Having hung onto my beard for nine years, I was in no hurry to emulate most of the others. I can wash my face and beard in a quarter of the time it would take to shave, and it does give protection in cold weather.

A magnificent performance that evening by the cooks to produce a really good dinner was a great success, and we had gigantic steaks and all the vegetables we could eat. It was just as well, for the wind got up again to gale force at dusk and we needed all the energy we had to keep changing sails. A force seven quickly became an eight, and then carried on rising until we had about sixty-five knots of wind. We ran down through our headsails as the wind rose until by 21.00 we had only the storm jib, out for the first time in nearly four months, and three reefs in the main. Even so, we surfed off the clock in short sharp seas that were not a bit smaller than those we had experienced in the Southern Ocean.

At the evening chat show we had 145 miles to go and *Pen Duik* 193. *Great Britain* had 315, and although most of the boats were reporting strong westerly winds, three were still almost becalmed close to the Azores. Barring accidents there was no way Tarbarly could sail fast enough to overtake us, but this meant we had to make no mistakes.

I had deliberately set a course up the middle of the Channel because that is where there is least shipping, and also to avoid the oil spill from the recently stranded *Amoco Cadiz* off France. But although I had taken sights during the day, and had managed a pretty good fix, there is nothing so reassuring as picking up a recognised shore light. Towards midnight I was called up from below for a light ahead. It grew in size until we realised that it was far more than a ship. No lights had been sighted to the north or south of us, and I wondered whether we had somehow missed seeing Start Point and were coming up on a supertanker sheltering in Lyme Bay. As we got closer the lights were even more confusing. The Major, who was on the helm, was steering to pass north of whatever it was, and we made an alteration even further to the north to make our intentions clear. I thought of taking out the radio direction finder, but it was extremely inaccurate on board *Heath's Condor*, due probably to the aluminium work in the deck, and gave differences in readings of over thirty degrees depending upon whether you were in the bow or the stern. We pressed on, and suddenly the two pairs of vertical white lights with one set of sidelights, and a pyramid of yellow lights astern, became clear. It was two tugs towing a large oil rig. The tugs were big fellows, but even so I do not think they were enjoying the seas very much. It was amazing that they were at sea at all, and it says much for recent developments, particularly the experience gained in the North Sea drilling operations, that they had put to sea with such an unwieldy tow with a poor forecast. This told us that we were probably well clear of land, and a little later the nearly full moon enabled Les and I to get sights of Polaris that agreed within two miles. We were further south than we thought, and I had the course hardened up twenty-five degrees.

At 02.45 on Thursday morning, between squalls, we picked up the loom of a light on the port bow. Within ten minutes the four flashes every twenty seconds identified it as Portland Bill, for many of the crew the first sight of England for seven months. The tide was now against us and against the wind, giving rise to even more unpleasant sea conditions. We were still surfing off the clock but now we had hardened up and much more spray was coming inboard making steering a cold, wet job. Not that anyone minded. Over the horizon, and getting closer every minute, lay Portsmouth, family, friends, hot baths and a pint.

As yet another grey dawn broke it revealed Anvil Head to the north of us, and then Paul was called on deck to pick out the Needles in the murk. We swept on and at 07.12 the log read that the Needles bore south.

The effect of the Isle of Wight on weather conditions in the Solent area has always been noticeable, but never more so than at about breakfast time on Thursday 23rd March. Once we were past the Shingles Bank and Hurst Castle and bore north, the wind eased right down and we were able to set the orange gale kite. As we passed Yarmouth, the Trinity House pilot vessel came out to greet us, and in no time at all we were off Egypt Point. With the wind still down at force five we decided to finish in style, and the big yellow spinnaker, the same one that had carried us away at the beginning of the race, was brought on deck. Willing hands hauled it quickly aloft, but perhaps through carelessness brought on by the nearness of the finish line, extra turns around the winch drum were not put on until the spinnaker had broken out, and as a result it took charge and ran out again. I had visions of our overrunning it, and jumped onto the halyard with Justin. Others joined us, and miraculously we hauled it up out of the water unharmed. It filled again as it went up which made hoisting it a little difficult. As we recovered our breath from this, we became aware of a small armada of boats that had joined us for the last run in. The first question we asked was 'Where is Tarbarly?' but he was well behind still, and was not expected in until the middle of the afternoon. I heaved a heartfelt sigh of relief. I do not think I had really allowed myself fully to believe his position reports all through the last days; perhaps I was trying to avoid too much disappointment by keeping myself from believing things were going our way.

We waved to the people in the boats close by as we headed for Gilkicker point. Spithead was not as well protected as the west Solent and a slop had built up, but this was nothing compared to the wash of the spectator fleet accompanying us. As the wind began to rise again we prepared to take the big spinnaker down as it was too light for the winds of force five or so. Everyone was in position when the situation took charge of itself. An over-zealous power boat opened its throttles and shot ahead and across our bow. As we hit its wash we began to roll. The rolling in itself was not dangerous, but it put additional strains on the spinnaker which just gave up at the weather clew and the whole sail blew out to leeward. We hauled it in and stowed it below. The running yankee was already hanked on, and it was the work of moments to hoist it and get it setting in the spinnaker's place.

We had decided to head straight for Elbow Spit buoy, the only mark in this leg, just one hundred yards from the finish line. This meant sailing over the shoals, but at high water it presented no danger. As we came up to the buoy a Dutch coaster was coming out of Portsmouth harbour, and I told everyone that we would have to gybe quickly to avoid getting in his way. We came up to the buoy and I was about to put the helm hard over when I saw that it had 'Bar' written on it, not 'Elbow Spit'. Had we cut the corner too tightly and missed the right mark? It seemed the logical thing to have happened although the transits we were using on the shore were all right. Still, there was no time to worry about that; we could see the finishing line quite clearly, but it would have been terrible to have crossed the line and then be told that we had to go back as we had failed to round a mark of the course. Then we were almost on top of the coaster. I swung the helm to starboard, and we turned away from the finishing line to go out to the next buoy in the channel. This one was called 'Ridge' which was what it should have been. Elbow Spit buoy did not seem to exist. We found out later that Bar buoy had replaced Elbow Spit the previous November. We swung round again to turn back to the finish line, but as we gybed the tired old mainsail gave up the ghost and split along its foot completely. What a time to happen with the shore of Southsea only 150 yards away to leeward. I yelled to Peter to put the second reef in, which would at least give us some mainsail and bring the huge flapping mass under control. In the meantime, we steadied up on course, hoping that we could make it without being blown off with just a headsail. If we could not, it meant putting the engine on and motoring clear, and this would have meant a penalty if nothing else. The boat came up into the wind and I found we could lay the course, although it was difficult, and Peter who was having trouble getting the reefs in suggested that we dispense with the main altogether and furl it on deck. I agreed as it would be less windage on deck than hoisted in the state it was in, and it came down for the last time.

Two minutes later we crossed the line, and the cannon at the Royal Albert Yacht Club boomed out. We were home, and first home at that. The crew gave a tremendous cheer, but we still had work to do, and we quickly got back to tidying up the mess on deck left by the sudden tearing of the spinnaker and the equally unexpected rip in the main, all within the last ten minutes. It is always the sailor's contention that it is much safer out at sea, and the risks lie close to the land. I have seldom had this point more emphatically driven home.

Under engine we took down the headsail and motored through the entrance to Portsmouth harbour, thronged on the town side by cheering people. Then we turned into Vernon Creek and made fast.

Heath's Condor was back from her maiden voyage. She had proved herself to those of us who sailed with her, and I think that most of us were a little sad that the voyage was over and the close team of friends that we had become would soon be breaking up as we returned to the normal task of making a living. One thing however would never be lost, and that is the memory of a great adventure, and the comradeship that existed during its course. This memory could be dusted off and re-lived for the rest of our lives; nothing could take that away from us.

The scene on deck within minutes of our arrival was chaotic as family, friends and scores of news- and cameramen scrambled on board. That moment is always for one's family, and outsiders seem a bit of an intrusion. But the race was not over yet, we still had our declaration to sign, which we did, and then for good measure we put in a final protest against the Race Committee over our rating.

It was heard a week later, after most of the rest of the fleet were home, and the appeal's committee found in our favour, reducing our rating from 68.8 feet to 65.9 for the last three legs of the race. This seemed a logical decision, and I was glad that the whole matter had been tidied up for the benefit of future races. It made no difference to the results, however; the time lost to get a new mast in the first leg had been too much to recover. In the previous race our progress on the last three legs would have won the race, but this time everyone had raced hard all the way, and overall on handicap, we finished last.

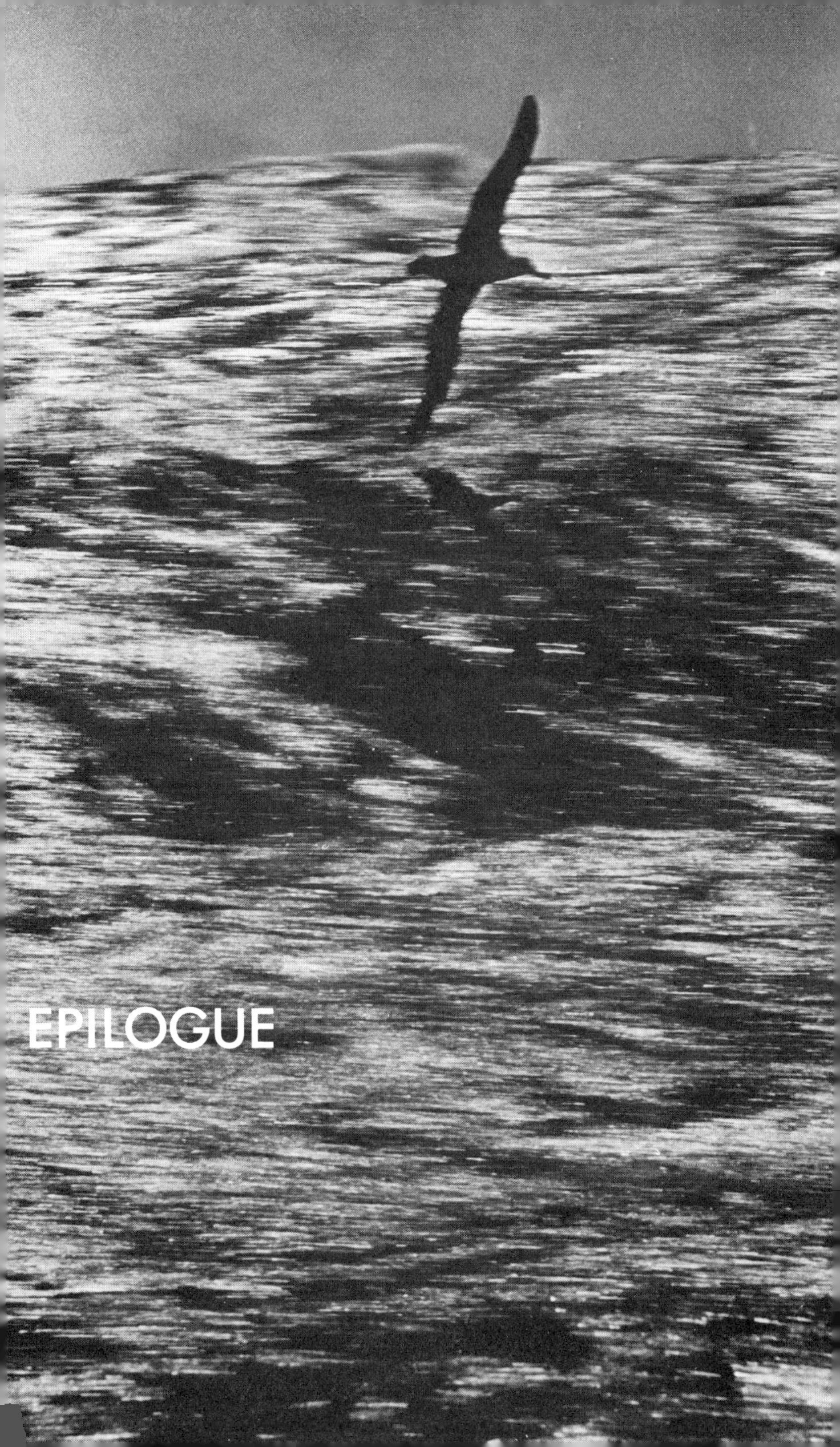

EPILOGUE

Although I had been determined to win, and had chosen the crew on the strength of their eagerness to be first across the line, we had finished last. However, as far as our own reactions to the race were concerned, it was a case of 'last but not least' for, despite our failure to win, we had all learnt a lot and enjoyed every minute of what turned out to be a fine race, which in the end was won by the best prepared of the new boats, *Flyer*. She had been designed and built for the race, had had four months for working up, and she was sailed hard. *Flyer*'s victory underlines the value of leaving time between the boat being finished and the start of a race, particularly a long race like this. Her success was all the greater because the race was a real race, with everyone pushing their boats and crews to the limit in waters that were avoided by yachtsmen whenever possible ten years before. The fact that the Southern Ocean did not throw up any really violent weather during the 1977–78 season meant that it was less risky to keep sail on the boats, but I think they would have been kept going whatever the weather. The times for this race were in some cases ten days faster than the previous race.

The good performance of the smaller boats is in part due to the excellent way they were sailed, but also it owes something to the method of handicap used. Where the race has a set handicap distance, but the boats all take a course that is shorter, the handicap favours the smaller boats. In the second leg, for instance, the handicap distance was 7,400 miles, but few boats logged more than 7,000. The extra four hundred miles would have taken a larger boat just over two days, but a smaller one would have needed at least two and a half to three days to cover the same distance. The smaller boats thus gained at least half a day at the expense of the large ones and this gave them better handicap results. A more satisfactory system in these circumstances would have been the time on time handicap arrangement.

This of course makes *Flyer*'s performance all the more outstanding, as she would have had an even greater win on the time on time system.

The race safety rules were tightened for the 1977–78 race, and this is perhaps the reason why no lives were lost, although there were four incidents of illness or injury. All the boats that started in Portsmouth sailed the whole course, and the only damage sustained was our broken mast, and *Gauloises*'s broken rudder. In both cases the boats rejoined the race as soon as they could complete repairs.

Our own result was disappointing. Even if the twelve days lost because of the mast are deducted from the overall times, we would still have finished only halfway down the fleet. More work up time would have made some difference, but not enough to have won the race. *Heath's Condor* proved able to hold any boat on handicap on a reach, especially in a strong wind, and her windward performance was good, although not as good as *Pen Duik*. Where we really lost out was in downwind performance. There was a hump at about twelve knots of speed which was very difficult to get over, and the trouble appeared to be that the stern dug in when running at speed and we were dragging a lot of water behind us as a result. The spectacular rooster tail was exciting to watch, but we only got it on the rare occasions we pushed the speed above twenty-five knots when surfing, and with the right stern it would not have been present. With more time, a solution to this transom drag might have been produced before the race started, but time was a commodity we were very short of. With more time for pre-race sailing, it is likely that the carbon fibre mast would have failed before the race, and we would have been spared the call into Monrovia, with all the loss of time and effect on morale it caused.

If I were to do it again, I would try and have the boat at least six months before the race, and then sail her and the crew as often and as hard as I could to ensure that any weaknesses were identified and eliminated before the race started. A lot of our problems could be traced to the pressure on everyone—the designer, builder and ourselves—to get the boat ready in time. A few extra months in the building programme would have made all the difference.

I do not think I would change the crew selection process. It would be easier now as I have most of the people who sailed on *Heath's Condor* to add to the list of those I would want as the hard core. It would be easy to find faults in individual crew members; in fact it would be remarkable if after a voyage of this length a few weaknesses had not shown. But the fact remains that with between fourteen and sixteen people crowded together for up to a month at a time in a small boat, very few tensions showed, and these quickly disappeared without leaving scars. Naturally some people developed more as sailors than others, but at the end of the race we had a good reliable crew who could be asked to take on anything and would willingly and competently tackle it. One cannot ask for more than that.

APPENDICES

FOOD APPENDIX

General notes

It is a major operation to plan, purchase and stow food for fifteen people on a race of this length where each leg lasts approximately one month. Allowances have to be made for emergencies, such as the unplanned detour to Monrovia, so the food was calculated for thirty-five to forty days, plus an additional small stock of dehydrated food. The main objective was to provide an interesting, well balanced, energy-producing diet.

On *Heath's Condor* we did not have a special cook, so one or two people were made commissar for each leg, and they were responsible for stocking or restocking with rations. The cooking and interior cleaning duties were divided up amongst the crew working in pairs. Weekly menus were prepared at the start of each leg and the quantities of food to be purchased were calculated on the basis of the requirements of one man and then multiplied. The menus obviously had to be based on what was available in the various ports and also on any foodstuffs that were donated. Slight variations were allowed in the menus to suit the conditions prevailing.

The crew were responsible for paying for their food, and it was generally agreed that it was worth paying extra for quality. In fact in Cape Town and Auckland the cost was less than expected, which was a pleasant bonus. The stops at the different ports allowed some welcome changes to be introduced into the diet, with the varied local fruits, vegetables and tinned foods.

In order to avoid confusion, a plan had to be made of where the food was stored around the boat. Tins were put in the bilges with their labels removed to avoid blocking the bilge pumps. A code was painted on them to make identification easy. On *Heath's Condor* we had a large stowage space in the after cabin for storing dry foods and fresh fruit and vegetables. Lockers were also used for this purpose. It was important to see that access was available relative to demand. The galley contained food in current use and items that needed to be constantly to hand. A close watch had to be kept on things that needed to be eaten quickly, or any items that were running low.

The deep freeze was situated in the galley. This was a tremendous success, and provided the meat to be stored there was delivered unfrozen, the thirty cubic feet of space was very adequate. Having fresh meat always available allowed for more varied and tasty meals to be served. It also provided a more nutritious diet.

As the voyage progressed people's likes and dislikes were established. One problem that occurred was that at some stages a particular item became very popular, so it was restocked in bulk in the next port, and then, after the delights of feeding ashore, that item would not be in demand.

Having fresh food available after each stop helped the crew to get adjusted to the more limited diet at sea, and once everyone had settled down, meals became an extremely important part of the day. Most of the cooks produced excellent meals to a critical clientele, with only a few notable exceptions. It was noticeable that as the race continued the cooking became more adventurous with progressively more exotic items being purchased and enjoyed. Bad weather made cooking difficult, and only simple meals of porridge and stews were produced on those days.

The food list given is roughly the amounts needed for the start of the race. Obviously some items lasted for more than one leg and a few even went the whole way round the world. There was some exchange between boats of surplus food.

There never seemed to be enough 'goodies' in the form of chocolate, sweets and so on. Some additional items such as Christmas puddings were put on board for special occasions like New Year's Day and Rounding the Horn. In New Zealand members of the Devonport Yacht Club kindly baked a number of fruit cakes which were much appreciated.

FOOD LIST: Example for one leg

Fresh meat

Rump steaks (8 oz)	lb: 156
Chicken portions	lb: 156
Mince	lb: 90
Bacon	lb: 40
Lamb chops	lb: 35
Liver	lb: 30
Gammon steaks	lb: 30
Stewing lamb	lb: 30
Large salami	6

Fresh fruit and vegetables

Apples	400
Oranges	400
Grapefruits	100
Bananas	100
Avocadoes	40
Green peppers	40
Papaws	40
Lemons	24
Cauliflowers	12
Cabbages	12
Potatoes	lb: 112
Onions	lb: 40
Plus assorted salads	

Dried meat (Cape Town) and soya

Vegimix	g: 20 × 350
Soyastew	g: 40 × 200
Soya Chunks	g: 40 × 200
Biltong	lb: 2

Tinned meat and fish

Pilchards	g: 25 × 450
Tuna	g: 20 × 200
Sardines	g: 20 × 125
Corned beef	g: 60 × 400
Steak and onion	g: 60 × 400
Meat balls	g: 20 × 400
Ham	tins: 24

Tinned vegetables	***Cases***
Baked beans	8
Peas	6
Carrots	4
Mushrooms	4
Tomatoes	4
Potatoes	4
Green beans	4
Peppercorn	2
Sweet corn	2
Dried potato	1

Bread and cereals

Loaves	70
Ryvita	packets: 200
Bread mixes	kg: 5
Porridge oats	kg: 16
Cornflakes	kg: 5
Alpen	lb: 5

Eggs dozen: 90

Sugar lb: 150

Packet soups

Oxtail	140
Tomato	120
Vegetable	120
Lentil	70
Chicken noodle	70

Pastas, etc

Spaghetti Vermicelli Macaroni Semolina	packets: 10
Vesta	packets: 50
Rice	lb: 40
Flour	lb: 10

Tinned fruit and puddings

Creamed rice	cases: 4
Peaches Fruit cocktail Apricots Ginger pudding Fruit pudding	cases: 2
Angel's Delight	packets: 40
Custard powder	lb: 6

Biscuits, sweets, etc

Ginger nuts	packets: 20
Mixed biscuits Lemon cream Cream crackers	packets: 15
Mint humbugs	tins: 15
Mixed boiled sweets Caramels	tins: 10
Quality Street	bags: 15
Mars bars	boxes: 15
Chocolate bars	boxes: 10
Assorted fruit cakes	

Preserves, etc

Marmalade	g: 20 × 900
Golden syrup	kg: 12 × 1
Honey	g: 10 × 500
Strawberry jam	g: 10 × 450
Peanut butter	g: 5 × 850
Maple syrup	bottles: 2

Sauces, spices, etc

Salt Pepper	lb: 6
Tomato sauce	litres: 4
Tabasco sauce	bottles: 4
Mayonnaise	g: 2 × 850
Chutney	g: 10 × 450
Tomato paste	tubes: 20
Mustard	jars: 6
Curry powder	tins: 5
Parmesan (grated)	jars: 6
Bisto	packets: 6
Chicken stock cubes Beef stock cubes	large boxes: 2
Beetroot Coleslaw	jars: 12
Cooking oil	litres: 2 × 2.5
Olive oil	litres: 1 × 10
Pearl barley	packets: 3
Ground nutmeg Cinnamon Caraway seeds Bay leaves	bottles: 6
Rosemary Thyme Parsley Garlic salt Steak spice Cloves Paprika	jars: 4
Barbecue sauce mix	packets: 5
Parsley sauce mix Onion sauce mix Cheese sauce mix	packets: 10

Dairy produce

Margarine	kg: 20
Butter	kg: 15
Cheddar cheese	
Edam	kg: 6
Brie	kg: 2

Dried fruit and nibbles

Mixed fruit	
Raisins	kg: 10
Peanuts	

Drinks

Tea bags	catering packs: 6
Coffee	
St Ivel milk powder	pint: 85 × 5
Drinking chocolate	kg: 10
Orange concentrate	litres: 6
Lime juice	bottles: 18
Pure fruit juice	litres: 50
Bovril	large jars: 4
Carnation Milk	tins: 24

Alcohol

Beer	dozen cans: 20
	boxes of 1 dozen each
Rum	5
Whisky	2
Brandy	2
Sherry	2
Wine	4

SAMPLE MENUS

Breakfast
- Fruit juice—tinned or packet
- Cornflakes
- Scrambled eggs, bacon, baked beans
- Toast and butter, marmalade/jam
- Tea/coffee, with sugar, milk

Lunch
- Tomato soup
- Tinned stewed steak, tinned carrots, fresh onions, red wine
- Fresh potatoes, tinned green beans
- Tinned pears and custard
- Tea/coffee, with sugar, milk

Dinner
- Vegetable soup
- Lamb chops, grilled/fried
- Tinned mixed vegetables, tinned potatoes
- Fruit pudding
- Biscuits and cheese
- Tea/coffee, with sugar, milk

Breakfast
- Fruit juice
- Porridge
- 2 fried eggs, bacon, baked beans
- Toast and butter, marmalade/jam
- Tea/coffee, with sugar, milk

Lunch
- Oxtail soup
- Fried hamburgers and tinned tomatoes
- Tinned potatoes, tinned mixed vegetables
- Tinned plums and custard
- Tea/coffee, with sugar, milk

Dinner
- Lentil soup
- Steak (grilled/fried) with fresh onions
- Fresh potatoes, tinned mushrooms, tinned carrots
- Rice pudding and tinned fruit
- Tea/coffee, with sugar, milk

MEDICAL APPENDIX

BUPA Medical Kit

DRUGS	*USE*	*QUANTITY*
Asilone	Indigestion	300
Multivite	Vitamin tablets	600
Panadol	Painkillers	500
Distalgesic		400
Omnopon		12
Lanoline		2
Ambre Solaire	Sun cream	5
Uvistat lipsalves		10
Bradosol lozenges	Antiseptic lozenges	100
Tinaderm	Antifungal cream	5
Septrin	Antibiotics	500
Crystapen		500
Penbriton		10
Streptotriad	Anti-diarrhoea	200
Lomotil		100
Dalmane	Sleeping tablets	100
Otosporin	Eye/ear drops	2
Chlormycetin		4
Maxolon	Anti-seasickness/vomiting	200
Dramamine		200
Hyoscine		10
Phenergan	Anti-histamines	50
Piriton		100
Dulcodos	Anti-constipation	200
Xylocaine	Local anaesthetics	2
Slow sodium	Salt tablets	500
Sodium bicarb paste	Burns	1

DRESSINGS, ETC

Cotton wool
Gauze swabs
Elastoplast bandages
Airstrips
Crepe bandages
Cotton bandages

Hexcelite splints
Ambulance dressings
Dressing packs (large and small)
Mediswabs
Steristrips

Nobecutaine spray
Hibitane antiseptic solution
Hibitane cream
Betadine skin cleanser
Cicatrin antibiotic powder

Scissors, forceps, scalpel
Syringes and needles
Sutures

Fitness

All the British crews in the race were examined by BUPA both before the departure and also at Portsmouth immediately after their return. For the most part this involved telling a collection of fit young men that they were just that. However, the physicians examining for BUPA did find that in general, crews were fitter after the race than before; most had lost weight, though increased muscle bulk, many had stopped smoking, and respiratory tests were better overall at the end of the race.

1977–78 WHITBREAD ROUND THE WORLD RACE

OVERALL RESULTS

HANDICAP POSITION	NAME OF YACHT	ELAPSED TIME	CORRECTED TIME
1	*Flyer*	3269.4769	2857.0083
2	*King's Legend*	3327.7894	2915.2938
3	*Treaty of Rome*	3716.9662	2922.8534
4	*Disque d'Or*	3408.6301	2938.9414
5	*ADC Accutrac*	3495.4664	3044.3129
6	*Gauloises II*	3767.0098	3055.9068
7	*Adventure*	3806.2133	3074.9191
8	*Neptune*	3653.5619	3131.8757
9	*B & B Italia*	3773.5831	3170.3817
10	*33 Export*	3951.5333	3192.5179
11	*Tielsa*	3565.3704	3192.5995
12	*Great Britain II*	3228.3764	3226.7239
13	*Debenhams*	3869.0935	3259.8289
14	*Japy-Hermes*	3937.4870	3438.0035
15	*Heath's Condor*	3433.6975	3456.1618

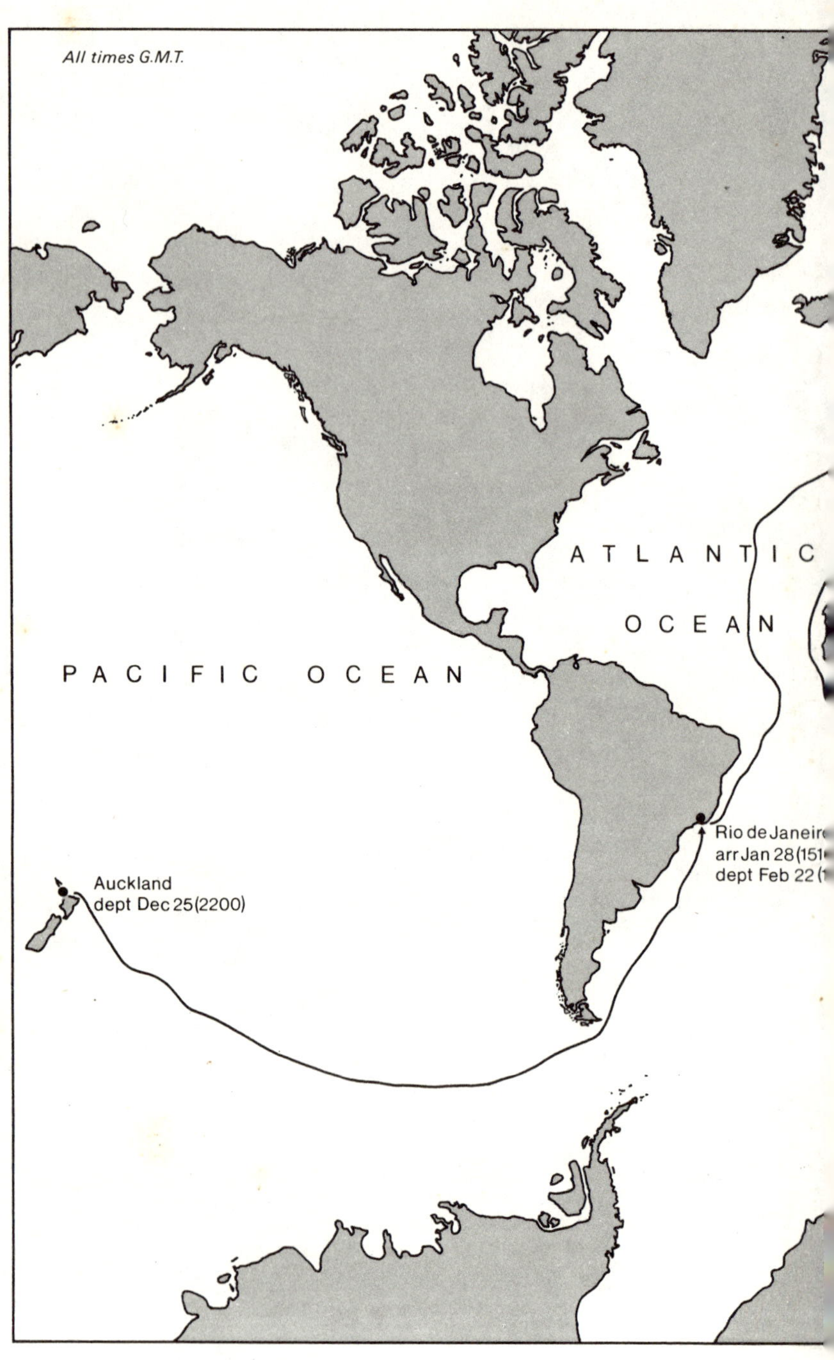

All times G.M.T.
ATLANTIC
OCEAN
PACIFIC OCEAN
Auckland
dept Dec 25(2200)